2015 Agricultural Productivity, Decentralisation, and Competitiveness Analysis for Provinces and Regions of Indonesia

NUS National University of Singapore

LKY Lee Kuan Yew School of Public Policy
ASIA COMPETITIVENESS INSTITUTE

In 2016 ACI was ranked 13th globally, 2nd in Asia and 1st in Singapore amongst 90 think-tanks world-wide under the "Best University Affiliated Think-Tank" category by Think-Tanks & Civil Societies Program at The University of Pennsylvania, USA

About ACI

The Asia Competitiveness Institute (ACI) was established in August 2006 as a research centre at the Lee Kuan Yew School of Public Policy (LKYSPP), National University of Singapore (NUS). It aims to build the intellectual leadership and network for understanding and developing competitiveness in the Asia region. ACI seeks to contribute to the enhancement of inclusive growth, living standards and institutional governance through competitiveness research on sub-national economies in Asia. It identifies mitigating issues and challenges for potential public policy interventions through close collaboration with regional governments, business corporations, policy think-tanks and academics. ACI's three key research pillars include (i) sub-national economies level competitiveness analysis and city-level liveability analysis, (ii) firm-level competitiveness analysis in 16 Asia economies, and (iii) Singapore's long-term growth strategies and public policy analysis.

ACI's value propositions may be encapsulated in its acronym:

Analytical inputs to initiate policies for policy-makers and business leaders in Asia

Capacity building to enable others through improvement in productivity and efficiency

Intellectual leadership to create pragmatic models of competitiveness and inclusive growth

The institute's core research competencies can also be encapsulated in this acronym describing our evidence-based assessments conducted on public policies for ASEAN in the context of the rise of China and India.

Vision and Mission

- ACI's over-arching vision is to build up its research credibility with policy impact, contributing as a professional, world-class think-tank.
- ACI's mission is to establish our niche as a leading policy think-tank by identifying competitiveness trends, opportunities and challenges, as well as promoting competition and synergising complementarities amongst Asian economies and business corporations.
- ACI endeavours to articulate sound recommendations, entice discourse, and shape agenda in the arena of public policy amongst Asian governments.
- ACI undertakes evidence-based analysis of public policy issues and decisions, in order to provide assessment of their effectiveness as well as economic and societal impact.

Research Initiatives and Collaborations

I. Identify trends of competitiveness and policy analysis on trade and investment of ASEAN, within the regional context of competition and complementarities with China and India.

II. Identify competitive strengths and conduct policy analysis on Singapore within the context of regional economies with international benchmarking.

III. We are regularly releasing three indices on liveability ranking including 64 Global Cities, 100 Greater China Cities and 17 Shandong Cities.

IV. We have established an Ease of Doing Business Index on Attractiveness to Investors, Business Friendliness and Competitive Policies for 21 states and federal territories of India and 33 provinces of Indonesia.

V. We have signed Memoranda of Understanding with The World Bank (2016 and 2015), SPRING Singapore (2014) and European Central Bank (2014).

VI. We have signed Memoranda of Understanding with various institutions in Greater China economies, including Shanghai Academy of Social Sciences (2016), Shandong Academy of Social Sciences (2015), Chongqing Municipal People's Government (2015), China Institute for Reform and Development, Haikou (2015), Counsellors' Office of the People's Government of Guangdong Province (LOI, 2014) and Chung-Hua Institution for Economic Research (2015), Taiwan.

VII. We have signed Memoranda of Understanding with six Chief Ministers' Offices in Andhra Pradesh (2015), Bihar (2015), Chhattisgarh (2015), Madhya Pradesh (2015), Odisha (2015) and Punjab (2015).

VIII. We have signed Memoranda of Understanding with Indonesia Investment Coordinating Board (2014), Indonesian Agency for Agricultural Research and Development at Ministry of Agriculture (2014), Indonesian President's Delivery Unit for Developing Monitoring and Oversight (2013) and Employer's Association of Indonesia (2013).

IX. We have signed Memoranda of Understanding with ASEAN think-tanks, including Centre for Strategic and International Studies, Indonesia (2015), Institute of Strategic & International Studies, Malaysia (2015), Philippine Institute for Development Studies (2015), Thailand Development Research Institute (2015) and Central Institute for Economic Management, Vietnam (2015).

About ACI's Research Pillars

ACI has consciously engaged in economic research that has significant relevance to Singapore and the Asian region. Over the years, ACI has focused on our expertise in quantitative competitiveness analysis and simulation, spinning off volumes of research output in the applications of our methodology and regional insight. At this stage, ACI has identified three core research pillars that will guide and define its research efforts moving forward. The three research pillars are as follows:

Pillar I. Sub-national Economies Competitiveness Analysis

ACI engages in systematic and methodical competitiveness analyses of the *sub-national economies* by using an evidence-based, empirical approach involving a comprehensive list of relevant indicators, which are categorised under multiple layers called the 'environments'. A number of our projects, including competitiveness analyses of Greater China, ASEAN-10, India, and Indonesia, as well as other thematic research projects, were conducted by adopting this common methodology, with potential variations in the specific environments and indicators. ACI's competitiveness analysis of Asian economies goes beyond the usual ranking to offer constructive policy recommendations on how individual member states can improve their rankings vis-à-vis their sub-national or regional peers through the application of the 'what-if' simulation, which provides the projected improvements of each state's ranking whereby the bottom one-fifth of its indicators are enhanced.

Pillar II. Micro-based Firm Level Competitiveness Analysis

Micro-based firm level competitiveness analysis is ACI's second research pillar that has been developed in view of the intrinsic importance of firm-level competitiveness in terms of productivity, efficiency, and governance. In the context of globalisation, mobility of economic activities, and blurring of borders, an understanding of the determinants and dynamics of firm-level competitiveness is paramount, in order for policy makers to make adjustments and prepare their industries for an increasingly competitive economic landscape. To this end, ACI has partnered with the European Central Bank to carry out research in this area, possessing a solid foundation in firm-level productivity research in the form of European Competitiveness Network database and methodology. ACI envisaged the expansion of CompNet into Asia, thereby pioneering the Asia CompNet research network encompassing 16 economies in Asia.

Pillar III. Singapore's Long-term Economic Growth Strategies and Public Policies Analysis

The third and imminent research pillar focuses on Singapore's long-term economic growth strategies in the context of changing circumstances, future trends, and emerging opportunities for Singapore in the decades ahead. In particular, ACI will take on the task of critically examining Singapore's public policy strengths and areas of improvement by assessing policy successes of the past, identifying new issues to address and the current policy gaps, through a systematic and evidence-based research inquiry using quantitative methodology and empirical data, leveraging on our network of policy experts.

Founding Patron and International Advisory Panel

Founding Patron: **Mr George Yeo**
Visiting Scholar, Lee Kuan Yew School of Public Policy, National University of Singapore & Former Minister of Foreign Affairs, Singapore

International Advisory Panel

Co-Chairs:

Professor Michael Porter (2006–2010)
Bishop William Lawrence University Professor

Ms Marjorie Yang (2006–2012)
Chairman, Esquel Group

Members:

Professor Kishore Mahbubani
Dean, Lee Kuan Yew School of Public Policy, National University of Singapore

Dr Kuntoro Mangkusubroto
Head, President's Delivery Unit for Developing Monitoring and Oversight (UKP4), Indonesia

Mr Narayana Murthy
Chairman, Infosys Technologies Limited

Mr Philip Yeo
Chairman, SPRING Singapore

Mrs Ow Foong Pheng
Permanent Secretary, Ministry of Trade and Industry

Ms Yong Ying-I
Permanent Secretary, Public Service Division

Professor Chan Kam Leung Alan
Dean, College of Humanities, Arts and Social Sciences,
Nanyang Technological University

Asia Competitiveness Institute

Co-Directors:

Associate Professor Tan Khee Giap (2011 till now)
Professor Tan Kong Yam (2011 till now)

Asia Competitiveness Institute - World Scientific Series

ISSN: 2424-9912

Series Editor: Tan Khee Giap (*Lee Kuan Yew School of Public Policy, NUS, Singapore)*

2014

2014 Annual Competitiveness Ranking and Simulation Study for ASEAN-10 and Development Strategies to Enhance Asia Economic Connectivity
by Tan Khee Giap, Sangiita Yoong Wei Cher, Sasidaran Gopalan & Nguyen Le Phuong Anh (Lee Kuan Yew School of Public Policy, NUS, Singapore)

2014 Annual Provincial and Regional Competitiveness Analysis for Greater China Economies: Development Strategies under the New Normal
by Tan Khee Giap, Yuan Randong & Sangiita Yoong Wei Cher (Lee Kuan Yew School of Public Policy, NUS, Singapore)

2014 Regional Competitiveness Analysis and a Master Plan on Regional Development Strategies for India: Annual Competitiveness Update and Evidence on Economic Development Model for Selected States of India
by Tan Khee Giap, Linda Low, Kartik Rao & Tan Kong Yam (Lee Kuan Yew School of Public Policy, NUS, Singapore)

2014 Provincial and Inaugural Regional Competitiveness Analysis: Safeguarding Indonesia's Growth Momentum
by Tan Khee Giap, Nurina Merdikawati, Mulya Amri & Tan Kong Yam (Lee Kuan Yew School of Public Policy, NUS, Singapore)

2014 Annual Competitiveness Analysis and Development Strategies for Indonesian Provinces
by Tan Khee Giap, Nurina Merdikawati, Mulya Amri & Blake Harley Berger (Lee Kuan Yew School of Public Policy, NUS, Singapore)

2015

2015 Annual Competitiveness Analysis, Agricultural Productivity and Development Vision for ASEAN-10
by Tan Khee Giap, Nguyen Le Phuong Anh, Sasidaran Gopalan & Luu Nguyen Trieu Duong (Lee Kuan Yew School of Public Policy, NUS, Singapore)

2015 Estimation of Agricultural Productivity and Annual Update of Competitiveness Analysis for Greater China: Optimising Agricultural Productivity and Promoting Innovation Driven Growth
by Tan Khee Giap, Yuan Randong & Xie Teleixi (Lee Kuan Yew School of Public Policy, NUS, Singapore)

2015 Agricultural Total Factor Productivity and Competitiveness Analysis for States and Federal Territories and Five Regions of India: Annual Competitiveness Update and Evidence on the Agricultural Development Models for Selected Indian States
by Tan Khee Giap, Sasidaran Gopalan & Anuja Tandon (Lee Kuan Yew School of Public Policy, NUS, Singapore)

2015 Agricultural Productivity, Decentralisation, and Competitiveness Analysis for Provinces and Regions of Indonesia
by Tan Khee Giap, Nurina Merdikawati, Mulya Amri & Tan Kong Yam (Lee Kuan Yew School of Public Policy, NUS, Singapore)

2015 Annual Competitiveness Analysis and Development Strategies for Indonesian Provinces
by Tan Khee Giap, Mulya Amri, Nurina Merdikawati & Nursyahida Binte Ahmad (Lee Kuan Yew School of Public Policy, NUS, Singapore)

The complete list of the volumes in the series published since 2013 can be found at
http://www.worldscientific.com/series/aciwss

Asia Competitiveness Institute - World Scientific Series

2015 Agricultural Productivity, Decentralisation, and Competitiveness Analysis for Provinces and Regions of Indonesia

Tan Khee Giap
Co-Director, Asia Competitiveness Institute
Lee Kuan Yew School of Public Policy, National University of Singapore

Nurina Merdikawati
Research Associate, Asia Competitiveness Institute
Lee Kuan Yew School of Public Policy, National University of Singapore

Mulya Amri
Research Fellow & Deputy Director (Research), Asia Competitiveness Institute
Lee Kuan Yew School of Public Policy, National University of Singapore

Tan Kong Yam
Co-Director, Asia Competitiveness Institute
Lee Kuan Yew School of Public Policy, National University of Singapore

Reviewers

Ir Alma Karma, MEM
Director of Regional Potential Development
Investment Coordinating Board (BKPM),
Indonesia

Dr Agung Wicaksono
Assistant Professor
School of Business and Management — Institut Teknologi Bandung and Special Assistant to Head of President's Delivery Unit for Development Monitoring and Oversight (UKP4) 2009–2014,
Indonesia

Mr Robert Na Endi Jaweng, MAP
Executive Director of Regional Autonomy Watch (KPPOD),
Indonesia

Dr Agung Hendriadi
Executive Secretary of Indonesian Agency for Agricultural Research and Development (IAARD)

APINDO
Lee Kuan Yew School of Public Policy
Asia Competitiveness Institute
NUS National University of Singapore
World Scientific

Published by

World Scientific Publishing Co. Pte. Ltd.
5 Toh Tuck Link, Singapore 596224
USA office: 27 Warren Street, Suite 401-402, Hackensack, NJ 07601
UK office: 57 Shelton Street, Covent Garden, London WC2H 9HE

British Library Cataloguing-in-Publication Data
A catalogue record for this book is available from the British Library.

Asia Competitiveness Institute - World Scientific Series
2015 AGRICULTURAL PRODUCTIVITY, DECENTRALISATION, AND COMPETITIVENESS ANALYSIS FOR PROVINCES AND REGIONS OF INDONESIA

ISBN 978-981-3148-34-5

Desk Editor: Jiang Yulin

Typeset by Stallion Press
Email: enquiries@stallionpress.com

Printed in Singapore

Contents

Foreword

Under President Joko Widodo's leadership, Indonesia is facing an interesting trajectory. The government has been keen to speed up infrastructure development and translated their words into action. A case in point was when a decades-old system of fuel subsidy was scrapped a few months after the presidential inauguration, allowing the government to have more fiscal room for infrastructure spending. Starting in 2015, more economic policy packages were introduced to boost more participation from the private sector and position Indonesia as an attractive investment destination. Understanding that such grand vision requires collaboration from multiple layers of government — central and local governments alike — Asia Competitiveness Institute's (ACI's) focus on conducting subnational analysis for broad topics such as competitiveness, governing institutions and agricultural productivity is very relevant and timely to push for reform and joint efforts at subnational level.

As pointed out by ACI's empirical analysis, regional disparity is still prevalent, especially between easternmost provinces and the rest of Indonesia. The government has been committed to improve connectivity between western and eastern part of Indonesia, paving the way for all provinces in Indonesia to unleash their utmost potential. Several projects in the president's flagship "sea toll" programme have started, as part of efforts to strengthen Indonesia's maritime connectivity. The government also set up a committee for acceleration of priority infrastructure delivery (KPPIP) to expedite the realisation of various strategic infrastructure projects such as construction of power plant, toll road, sewerage system, railway, airport and development of seaport in various locations in Indonesia.

To achieve such ambitious infrastructure target, the government requires substantial funding. Based on studies by Ministry of National Development Planning/BAPPENAS, the funding needed for infrastructure projects from 2015 to 2019 is around 511 billion US Dollars, of which only 124 billion US Dollars will be covered by the government budget. Therefore, it is crucial for the government to encourage participation from private sector and multilateral institutions such as the Asian Infrastructure Investment Bank (AIIB) to close the financing gap.

I hope ACI will continue its excellent work on Indonesia's provincial and regional competitiveness study. I also applaud ACI's ardent efforts in providing evidenced-based insights from its empirical analysis of various strategic development themes at subnational level. I extend my wholehearted support for ACI's research projects and look forward to collaborating with ACI in the future.

Luky Eko Wuryanto
Vice President and Chief Administration Officer, AIIB
Deputy Minister for Infrastructure and Regional Development,
Coordinating Ministry for Economic Affairs, Indonesia

Preface

The Asia Competitiveness Institute (ACI) has been at the forefront of subnational studies, not only actively conducting research on Indonesia, but also on China and India. Its extensive achievement has been widely regarded, as the ACI is recently ranked 13th for Best University Affiliated Think Tanks according to the 2015 Global Go To Think Tank Index by The Think Tanks and Civil Society Programme at the University of Pennsylvania. Its subnational studies have been extended beyond competitiveness analysis as can be seen from this book where the ACI's researchers rigorously analysed the governing institutions and agricultural productivity across Indonesian provinces.

During the course of its research cycle, the ACI has created significant footprints in Indonesia by engaging national and provincial stakeholders. Given Indonesia's vast diversity, opportunities and challenges abound as the country is facing a more open and integrated world's economy. As an archipelagic country, the current focus on strengthening maritime infrastructure is a step in the right direction. Connecting Indonesia's sparse islands is crucial to address the regional and price disparity between the western and eastern part of Indonesia, to make each and every island an active contributor and participant of nation-wide economic production and distribution process. President Joko Widodo has been progressive in pushing for more reforms to pave the way for executing the strategic infrastructure projects and making Indonesia as an attractive investment destination.

Indonesia should remain resilient in its growth trajectory amidst uncertainty in the global economy. With a persistent plunge in commodity prices, the government has to find alternative engines for growth. More efforts on building a strong manufacturing sector should be seriously considered as it has been touted as the key sector for advancing the country's economic development and an important source of formal employment.

Indonesia's role in the region, especially in the Association of Southeast Asian Nations (ASEAN), remains foremost. Indonesia is expected to take more leadership position in ASEAN, stirring ASEAN to assume its rightful competitive place in the world. In a globalised world, more openness and integration prevail as shown in a variety of regional initiatives to encourage stronger collaboration among nations, such as ASEAN Economic Community (AEC), Regional Comprehensive Economic Partnership (RCEP), and Trans-Pacific Partnership (TPP).

As the ACI continues to grow in expanding its evidenced-based assessments to public policies in ASEAN, China and India, more insights will be generated to spearhead the policies to raise the standards of governance, improve the lives of the people and contribute to the transformation of the region. This is in line with the Lee Kuan Yew School of Public Policy's vision and mission. Indonesia's growth and advancement not only will benefit its neighbours, but also the region at large. I hope this study contributes to the ongoing policy discussions in Indonesia on what can be done to spur faster economic growth.

Professor Kishore Mahbubani
Dean
Lee Kuan Yew School of Public Policy
National University of Singapore

Acknowledgments

In this book, *2015 Annual Provincial and Regional Competitiveness Analysis in Indonesia: Optimising Layers of Government and Agricultural Productivity*, we updated our previous provincial and regional competitiveness studies with the latest available data. Leveraging on Asia Competitiveness Institute's (ACI) rich database, we also conducted provincial analysis on governing institutions and agricultural productivity, in collaboration with other ACI's researchers. We benefited immensely from the feedback and comments on our preliminary findings during the past two Review Seminars held at Lee Kuan Yew School of Public Policy, National University of Singapore, on 4th August 2014 and 8th September 2015. For that, we would like to thank the following experts and reviewers:

- Ir Alma Karma, MEM
  Director of Regional Potential Development, Investment Coordinating Board (BKPM), Indonesia
- Dr Agung Wicaksono
  Assistant Professor, School of Business and Management — Institut Teknologi Bandung and Special Assistant to Head of President's Delivery Unit for Development Monitoring and Oversight (UKP4) 2009–2014, Indonesia
- Mr Robert Na Endi Jaweng, MAP
  Executive Director of Regional Autonomy Watch (KPPOD), Indonesia
- Dr Agung Hendriadi
  Executive Secretary of Indonesian Agency for Agricultural Research and Development (IAARD)

We, in particular, would like to extend our appreciation for encouragement and solid support from our adjunct professors at various stages of this research:

- Dr Luky Eko Wuryanto who is also a Deputy Minister for Infrastructure and Regional Development, Coordinating Ministry for Economic Affairs, Indonesia and recently appointed as Vice President and Chief Administration Officer, Asian Infrastructure Investment Bank; and
- Mr Mahendra Siregar, MA, former Chairman of BKPM (2013–2014), Vice Minister of Finance (2011–2013), and Vice Minister of Trade (2009–2011), Indonesia.

We are grateful for the involvement of Professor Ramkishen S. Rajan, ACI's adjunct senior research fellow, as a co-author of Chapter 5 on "Agricultural Productivity in Indonesian

Provinces." We also invited ACI research fellows, Assistant Professor Li Hui and Assistant Professor Yee Wai-Hang, to contribute Chapter 4 on "Decentralisation, Governing Institutions, and Economic Development in Indonesia".

This report is the result of a strong partnership among the business sector, government, and academia. We are grateful for the partnership with the Indonesian Employers' Association (APINDO) in conducting the business perception surveys across Indonesian provinces. We would also like to extend our gratitude to various local government offices and universities for their cooperation in hosting forums in their premises and participating in our perception surveys.

The coordination and execution of field trips would not have been possible without the excellent work by Yap Xin Yi, Shanty Citra Eka Vebriani Yusup, Rizky Novrianto, Ririn Radiawati Kusuma, Faizal Rianto, Bonifasius Agung Nugroho, Fenny Karlavita Siregar, Raisa Annisa, Dessy Septiane Sukendar, Edwina Frisdiantiny, Muhammad Fadhel Jamali, Vincent Kwan Wen Seng, Kartik Rao and Sujata Kaur. We would also like to place on record our appreciation for the encouragement of ACI's extended researchers and administration staff as well as other colleagues at LKYSPP.

Finally, we are immensely grateful to Dean Kishore Mahbubani and for the research funding from the Ministry of Trade and Industry, Singapore, in supporting this unprecedented effort, without which, such extensive book would not have been possible.

Tan Khee Giap, Nurina Merdikawati,
Mulya Amri and Tan Kong Yam
Asia Competitiveness Institute
Lee Kuan Yew School of Public Policy
National University of Singapore

About the Authors

Tan Khee Giap is a Co-Director of the Asia Competitiveness Institute (ACI) and Associate Professor at the Lee Kuan Yew School of Public Policy, National University of Singapore. He is also the Chairman of the Singapore National Committee for Pacific Economic Cooperation. Upon graduating with a PhD from University of East Anglia, England, in 1987 under the Overseas Research Scheme awarded by the Committee of Vice-Chancellors and Principals of the Universities of the United Kingdom. He joined the banking sector as a treasury manager. Thereafter, he taught at the Department of Economics and Statistics, National University of Singapore, 1990–1993. Dr Tan joined Nanyang Technological University in 1993 and was Associate Dean, Graduate Studies Office, 2007–2009. Dr Tan has consulted extensively with the various government ministries, statutory boards and government-linked companies of Singapore government. He has also served as a consultant to international agencies such as the Asian Development Bank, Asian Development Bank Institute, United Nations Industrial Development Group, World Gold Council, ASEAN Secretariat, Central Policy Unit of Hong Kong, Kerzner International, Las Vegas Sands and Marina Bay Sands. Dr Tan is the lead author of twenty books, serves as journal editors and published widely in international refereed journals. His current research interests include econometric forecasting, cost of living index, global liveable cities index, ease of doing business index and competitiveness analysis on sub-national economies of China, India, Indonesia and ASEAN. Dr Tan was Deputy President of the Singapore Economic Society, 2004. He served in the 2002 Economic Review Committee (ERC), served as the Deputy Chairman of the IPS Forum for Economic Restructuring (IFER) in 2003 and served as a member of the Resource Panel of the Government Parliamentary Committee for Transport and Government Parliamentary Committee for Finance and Trade since 2007. Dr Tan has extensively advised and guided multinational corporations leading to public listings, especially those companies from Mainland China and Taiwan. He is also currently an Independent Director of the publicly listed Artivision, BreadTalk Group, Boustead Projects and TEE Land.

Nurina Merdikawati is a Research Associate at the Asia Competitiveness Institute (ACI) at the Lee Kuan Yew School of Public Policy (LKYSPP), National University of Singapore. At ACI, Nurina is coordinating and leading the research on Indonesia's competitiveness analysis at the provincial and regional levels as well as provincial studies on agriculture productivity and ease of doing business. She has written widely on the abovementioned subjects and published books, journal, and working papers for ACI. Prior to ACI, she spearheaded data management, collection, and analysis for INSEAD eLab projects and the Global Talent Competitiveness Index. Additionally, Nurina conducted firm-level studies on building business performance and competitiveness with new information and communications technology (ICTs), country-level studies on payment systems, and talent competitiveness. Nurina graduated with a Master's degree in Public Policy from the LKYSPP with a specialisation in economic policy analysis. She was a Mochtar Riady Scholar and on the Dean's list. Nurina received her Bachelor's degree in Economics (Second Upper) from Nanyang Technological University, Singapore. She has worked with the Central Bank of Indonesia as a visiting researcher and held an internship at the Centre for Strategic and International Studies (CSIS) in Jakarta.

Mulya Amri is a Research Fellow at the Asia Competitiveness Institute (ACI), Lee Kuan Yew School of Public Policy, National University of Singapore. He has held a key role in ACI's research on Indonesian sub-national competitiveness since 2011, including co-writing three books on the topic, the latest one titled "2014 Annual Competitiveness Analysis and Development Strategies for Indonesian Provinces". He is also closely involved in ACI's research on city live-ability and competitiveness, and has written widely on the topic of urban development and city-level governance. Mulya has 15 years of working experience in the private, public, and non-profit sectors. Upon moving to Singapore in 2008, he worked with HOK (a global planning and architecture consultancy firm) on city planning projects throughout Asia and with Jurong Consultants (the consultancy arm of Singapore's JTC Corporation) on the planning of industrial zones in the Middle East. Prior to that, Mulya worked with international development agencies such as the World Bank, UNDP and UN-HABITAT on projects related to urban and housing development, local governance, as well as community-driven development in various Indonesian regions. He is also a co-founder and sits on the advisory board of COMBINE Resource Institution, a non-profit organization based in Yogyakarta, Indonesia. Mulya has a PhD degree in Public Policy from the National University of Singapore. Prior to that, he graduated with a bachelor's degree from Institut Teknologi Bandung, Indonesia, and was awarded the Fulbright scholarship to study for a Master's degree in Urban Planning at the University of California, Los Angeles and a Chevening award to study at the London School of Economics and Political Science.

Tan Kong Yam is a Co-Director of the Asia Competitiveness Institute (ACI) at the Lee Kuan Yew School of Public Policy, National University of Singapore. He is also Professor of Economics at the Nanyang Technological University. From June 2002 to June 2005, he was a senior economist at the World Bank office in Beijing. In 2004, he was a member of the World Bank expert group on the eleventh five-year plan (2006–2010) for the State Council in China. The expert group provided the Chinese Government with analyses and policy recommendations. Prior to that, he was the chief economist of the Singapore Government (1999–2002) and Head, Department of Strategy and Policy, NUS Business School at the National University of Singapore. He is a graduate of Princeton (1975–1979, class of 1931 scholar, Paul Volcker Thesis prize) and Stanford University (1980–1983), where he completed his Master's and PhD in three years. Prior to joining NUS, he has worked at the Hoover Institution at Stanford University, World Bank, the Monetary Authority of Singapore and was the Director of Research at the Ministry of Trade and Industry in Singapore. His research interests are in international trade and finance, economic and business trends in the Asia Pacific region and economic reforms in China.

He has published 10 books and numerous articles in major international journals including American Economic Review, World Bank Economic Review, Long Range Planning, Australian Journal of Management, etc. on economic and business issues in the Asia Pacific region. He served as a board member at the Singapore Central Provident Fund Board (1984–1996) and the National Productivity Board (1989–1990). He has also consulted for many organizations including Temasek, GIC, Citigroup, IBM, ATT, BP, ABN-AMRO, Ikea, Bank of China, China Construction Bank, People's Bank of China, EDB, Areva, Capitaland, Guangdong provincial government, Samsung, Mauritius Government, Ministry of Trade and Industry, Mobil and Singapore Technology, amongst others.

List of Abbreviations

AAHRD	Agency of Agricultural Human Resource Development
ACI	Asia Competitiveness Institute
AE	Administrative efficiency
AEC	ASEAN Economic Community
AECV2030	Asia Economic Connectivity Vision 2030
AFC	Asian Financial Crisis
AFI	Attractiveness to Foreign Investors
AIAT	Assessment Institutes for Agricultural Technology
AIIB	Asian Infrastructure Investment Bank
AMFR	Agency for Marine and Fisheries Research
APBN	State budget (*Anggaran Pendapatan dan Belanja Negara*)
APINDO	Indonesian Employers' Association (*Asosiasi Pengusaha Indonesia*)
AR	Administrative Region
ASEAN	Association of Southeast Asian Nations
BI	Basic infrastructure
BIMP-EAGA	Brunei Darussalam-Indonesia-Malaysia-Philippines East ASEAN Growth Area
BKPM	Investment Coordinating Board (*Badan Koordinasi Penanaman Modal*)
BPK	Supreme Audit Agency (*Badan Pemeriksa Keuangan*)
BPMPTSP	Investment Board and One Stop Services (*Badan Penanaman Modal dan Pelayanan Terpadu Satu Pintu*)
BPS	Indonesia's Central Statistical Agency (*Badan Pusat Statistik*)
CRSRL	Competition, Regulatory Standards, and Rule of Law
DAK	Special allocation fund (*Dana Alokasi Khusus*)
DAU	General allocation fund (*Dana Alokasi Umum*)
DPRD	Local parliament (*Dewan Perwakilan Rakyat Daerah*)
EDB Index ABC	Ease of doing business index on attractiveness to investors, business friendliness, and competitive policies
FAO	Food and Agricultural Organisation
FBMC	Financial, Businesses, and Manpower Conditions
FDBE	Financial Deepening and Business Efficiency
FDI	Foreign domestic investment
FORDA	Forestry Research and Development Agency
GDP	Gross domestic product
GG	Good governance

GIS	Government and Institutional Setting
GPFS	Government Policies and Fiscal Sustainability
GRDP	Gross regional domestic product
IAARD	Indonesian Agency for Agricultural Research and Development
ICAR	Indian Council of Agricultural Research
ICATAD	Indonesian Centre for Agricultural Technology Assessment and Development
ICT	Information, communications, and technology
IGL	Institutions, Governance, and Leadership
IMD	International Institute for Management Development
INDO-DAPOER	Indonesia Database for Policy and Economic Research
IPARD	Indonesian Planters Association for Research and Development
IRIEC	Indonesian Research Institute for Estate Crops
ISIS	Islamic State of Iraq and Greater Syria
ITB	Institut Teknologi Bandung
KEIN	National Economic and Industry Committee (*Komite Ekonomi dan Industri Nasional*)
KPK	Corruption Eradication Commission (*Komisi Pemberantasan Korupsi)*
KPPIP	Committee for acceleration of priority infrastructure delivery (*Komite Percepatan Penyediaan Infrastruktur Prioritas*)
KPPOD	Regional Autonomy Watch (*Komite Pemantauan Pelaksanaan Otonomi Daerah*)
KPU	General elections commission (*Komisi Pemilihan Umum*)
LAPOR	Layanan Aspirasi dan Pengaduan Online Rakyat
LGC	Local government coordination
LKYSPP	Lee Kuan Yew School of Public Policy
LMF	Labour Market Flexibility
LO	Liaison officer
LOI	Letter of intent
LPI	Logistics Performance Index
MIFEE	Merauke Integrated Food and Energy Estate
MNC	Multinational companies
MOU	Memorandum of understanding
MP3EI	Master Plan for Acceleration and Expansion of Indonesia's Economic Development (*Masterplan Percepatan dan Perluasan Pembangunan Indonesia*)
MPAC	Master Plan on ASEAN Connectivity
MS	Macroeconomic Stability
MW	Megawatt
NGO	Non-government organisation
NUS	National University of Singapore
O&S	Order and security
OR	Autonomous Region
OSS	One stop service (*Pelayanan Terpadu Satu Pintu*)

OTS	Openness to Trade and Services
PI	Physical Infrastructure
PP	Productivity Performance
PPP	Public private partnership
PT PLN	State-owned electricity company (*Perusahaan Listrik Negara*)
PTT	Integrated crop management (*Pengelolaan Tanaman Terpadu*)
QLID	Quality of Life and Infrastructure Development
R&D	Research and Development
RCEP	Regional Comprehensive Economic Partnership
REV	Regional Economic Vibrancy
RPJMD	Local medium term development plan (*Rencana Pembangunan Jangka Menengah Daerah*)
RPJMN	National medium term development plan (*Rencana Pembangunan Jangka Menengah Nasional*)
RPJPD	Local long term development plan (*Rencana Pembangunan Jangka Panjang Daerah)*
SAU	State agricultural universities
SEZ	Special Economic Zone
SINCPEC	Singapore National Committee for Pacific Economic Cooperation
SLESS	Standard of Living, Education, and Social Stability
SMS	Short message service
TC	Technological change
TEC	Technical efficiency change
TEU	Twenty-foot equivalent unit
TFP	Total Factor Productivity
TFPC	Total Factor Productivity Change
TI	Technological Infrastructure
TPP	Trans-Pacific Partnership
UKP4	President's Delivery Unit for Development Monitoring and Oversight (*Unit Kerja Presiden Bidang Pengawasan dan Pengendalian Pembangunan*)
UP4PB	Unit for acceleration of development in Papua and West Papua (*Unit Percepatan Pembangunan Papua dan Papua Barat*)
VOC	Dutch East India Company (*Vereenigde Oost-Indische Compagnie*)
VRS	Variable returns to scale
WTP	Reasonable without exceptions (*wajar tanpa pengecualian*)
YOY	Year-on-year

List of Tables and Figures

Chapter 1

Chapter 2

Chapter 3

Chapter 4

Discussant Notes 1

Discussant Notes 2

Chapter 5

Chapter 1

Introduction

1.1 WHY THIS BOOK AND FOR WHOM?

In the tradition of the Asia Competitiveness Institute (ACI) at the Lee Kuan Yew School of Public Policy (LKYSPP), National University of Singapore (NUS), our work and publications make a distinctive contribution to the literature by first, focusing on competitiveness analysis and ranking at both national and sub-national levels, over and above those at the traditional national level. Second, it is in this spirit that we at the ACI have crafted a comprehensive methodology to annually assess competitiveness at the sub-national level, which is employed here in this book, as well as in ACI's previous publications reporting research findings on Indonesia, Greater China, India and the Association of Southeast Asian Nations (ASEAN) countries.[1] Since the inaugural volume of the *Competitiveness Analysis and Development Strategies for 33 Indonesian Provinces* (Tan *et al.* 2013c), the comprehensive competitiveness index developed by ACI has been used to rank the 33 Indonesia provinces in various dimensions.[2] As ACI aims to provide an update by extending all studies, this updated book thus includes 2012 data from official sources and 2014 data from ACI's perception surveys.

As ACI works on evidence-based analysis, it is supported by quantitative methodologies scientifically presented to be useful to policy-makers. They, together with other academics, practitioners, business interests and non-government organisations (NGOs) are among the ACI's target audience. To facilitate multidisciplinary and cross-border dialogues among the relevant stakeholders, the ACI holds Review Seminars prior to any book publication, also for comments and suggestions as peer review.

The rest of Chapter 1 is organised as follows. Section 1.2 presents the structure of the book with brief summaries of each chapter. Section 1.3 briefly discusses the Maritime Vision proposed by President Joko Widodo as a key proposed policy to be implemented during his leadership. Section 1.4 extends the discussion on how Maritime Vision plays a role in strengthening domestic and global connectivity. Section 1.5 provides brief concluding remarks on Indonesia's Maritime Vision going forward.

---

[1]See Tan *et al.* (2013a, 2013b, 2013c, 2013d; 2015a, 2015b, 2015c, 2015d), and Tan, Yuan and Yoong (2015e). For ASEAN, the analysis is conducted at national level.

[2]As of 2016, there are 34 provinces in Indonesia. North Kalimantan, the newly created province being carved out of East Kalimantan in 2012, is not yet included pending availability of data.

1.2 STRUCTURE OF THE BOOK

This book comprises six chapters, inclusive of this introductory chapter as the roadmap for readers. Chapter 2 details 2015 Annual Update on Provincial Competitiveness Ranking and Simulation for Indonesia. Chapter 3 features the competitiveness analysis framework for the six regions proposed by the Master Plan for Acceleration and Expansion of Indonesia's Economic Development 2011–2025 (MP3EI). Chapter 4 offers distinct insights into the decentralisation, governing institutions and economic development in Indonesia. Chapter 5 presents our evidence-based study on assessing agricultural productivity in Indonesia's provinces. Chapter 6 is the concluding chapter with a brief overview of ACI's future research agenda.

1.3 OVERVIEW OF INDONESIA'S MARITIME VISION

As the largest archipelagic nation, the fourth most populous country with the largest Muslim population, and the third largest democracy in the world, Indonesia has received regional and global attention. The most recent call from ruling President Joko Widodo (Jokowi) to transform Indonesia as a global maritime axis has intrigued regional and local community alike who are hopeful that such policy brings higher prosperity to the nation.

President Jokowi first sounded his Maritime Vision in his election manifesto, with the word 'maritime' appearing in three out of seven missions to be submitted to the General Elections Commission (KPU).[3] The emphasis is not only on economic aspects, but also on boosting Indonesia's identity as an archipelagic country by strengthening maritime defence and diplomacy. These include but not limited to protecting maritime interest concerning borders and natural resources, strengthening naval capabilities and resolving territorial disputes in the Indo-Pacific region through maritime diplomacy. During his inauguration in October 2014, he further reaffirmed his vision, "We have to work hard to restore Indonesia as a maritime country. The oceans, the seas, the bays and the straits are the future of our civilisation. We have far too long turned our back on the seas, the oceans, the straits and the bays. It is time for us to restore everything so that *Jalesveva Jayamahe* (in the ocean we will triumph), a slogan used by our forefathers, will echo again."[4]

It did not take long for Indonesia to announce its Maritime Vision to the world. In November 2014, during the East Asia Summit in Naypyitaw, President Jokowi outlined his maritime doctrine that covered five pillars: (i) reviving Indonesia's maritime culture; (ii) revitalising management of maritime resources; (iii) prioritising infrastructure for maritime connectivity; (iv) focusing on maritime diplomacy for resolving conflicts and (v) strengthening maritime defence power.[5] All in all, the president's maritime axis is as important for Indonesia as it is Indonesia prospering within ASEAN as the ASEAN Economic Community (AEC) is to be completed by end of 2015.

[3] For further details, please see General Elections Commission (2014).

[4] The speech was retrieved from Ministry of State Secretariat of the Republic of Indonesia (2014).

[5] More details can be found in Neary (2014).

The next section will briefly discuss on how the shift towards maritime-based policies, especially those related to the third pillar of improving maritime connectivity, affects the internal dynamics within Indonesia and external dynamics with other countries. Most of the discussions will centre on how Maritime Vision can enhance Indonesia's economic prosperity and improve the lives of its people.

1.4 STRENGTHENING DOMESTIC AND GLOBAL CONNECTIVITY THROUGH MARITIME VISION

It is uncommon for a maritime agenda to turn into a mainstream policy discourse. The legacy of President Soeharto's era to concentrate economic activities in Java Island left Indonesia's maritime connectivity between the islands lagging behind. The Asian financial crisis (AFC) in 1997 witnessed a sharp reduction in infrastructure investment in Indonesia, from 5 to 6% of the gross domestic product (GDP) before 1997 to as low as 1–2% of the GDP in 2000. Infrastructure investment only picked up to 3.4% of the GDP in 2007,[6] further exacerbating the country's limited capacity to keep up with rising economic demand.

Land connectivity within an island is often prioritised over sea-based connectivity. Many islands have turned into subsistent economies, but remain isolated from the nation-wide economic processes; a situation commonly found in the islands of eastern Indonesia.[7] As a result, regional development is often imbalanced with the easternmost islands such as Maluku and Papua suffering from rudimentary hard and soft infrastructure. Price disparity occurs as an inevitable consequence, with the price of basic goods varying by a factor of 20 between the western and eastern regions.[8]

Poor connectivity also contributes to inefficient logistics system, with container shipping cost from Padang (West Sumatra) to Jakarta more than three times than the cost from Jakarta to Singapore. It is also equally challenging to unleash the maritime resources in eastern Indonesia as high quality sea-based products become too expensive to be processed in Java or exported to international market.[9] Anecdotal evidence also found that local tuna fishers would prefer going to the Philippines to sell their catch rather than rely on Indonesia's fledgling port infrastructure.[10] Hence, it is not surprising that Indonesia is ranked 53rd in logistics performance index (LPI) in 2014, below Singapore (5th), Malaysia (25th), Thailand (35th) and Vietnam (48th). Across LPI's evaluation components, the lowest performance is found in Indonesia's international shipments which is ranked 74th.[11]

While inter-island connectivity is not seamless, as seen from the poor quality of roads and traffic congestion across Java as Indonesia's main island, the impetus for inter-island and

---

[6] Under-investment in infrastructure has severely affected water, electricity and sectors, partially due to lower private investment commitments as a result of uncertainties in the legal system. More can be found in World Bank (2008).

[7] See Shekhar and Liow (2014).

[8] See Hutchinson (2013).

[9] See Sandee (2011).

[10] See Pisani (2014).

[11] See World Bank (2014).

eventually international connectivity is even more relevant in a globalised world. Inter-island connectivity is required for the government to achieve a more balanced regional growth:[12] between Java and non-Java; western and eastern Indonesia; and urban and rural areas. During the presidential campaign, Mr. Jokowi was championing maritime highways in the form of ships serving frequent routes connecting western and eastern Indonesia. If implemented, such programme is expected to reduce the high price disparity across Indonesia's regions.

Beyond that, a better maritime connectivity will induce greater inter-provincial trade facilitated by improved port infrastructure, with more provinces taking part in domestic value-chain activities and distribution processes. Agriculture-based provinces can prosper as their agricultural products are absorbed where demand is the highest.[13] For instance, surplus of rice from Sulawesi and beef from West Nusa Tenggara and East Nusa Tenggara can be shipped to Java to meet rising food demand in the country's most populous island. The implementation of MP3EI that aimed to spread growth centres across Indonesia's archipelago further emphasises the importance of sea-lane connectivity. While each economic corridor has been designated special themes, the goods they produced are not necessarily for their own consumption but to be traded with other corridors and even shipped to international market.

On top of inter-island connectivity, international connectivity is equally important. Despite Indonesia's strategic location in proximity to Singapore and the Straits of Malacca as one of the world's busiest shipping hubs, the country is yet to optimise the growing opportunities that lie ahead. President Jokowi's Maritime Vision paves the way for Indonesia's increasing role in international trade as better port infrastructure facilitates seamless goods going in and out of the country. Average dwelling time[14] in Jakarta's Tanjung Priok Port, which handles more than two-thirds of Indonesia's international trade, was 5.98 days in mid-2014, substantially behind the performance of other countries, such as Singapore (1.5 days), Malaysia (3 days) and Thailand (4–5 days).[15] Hence, it is not surprising that logistics cost accounted for 18–22% of firms' production cost,[16] further increasing the cost of doing business in Indonesia. Improvement in Tanjung Priok Port will contribute to lower logistics cost, positively affecting Indonesia's global competitiveness. Hence, it is encouraging to see progress in the making when average dwelling time in Tanjung Priok Port has been reduced to 4.5 days in October 2015.[17] On top of improvement in existing ports, the Maritime Vision also highlights the needs to build new ports,

[12]Please see Chapters 2 and 3 that cover competitiveness landscape across provinces and regions in Indonesia.

[13]Chapter 5 provides more detailed discussions on agricultural productivity in Indonesia's provinces. For this research, the ACI has collaborated with Indonesian Agency for Agricultural Research and Development (IAARD) in the form of Memorandum of Understanding (MOU) comprising collaboration in research and knowledge sharing activities; knowledge and technology transfer to increase the capacity of researcher in both institutions on methodologies related to agricultural studies; joint or individual publications to enhance knowledge about agricultural research and development (R&D); and human resources development of IAARD staff through training and higher education related to management of public administration and policy development in agriculture.

[14]Measures the time for a vessel to unloaded its containers and leave the port.

[15]See *The Jakarta Post* (2014).

[16]See Indonesia-Investments (2014).

[17]See *The Jakarta Post* (2015).

altogether will allow more cargos to pass through which will attract more manufacturers to further develop the processing industry in Indonesia.

The construction of Jakarta's New Priok Port next to the existing port, to be fully operational in 2023, is expected to become an international hub for seaborne trade, further strengthening the country's logistics chain. The port, with capacity to serve 18 million 20-foot equivalent units (TEUs) of containers, is also envisioned to reduce the time and cost of existing practice where many container shipping companies have to use transhipment facilities in Singapore and Malaysia to feed the second tier ports in Indonesia. Another plan in the pipeline is to develop two international hub ports as the sea gate into Indonesia, Kuala Tanjung in North Sumatra (western Indonesia) and Bitung in North Sulawesi (eastern Indonesia).

As the biggest archipelagic country, a well-connected Indonesia also supports regional and global connectivity, including the ACI's Asia Economic Connectivity Vision 2030 (AECV2030) that promotes connectivity across Asia, driven by ASEAN leadership.[18] Acknowledging the importance of maritime connectivity, AECV2030 offers five proposals, ranging from positioning ASEAN as the leading manufacturing base; increasing infrastructure investment to spearhead export-oriented growth; improving agricultural productivity for Asia to be the food basket of the world; enhancing regional cooperation for promoting liveability ecosystems; and positioning ASEAN as regional trade, business and service hub for Asia.

Indonesia's revived maritime posture is also in line with the Master Plan on ASEAN Connectivity (MPAC) which seeks to achieve inter-island connectivity by developing a "nautical high system" or proposed "ring shipping route" in Southeast Asia. The MPAC highlighted the development of 42 priority ports in ASEAN, of which 14 are located in Indonesia.[19] Indeed, Indonesia's maritime axis may inspire the Philippines as the other big archipelagic ASEAN member state with some 7,000 islands to follow suit, thus making maritime ASEAN as a whole more credible and connected with the MPAC.

The Chinese Foreign Minister iterated that "Indonesia is a key partner in the construction of a 21st century Maritime Silk Road,"[20] a vision attempting to revive a trade route linking China to Europe through the South China Sea and the Indian Ocean. With ASEAN and China as Indonesia's major trading partners, increased connectivity will further facilitate the ascension of Asia as a major global economic player. Plenty of opportunities are abound for Indonesia to assume greater role in the global value chain, offering the world with an alternative manufacturing base.

1.5 GOING FORWARD

The vision to enhance Indonesia's maritime infrastructure certainly looks promising. It is through sea that goods are traded across Indonesia's vast archipelago and eventually across the world. Various plans to build new ports and modernise existing ports are necessary to boost Indonesia's

[18]See Chapter 1 on "ACI Proposed Master Plan for Asia Economic Connectivity Vision 2030 (AECV2030)" in Tan *et al.* (2015d).

[19]See ASEAN Secretariat (2013).

[20]See Hussain (2014).

competitiveness. Beyond that, maritime development also involves revitalisation of the shipyard industry, improvement of more than 60 crossing ports, and procurement of a substantial number of vessels. Nevertheless, the success of such vision hinges upon the implementation.

For the Maritime Vision to be realised, the government has to secure investments, given limited state budget to fund the infrastructure projects. Involvement of private sector is required, which further raises the impetus for Indonesia to improve its business and regulatory environment. Accessing concessionary loans from international development banks can serve as an additional source of funding. Even with political will and funding in place, bureaucracy still becomes a hurdle and stumbling block for many infrastructure projects. Hence, cutting through the stifling bureaucracy is another key task.

Indonesia achieved a period of political stability and respectable GDP growth which averaged at 5.7% annually between 2004 and 2013. Behind this growth, however, is a story of dependence on commodity exports. As global demand slowed down and commodity prices fell in recent years, Indonesia was left with a meagre 4.7% growth in 2015; much lower than the 5.7% initially targeted by the state budget, and well below that achieved by Myanmar (8.3%), Vietnam (6.5%) and the Philippines (6.0%).

Analyses conducted by the ACI confirmed that Indonesia has substantially increased its competitiveness *vis-à-vis* other ASEAN countries between 2005 and 2010, but such advantage has declined steadily from 2010 onwards. In the meantime, the Philippines and Vietnam are quickly catching up (see Figure 1.1).

Figure 1.1: Indonesia's Overall Competitiveness Increased Substantially *vis-à-vis* Other ASEAN Countries Between 2005 and 2010, but Has Deteriorated Since Then

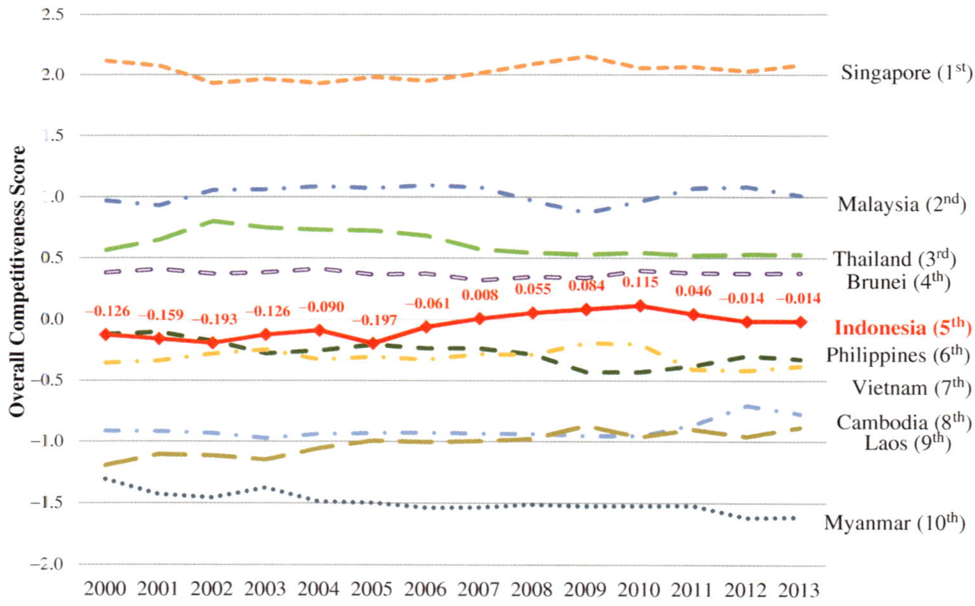

Note: Value in the parenthesis denotes the 2015 competitiveness ranking amongst ASEAN-10.
Source: Asia Competitiveness Institute.

Indonesia's pronouncement to achieve 7% growth by 2018 was followed by a series of stimulus such as tax amnesty and major policy revisions to trim the negative investment list, all in a bid to attract investment into Indonesia. In February 2016, Indonesia announced that 35 sectors have been taken out of the negative investment list, and the "recommendation" previously required for 83 other sectors have been removed. Beyond structural reforms, Indonesia is also mobilising more efforts towards the development of infrastructure, including those aimed at fostering better maritime linkages between the country's many islands.

In this regard, ACI's annual competitiveness analysis and simulation study for Indonesia *vis-à-vis* its ASEAN peers, as well as for Indonesia's 34 provinces, offers an instructive roadmap for Indonesia's policy-makers. Drawing on 121 variables over a period of 13 years, an objective identification of Indonesia's top 20% weakest indicators can provide much insight into the priority issues that the country needs to deal with to improve its competitiveness. Our findings highlight three critical issues for the development of Indonesia's manufacturing industries: infrastructure, bureaucracy and human resources.

1.5.1 Expanding Infrastructure

Indonesia's infrastructure condition is largely inadequate for both its least competitive as well as most competitive provinces. Power blackouts and brownouts occur throughout the country but happen alarmingly frequently outside of Java. Meanwhile, traffic congestion remains the norm in some of Indonesia's largest cities such as Jakarta, Surabaya and Makassar, with development of mass public transportation trailing behind an aggressive growth in the number of private vehicles. The ACI's studies found that high costs of logistics, including inadequate roads, uncertainty of traffic, and inefficient handling of ports are hampering businesses, even in Indonesia's 10 most competitive provinces. The State of Logistics Indonesia 2013 argued that Indonesia's logistics cost makes up 27% of the GDP in 2012, whereas such cost only makes up 20% in Thailand and 13% in Malaysia.[21] Also, reliable internet access remains a key distinguishing feature between the most competitive and the least competitive provinces.

The government is taking infrastructure development seriously, i.e. by amending the law to enable more public-private partnerships (PPPs), passing a law that eases land acquisition for public purposes, and more recently increasing its infrastructure budget by 50% between 2014 and 2015. Indonesia has identified a need for "Strategic Infrastructure Investment" worth almost USD 400 billion, wherein 41% would be financed by the state budget, and the remaining 59% by state-owned enterprises and the private sector.[22] To enable the PPP's to take place, the Ministry of Finance is providing fiscal support, among others in the form of Viability Gap Fund and the Indonesia Infrastructure Guarantee Fund. Despite good intentions, PPP in Indonesia is unfolding much slower compared that that taking place in the Philippines, for example. Due to coordination problems both among central government-level agencies as well as between the central and local governments, *The Economist* recently pointed out that, "too few shovels have hit dirt".

[21] See Bahagia, Sandee and Meeuws (2013).

[22] See Saragih (2015).

1.5.2 Improving Bureaucracy

The ACI's competitiveness analysis of Indonesia's 34 provinces found that corruption and bureaucracy-related issues feature prominently among the weakest indicators of the 10 least competitive provinces. Corruption is perceived as a major issue in eight out of 10 provinces, while seven out of 10 are facing problems in either Regulatory Governance or Rule of Law. Additionally, Inclusiveness and Accountability as well as Coordination of Local Governments each demand attention in six out of 10 least competitive provinces.

Indonesia in 2010 issued a "grand design" for bureaucracy reform[23] which aims to achieve three major goals: (1) a clean government free of corruption, collusion and nepotism, (2) increase in the quality of public services and (3) improvements in the performance and accountability of the public sector. Despite some progress in achieving better bureaucracy, most of the grand design's targets for 2014 have not been achieved. For example, Transparency International's Corruption Perception Index for Indonesia improved from 28 (2009) to 34 (2014), but still short of 50 targeted for 2014. Similarly, in terms of the World Bank's Doing Business ranking, Indonesia's position improved from 122nd (2009) to 109th place (2016). Again, this is still far from the 75th place originally aimed for 2014. To expedite achievement of the targets, President Joko Widodo's administration is focusing on streamlining business licensing procedures, implementing open recruitment for civil servants and closely monitoring and interacting with street-level bureaucracy.

Bureaucracy reform involves strengthening audits and law enforcement and institutionalising changes in more productive working norms and procedures. The Corruption Eradication Commission (KPK) has been playing a much needed role in dealing with high-level corruption cases and is slowly building a deterrent effect. However, the KPK's reach is limited and perpetrators have a larger chance of not being caught. Instead of heeding to some politicians' demand to regulate and weaken the KPK, Indonesia should instead expand the KPK model to its regions and instill higher transparency requirements for government projects.

1.5.3 Increasing Labour Productivity

The substantial rise in minimum wage across Indonesian provinces over the years has been worrying, but interestingly has caused business owners less concern compared to the fact that the labour force has not increased its productivity to match its cost. ACI's research found that firms are willing to invest in labour cost if their productivity justifies it. Ironically, as many as six out of Indonesia's 10 least competitive provinces cited Firms' Human Resource Capacity as among its top 20% weakest indicators, and the same proportion reported alarmingly low Net School Enrolment Rate for Secondary Schools. Despite Indonesia's achievement in expanding access to primary education, more is needed to bring the country to greater productivity and prosperity. In 2014, almost one half of the labour force only had primary school education and only about

---

[23] See Ministry of State Apparatus and Bureaucracy Reform of Indonesia (2010).

one-third were working in the formal and skilled sector. Lack of skilled labour has been argued to be Indonesia's biggest challenge in achieving economic development.[24]

In this context, Indonesia has turned to place more attention on its vocational and technical education system. In 2012, vocational secondary school students made up 49% of all secondary school students (the other 51% being enrolled in general secondary schools). This is an improvement compared to 2001, when vocational school students made up merely 36%. Now Indonesia is hoping to bring the proportion up to 60% by 2020. Graduates of vocational secondary schools tend to be more job-ready (an Organisation for Economic Co-operation and Development (OECD) report on Education in Indonesia reported that 94% of vocational school graduates entered the job market immediately upon completion), signalling high actual demand for skilled labour.[25]

The management of Indonesia's vocational education, however, still leaves plenty of room for improvement. Its success depends on the coordination of at least three ministries (Ministry of Education and Culture, Ministry of Manpower and Ministry of Industry) and employers have complained about the mismatch between vocational school curriculum and actual demand of industries. Few industries have been involved in the planning and development of curriculum and in the provision of facilities, equipment and trainers.

1.5.4 Adopting a More Regional Orientation

While Indonesia has achieved some progress in dealing with the issues described above, we argue that the speed and quality of such improvements are not enough to keep up with growing demand and economic growth potential, as well as the progress made by other countries in the region. Internal geographic disparity is rightly a concern in Indonesia with most of the GDP (61%) generated in Java. However, pragmatically speaking, if Indonesia were to seriously attract investment in the manufacturing sector, such investment is most likely to be attracted to cities in Java and a few other competitive cities outside the island, such as Makassar in South Sulawesi.

The province of East Java, in particular, has been ranked by ACI to be Indonesia's most competitive province outside of Jakarta for three years in a row. Even so, East Java potential is underutilised. As one of the country's major economic locomotives, East Java's growth in 2015 was 5.25% or only slightly above Indonesia's 4.7%. If President Jokowi's target of achieving 7% growth nationwide were to be achieved, East Java needs to grow by substantially more than 8%. In effect, it needs to play the role that Guangdong Province holds in China's growth, and it has the potential to do so. History shows that development and progress does not take place evenly across the lands, but starts initially in some places and spreads later to others. East Java should be allowed to grow faster and compete head-to-head with Southeast Asia's major growth centres. To ensure other places in Indonesia could follow in its footsteps, maritime connectivity between Java and the other main islands should be improved.

[24] See Asian Development Bank (2015).

[25] See OECD/Asian Development Bank (2015).

As Southeast Asia's largest economy and most populated country, Indonesia's growth helps determine the level of growth in the region. Indonesia shares Singapore's interest to maintain stability in the region and continue to prosper for that stability. By increasing its competitiveness, Indonesia is more likely to have an optimistic outlook and actively participate in the ASEAN Economic Community, which will ultimately benefit all the member countries. We look forward for Indonesia to regain its competitiveness and resume its economic momentum.

REFERENCES

ASEAN Secretariat. 2013. *Master Plan on ASEAN Connectivity*. Jakarta: ASEAN Secretariat.

Asian Development Bank. 2015. *Indonesia: Vocational Education Strengthening Project (ADB Completion Report)*. http://www.adb.org/sites/default/files/project-document/179095/33409-013-pcr.pdf (accessed February 2016).

Bahagia, Senator Nur, Henry Sandee and René Meeuws. 2013. *State of Logistics Indonesia 2013*. The World Bank Office Jakarta, Center of Logistics and Supply Chain Studies — Institut Teknologi Bandung (ITB), Asosiasi Logistik Indonesia, Panteia/NEA. http://documents.worldbank.org/curated/en/2013/09/18197499/state-logistics-indonesia-2013 (accessed February 2016).

General Elections Commission. 2014. "Vision and Mission of Ir. H. Joko Widodo and Drs. H.M. Jusuf Kalla: Presidential and Vice Presidential Election 2014." http://www.kpu.go.id/koleksigambar/Visi_Misi_JOKOWI-JK.pdf (accessed July 31, 2015).

Hussain, Zakir. 2014. "Indonesia 'Key in China's Vision of Maritime Silk Road'." *The Straits Times*, November 4. http://www.straitstimes.com/st/print/3025463 (accessed July 31, 2015).

Hutchinson, Francis. 2013. "Singapore Asia's Largest Economy Needs Vast Improvements in Infrastructure." *ISEAS Perspective* No. 23/2013.

Indonesia-Investments. 2014. "Sea Toll Road of Indonesia will Reduce Country's Logistic Costs Sharply." November 30. http://www.indonesia-investments.com/news/todays-headlines/sea-toll-road-of-indonesia-will-reduce-countrys-logistics-costs-sharply/item2665 (accessed July 31, 2015).

Ministry of State Apparatus and Bureaucracy Reform of Indonesia. 2010. *Grand Design Reformasi Birokrasi 2010–2025 (Lampiran Peraturan Presiden Republik Indonesia Nomor 81 Tahun 2010)*. http://dpr.go.id/doksetjen/dokumen/reformasi-birokrasi--PERPRES-NOMOR-81-TAHUN-2010-TENTANG-GRAND-DESIGN-REFORMASI-BIROKRASI-2010-2025-1442913779.pdf (accessed February 2016).

Ministry of State Secretariat of the Republic of Indonesia. 2014 "Inaugural Address of President Joko Widodo at the MPR Building, Jakarta. 20 October 2014." http://www.setneg.go.id/index.php?lang=en&option=com_content&task=view&id=8267&Itemid=26 (accessed July 31, 2015).

Nazeer, Z. 2015. "Upbeat Jokowi Plans to Woo Singapore Investors during Visit." *The Straits Times*, July 27. http://www.straitstimes.com/singapore/upbeat-jokowi-plans-to-woo-singapore-investors-during-visit (accessed July 31, 2015).

Neary, Adelle. 2014. "Jokowi Spells Out Vision for Indonesia's Global Maritime Nexus." *Centre for Strategic and International Studies: Southeast Asia from Scott Circle* 5(24): 1–4.

OECD/Asian Development Bank. 2015. *Education in Indonesia: Rising to the Challenge*. Paris: OECD Publishing. http://dx.doi.org/10.1787/9789264230750-en.

Pisani, Elizabeth. 2014. *Indonesia, Etc.: Exploring the Improbable Nation*. New York: W. W. North and Company.

Sandee, Henry. 2011. "Promoting Regional Development in Indonesia through Better Connectivity." *World Bank*, March 13. http://www.worldbank.org/en/news/opinion/2011/03/13/promoting-regional-development-indonesia-through-better-connectivity (accessed July 31, 2015).

Saragih, Freddy R. 2015. *Indonesia Infrastructure Development*. Powerpoint Presentation of the Ministry of Finance, Republic of Indonesia. http://www.iesingapore.gov.sg/~/media/IE%20Singapore/Files/Events/iAdvisory%20Series/Indonesia_29Apr15/420Opportunities20in20Indonesias20PPP20sector.pdf (accessed February 2016).

Shekhar, Vibhanshu and Joseph Chinyong Liow. 2014. "Indonesia as a Maritime Power: Jokowi's Vision, Strategies, and Obstacles Ahead." *Brookings*, November. http://www.brookings.edu/research/articles/2014/11/indonesia-maritime-liow-shekhar (accessed July 31, 2015).

Tan Khee Giap, Linda Low, Tan Kong Yam and Kartik Rao. 2013a. *Annual Analysis of Competitiveness, Simulation Studies and Development Perspective for 35 States and Federal Territories of India: 2000–2010*. Singapore: World Scientific.

Tan, Khee Giap, Linda Low, Tan Kong Yam and Lim Lijuan Amanda. 2013b. *Annual Analysis of Competitiveness, Development Strategies and Public Policies on ASEAN-10: 2000–2010*. Singapore: Pearson.

Tan, Khee Giap, Mulya Amri, Linda Low and Tan Kong Yam. 2013c. *Competitiveness Analysis and Development Strategies for 33 Indonesian Provinces*. Singapore: World Scientific.

Tan, Khee Giap, Linda Low, Kartik Rao and Tan Kong Yam. 2015a. *2014 Regional Competitiveness Analysis and a Master Plan on Regional Development Strategies for India*. Singapore: World Scientific

Tan, Khee Giap, Nurina Merdikawati, Mulya Amri and Blake Harley Berger. 2015b. *2014 Annual Competitiveness Analysis and Development Strategies for Indonesian Provinces*. Singapore: World Scientific.

Tan, Khee Giap, Nurina Merdikawati, Mulya Amri and Tan Kong Yam. 2015c. *2014 Provincial and Inaugural Regional Competitiveness Analysis: Safeguarding Indonesia's Growth Momentum*. Singapore: World Scientific.

Tan, Khee Giap, Sangiita Yoong Wei Cher, Sasidaran Gopalan and Nguyen Le Phuong Anh. 2015d. *2014 Annual Competitiveness Ranking and Simulation Study for ASEAN-10 and Development Strategies to Enhance Asia Economic Connectivity*. Singapore: World Scientific.

Tan, Khee Giap, Yuan Randong, Sangiita Yoong Wei Cher and Yang Mu. 2013d. *Annual Analysis of Competitiveness, Simulation Studies and Development Perspective for 34 Greater China Economies: 2000–2010*. Singapore: World Scientific.

Tan, Khee Giap, Yuan Randong and Sangiita Yoong Wei Cher. 2015. *2014 Annual Provincial and Regional Competitiveness Analysis for Greater China Economies: Development Strategies under the New Normal*. Singapore: World Scientific.

The Jakarta Post. 2014. "Priok Dwelling Time Could be Cut to Four Days this Year." June 5. http://www.thejakartapost.com/news/2014/06/05/priok-dwelling-time-could-be-cut-four-days-year.html (accessed July 31, 2015).

The Jakarta Post. 2015. "Improvement in Dwelling Time Seen at Priok Port." October 27. http://www.thejakartapost.com/news/2015/10/27/improvement-dwelling-time-seen-priok-port.html (accessed February 2, 2016).

World Bank. 2008. "Spending for Development: Making the Most of Indonesia's New Opportunities." *Indonesia Public Expenditure Review.* Washington, DC: World Bank.

World Bank. 2014. *Connecting to Compete 2014: Trade Logistics in the Global Economy, the Logistics Performance Index and Its Indicators.* Washington, DC: World Bank.

Chapter 2

2015 Provincial Competitiveness Ranking and Simulation Study for Indonesia: An Annual Update

2.1 INTRODUCTORY REMARKS

Expectations ran high when Mr. Joko Widodo (Jokowi) was inaugurated as Indonesia's seventh president in October 2014. He started from humble beginnings as a furniture businessman turned mayor of Surakarta in Central Java and eventually Governor of the nation's capital, DKI Jakarta. His meteoric rise to the top was far from that of a typical politician supported by the entrenched oligarchs. President Jokowi was hailed as 'the people's president', owing to his casual approach in initialising public dialogues and popularising impromptu visits (*blusukan*) to keep track of the implementation of his policies.

His appointment was also welcomed by the international community, hoping that the new leader would transform Indonesia to greater heights. Within his first 100 days, he implemented structural reforms to reduce fuel subsidies, a necessary move to reallocate public funding to productive activities. There was no major public upheaval as anticipated, given such an opportune moment when public trust to the government was high and the world's oil price plunged.

The Jokowi administration pledged to boost the economy's annual growth rate to 7% from around 5% by 2016 (Parlina 2014). Nevertheless, challenges abound in 2015 especially when the country faced challenging external factors. Lower global commodity prices affected Indonesia's revenue especially when palm oil, metal and fossil fuels accounted for half of country's exports (Bank Indonesia 2015). The country's currency, Rupiah, also further weakened given the strengthening US Dollar as the prospect of a rate hike by the US Federal Reserve became imminent. Instead of closing the gap to reach the 7% annual growth target, the reported growth rate in 2014–2015 still hovered around 5%. The fourth quarter of 2015 recorded a 5.04% year-on-year (YOY) growth rate, the highest compared to the previous quarters of the same year (Table 2.1).

At the first and second quarters of 2015, growth was mainly supported by strong household consumption and gross fixed capital formation. Government consumption became the main engine of growth in the third and fourth quarter of 2015 as most public funds had been disbursed.[1] This also positively affected gross fixed capital formation which grew at 6.90% in the fourth

[1] Such sequencing in public funding disbursement — relatively small in the first two quarters and peak at the last two quarters — has been an annual phenomenon. In 2015, such slow disbursement was attributed to the fact that the revised budget only received parliamentary approval in February with accompanying regulations enacted in March 2015. The reorganisation of a number of ministries (e.g. establishment of new coordinating ministry for the maritime sector; transfer of higher education portfolio from ministry of education and culture to ministry of research, technology and higher education; etc.) also contributed to such delay (Sato and Damayanti 2015).

Table 2.1: Indonesia's Economic Performance (2010 Prices; % YOY)

	2014				2015			
	Q1	**Q2**	**Q3**	**Q4**	**Q1**	**Q2**	**Q3**	**Q4**
GDP	5.14	4.96	4.97	5.04	4.73	4.66	4.74	5.04
By expenditure								
Household consumption	5.25	5.14	5.13	5.11	5.01	4.97	4.95	4.92
Government consumption	6.06	−1.84	1.17	0.87	2.91	2.61	7.11	7.31
Gross fixed capital formation	5.16	4.08	4.48	4.59	4.63	3.88	4.79	6.90
Exports	3.16	1.37	4.84	−4.59	−0.62	−0.01	−0.60	−6.44
Imports	5.04	0.41	0.28	3.23	−2.19	−6.97	−5.90	−8.05

Source: Asia Competitiveness Institute as compiled from CEIC Indonesia Premium Database.

quarter of 2015. Exports plunged by –6.44%, owing to continued decline of global commodity prices and China's growth slowdown. Imports declined for the first time since 2014 and even dropped by –8.05% in the fourth quarter of 2015, showing a sign of sluggish domestic demand.

Despite the slowdown, there is still reason for optimism if the government's wide-ranging infrastructure projects began to materialise and other progressive policies to attract investment and resolve bottlenecks were well executed. President Jokowi has actively promoted Indonesia as an attractive investment destination in various local and international fora. He urged the Investment Coordinating Board (BKPM) to adopt major reforms in streamlining business processes. Though the full-fledged one-stop investment service had been implemented at the national level, further synchronisation has to be put in place for local licences under the jurisdiction of provinces, districts, and cities.[2]

The central government has allocated a record 290 trillion Rupiahs in the 2015 revised budget targeted for infrastructure projects. In the pipeline, there is a mega power plant project to produce an additional 35,000 megawatt (MW) of electricity by 2019 in more than 200 places across Indonesia (Susanto 2015). Reliable energy infrastructure is required for Indonesia to spearhead its downstream industries. The government also emphasised on using renewable resources such as geothermal and wind power to lower Indonesia's dependence on fossil fuels. The accomplishment of the target requires participation from the private sector, with roughly 10,000 MW produced by the state-owned electricity company (PT PLN) and 25,000 MW by the private enterprises.

President Jokowi's vision to improve maritime connectivity[3] is hoped to improve the flow of goods from one province to another, and also reduce logistic costs by 20% in the next five years. Better connected infrastructure throughout Indonesia's vast islands is also hoped to bridge economic disparity, especially between the easternmost provinces, Papua and West

[2] More of forthcoming research on ease of doing business in Indonesia will be briefly described in Chapter 6.

[3] Indonesia's maritime vision will certainly level up ASEAN maritime integration, as elaborated in Chapter 1 on "ACI Proposed Master Plan for Asia Economic Connectivity Vision 2030 (AECV2030)" in Tan *et al.* (2015d).

Papua, and the rest of Indonesia. In our previous competitiveness analysis (Tan *et al.* 2015b, 2015c), in spite of more provinces from Kalimantan and Sulawesi joining the top 10 group, there was still a tendency that competitiveness is skewed towards Java Island. Lifting Indonesia's competitiveness as a whole requires development to be geared towards unleashing the potential of each province.

In line with the above objective, Asia Competitiveness Institute (ACI) has tracked the competitiveness of Indonesia's provinces across the years, enabling policy-makers to assess the competitiveness profile of each province in Indonesia *vis-à-vis* their peers.[4] This chapter is organised as follows. Section 2.1 provides a snapshot to Indonesia's economic development. Section 2.2 outlines the methodology comprising the broad sweep of competitiveness review, the competitiveness framework, indicators, data sources, standardised score, and *what-if* competitiveness simulation. Section 2.3 discusses the empirical findings and Section 2.4 concludes by drawing out some policy implications.

2.2 RESEARCH METHODOLOGY

2.2.1 Broad Sweep of Competitiveness Review

Initially, the term "competitiveness" was closely associated to firms' performance (Porter 1980) with a notion that it was primarily firms that competed with each other. Over time, the discourse expanded into the national level (Porter 1990), as shown by the establishment of "Council on Competitiveness" or similar institution in various advanced industrialised countries. After all, the performances of those firms depend on various factors that are embedded in the firms' location that include, but not limited to, quality of labour and infrastructure, governance, costs of doing business, as well as the performance of competing and complementary firms around the area (Bristow 2010; Camagni 2002; Kitson, Martin and Tyler 2004).

The more common approach to measure a country's competitiveness is by constructing a benchmarking index, as adopted by the two highly cited cross-country competitiveness studies, *World Competitiveness Yearbook* by International Institute for Management Development (IMD) and *Global Competitiveness Report* by World Economic Forum. The benchmarking index is effective at summarising complex and multi-dimensional factors in a user-friendly and easily digestible platform. The information from the ranking, score, and progress over time can facilitate discussion with general public to promote key reforms that often require multi stakeholders efforts.

Beyond country-level competitiveness, there are more studies delving into the sub-national level, either at state/provincial level, or district/city level. For instance, the Beacon Hill Institute at Suffolk University has been publishing the annual competitiveness report for 50 states in US since 2001. As previously mentioned in Chapter 1, the ACI has also been analysing the sub-national competitiveness not only in Indonesia, but also in India and China (Tan *et al.* 2015a; 2015b; 2015c; 2015d; Tan, Yuan and Yoong 2015). Going deeper into a smaller subset

[4]For Indonesia's competitiveness *vis-à-vis* the rest of countries from Association of Southeast Asian Nations (ASEAN), please see Tan *et al.* (2015d).

of economic entity allows us to suggest development strategy which are relevant to stimulate productive discussion among key stakeholders at the sub-national level in the first instance, before engaging them at the national level.

2.2.2 The ACI's Competitiveness Framework

The ACI's approach to competitiveness is integrated and systemic, encompassing different factors that collectively shape the ability of an economy to achieve substantial and inclusive economic development over a sustained period of time.

In line with this comprehensive approach, the ACI defines competitiveness through four different environments and 12 sub-environments as the following:

1. Macroeconomic Stability

This environment encompasses aggregated economic conditions that underline the comparative and competitive advantage of each province based on classical macroeconomic indicators.

(a) *Regional Economic Vibrancy*

This sub-environment captures the size of each province's economy and its growth trajectory according to different characteristics in their economic structure. Beyond gross regional domestic product (GRDP), this sub-environment also takes into account inflation rate as well as capital formation.

(b) *Openness to Trade and Services*

This sub-environment measures the degree of openness to international trade for each province. All indicators related to exports, imports, and the ratio of openness are included.

(c) *Attractiveness to Foreign Investors*

This sub-environment measures to what extent each province manages to attract both foreign and direct investment. Considering that both foreign and direct investment may fluctuate on a yearly basis, we use the average value of the last three years of investment for each province.

2. Government and Institutional Setting

This environment covers the efficacy of government institutions as well as expectations of progress in the public sector.

(a) *Government Policies and Fiscal Sustainability*

This sub-environment captures the financial capacity of each provincial government to ensure fiscal sustainability to undertake various policies under their jurisdiction. All fiscal related indicators, such as provincial government's revenue, tax collection, expenditure and fiscal balance are included.

(b) *Institutions, Governance and Leadership*

This sub-environment covers the broad spectrum of governance quality ranging from how prevalent the corruption practice to how well the provincial government coordinate among different layers of local governments.

(c) *Competition, Regulatory Standards and Rule of Law*
This sub-environment covers to what extent each province is able to create and enforce consistent rule of law and regulation that allow competition and ease of doing business to thrive.

3. Financial, Businesses and Manpower Conditions
This environment encompasses the performance and potential of firms as well as conditions that managers face in running their companies.

(a) *Financial Deepening and Business Efficiency*
This sub-environment captures the availability of sound financial system to support the growing firms. Additionally, wide-ranging assessments to firms' performance, strategy, human resource and equipment capacity, application of information technology and innovation are included.

(b) *Labour Market Flexibility*
This sub-environment covers the size of each province's labour force, employment, and unemployment rate, as well as the stickiness of labour market as measured by minimum monthly wage, ease of recruiting managerial and technical workers and relationship between labour unions and management.

(c) *Productivity Performance*
This sub-environment covers all indicators related to productivity as measured by the output per worker, both in general term and specific to each economic structure.

4. Quality of Life and Infrastructure Development
This environment covers wide-ranging indicators related to physical and technological infrastructure as well as provision of basic social services.

(a) *Physical Infrastructure*
This sub-environment not only captures the market size as measured by population and urbanisation rate but also the physical infrastructure including, air, sea and land connectivity as well as access to water and electricity services.

(b) *Technological Infrastructure*
This sub-environment captures the rate of information, communications and technology (ICT) adoption in each province. All indicators related to telephone, hand phone, desktop and laptop ownership as well as internet access at various location points are included.

(c) *Standard of Living, Education, and Social Stability*
This sub-environment encompasses access to education and healthcare, as well as broader set of measurement for quality of life such as equality of income distribution, environmental sustainability, and accessibility of goods and services.

As visualised in Figure 2.1, each environment contributes the same weight (25%) to the Overall Competitiveness index. The ACI's competitiveness framework further drills down to nested approach, wherein each of the four environments is further divided into three

Figure 2.1: The ACI's Competitiveness Framework

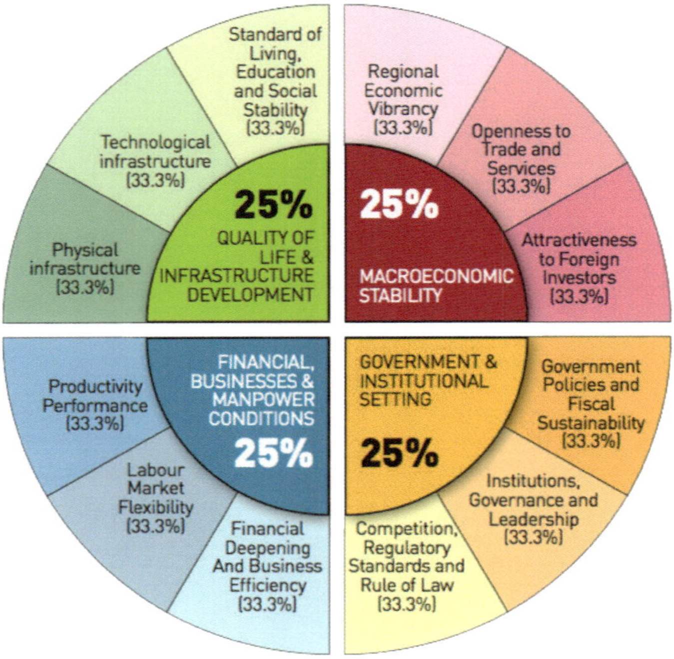

Source: Asia Competitiveness Institute.

sub-environments. Therefore, there are 12 sub-environments altogether. Each sub-environment contributes the same weight (33.3%) towards its respective environment's index.

In aggregating sub-environments into environments, and environments into an overall ranking, ACI uses a simple averaging mechanism with equal weights. While assigning different weights for different indicators with varying levels of importance may seem appropriate, the implementations are as controversial. Thus, to achieve a balanced view towards the different factors that make up an overall notion of competitiveness, we use equal weights across all indicators.

2.2.3 Indicators and Data Sources

The ACI's 2015 index for both provincial and regional ranking uses a combination of secondary and primary data, with a total of 103 indicators. Although the weight assigned to the four environments is equal (25% each), the weight of each indicator depends on the number of indicators present in each sub-environment. Depending on the availability of data, some environments and sub-environments have more indicators than others. See Appendix 1 for the complete list of indicators.

The uneven distribution of indicators across sub-environments due to data availability is acknowledged, but it is not an issue. Regardless of the number of indicators in a sub-environment, they will simply average out. This also allows a certain amount of flexibility in adding or removing indicators when updating the index in the future, as long as the overall structure of the 12 sub-environments nested within the four environments does not change.

Secondary Data

Secondary data (78 out of 103 indicators) were drawn from various government agencies, such as Indonesia's Central Statistical Agency (BPS), Bank Indonesia, Ministry of Trade, Ministry of Health, and Ministry of Environment and Forestry. We also collected data from other sources, such as World Bank's Indonesia Database for Policy and Economic Research (INDO-DAPOER) and CEIC Indonesia Premium Database which cited BPS as their original sources. In addition, we collaborated with data providers closely to ensure the accuracy, continuity and consistency of the data. Since Corruption Perception Index generated by Transparency International Indonesia has revamped its methodology significantly and would only release its updated study based on a smaller number of cities from selected provinces in 2015, we decided to drop this indicator. Hence, we have a total of 103 indicators in the 2015 index as compared to 104 indicators in the 2014 index. Due to lag in data availability, the latest available data at the time of collection in mid-2014 came from 2012.

Primary Data

A smaller portion of the data (25 out of 103 indicators) was based on primary data, through perception surveys conducted in each province in the second half of 2014. Survey questions are drafted to capture subjective perceptions on specific topics related to competitiveness that are not easily quantifiable. For instance, provincial governance system, quality of public services and firms' innovation and human resource capacity. The survey results allow us to capture the more recent dynamics of competitiveness in each province, to complement the secondary data where time lags are inevitable.

Three categories of stakeholders were surveyed separately in each province, namely, business owners and operators, provincial government officials and academicians. Responses from the three different stakeholders were aggregated at the province level, with the intention that one stakeholder group can provide a balancing view for the other stakeholders.

Due to resource limitations, the sampling method was purposive sampling, instead of random sampling. The ACI collaborated with local partners representing the three types of stakeholders. For business owners and operators, the surveys were done in collaboration with the Indonesian Employers' Association (APINDO), which has chapters in each province and invited their members to participate in the survey. For government respondents, the surveys were supported by the Coordinating Ministry for Economic Affairs, which provided reference letters to the governors of the 33 provinces.[5] The provincial government, in turn, invited representatives from various

[5]North Kalimantan became Indonesia's newest province in 2012, bringing the total number of provinces up to 34. However, as formal statistics between North Kalimantan and East Kalimantan has not been disaggregated, the discussion on North Kalimantan is included in the chapter on East Kalimantan.

Figure 2.2: Characteristics of Survey Respondents

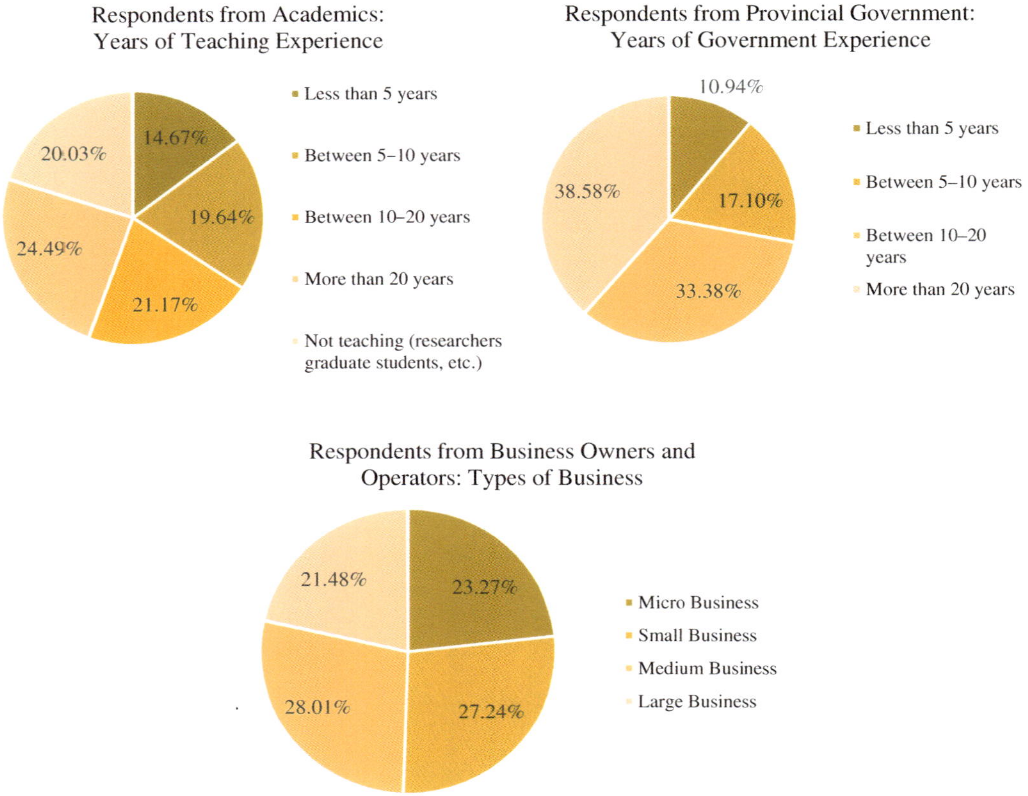

Source: Asia Competitiveness Institute.

provincial government agencies to participate in the survey. For academics, the ACI collaborated with universities in each province, most often with the school of economics and business, but not exclusively so. The university or school then invited their lecturers, researchers and graduate students to participate in the survey.

Figure 2.2 illustrates the characteristics of our respondents. From academic stakeholders, almost one-fourth (24.5%) of our respondents were senior lecturers with more 20 years in teaching experience. Comparable trend was also observed for respondents from provincial government, with more than one-third (38.6%) of our respondents have been working for more than 20 years in the government. For business owners and operators, we have equal representations from micro, small, medium, and large businesses. This classification is based on Law No. 20/2008 on micro, small, and medium enterprises that defines micro enterprise as a business unit which has annual sales of less than 300 million Rupiahs; small enterprise with annual sales of 300 million Rupiahs to 2.5 billion Rupiah; medium enterprise with 2.5 billion Rupiahs to 50 billion Rupiahs; and large enterprise with more than 50 billion Rupiahs.

The surveys were conducted using an electronic response system, where questions were presented on a computer projector and participants were to key in their answers using keypads or "clickers". Facilitators from ACI were present in each survey to read the questions and give clarifications when needed. In a rare case where an electronic survey could not be conducted, respondents were given paper-based survey forms to fill in. The fact that the surveys were done in face-to-face manner also provided good opportunity for ACI to discuss specific topics in more detail with relevant parties who are knowledgeable about their province.

The surveys managed to capture a total of 2,331 respondents. Of these, 790 were business owners and operators (33.9%), 806 were academics (34.6%) and 735 were provincial government officials (31.5%). The number of respondents is equivalent to about 70 respondents per province on average (2,331 respondents divided by 33 provinces). Out of these 70 respondents, typically 24 were business owners and operators, 24 were academics and 22 were provincial government officials.

2.2.4 Standardised Score

Upon completion of data collection, the next step is to determine how to aggregate the different types of data into one coherent way of analysis. There are 103 different indicators used in this research, each in different value or quantity terms, such as Government Revenue in thousands of Rupiahs or Cargo at International Seaport in tonnes and survey results in Likert Scale. How do we resolve these differences in the measurement units?

We use a statistical methodology of 'standardised score'. The standardised score is a relative comparison to see how well the performance of a certain province is, in comparison to the average province. Therefore, the unit of measurement is no longer relevant. The standardised score has no unit of measurement because it simply measures relative performance among provinces, whatever the indicator is. In statistical terms, it measures how many standard deviations away is each province from the average province. See Appendix 2 for technical explanation on computing the rankings.

If a province has a standardised score of zero, it is basically an average performer in terms of that particular indicator. Having a negative score means the province performs below average. Having a positive score, on the other hand, means above-average performance. The further away the score is from zero, the further away is the performance of said province from the national average. There were four standardisations conducted: (1) at the indicator level, (2) after aggregating indicators into sub-environments, (3) after aggregating sub-environments into environments and (4) after aggregating environments into overall competitiveness.

The standardised scores for each indicator are then systematically aggregated, firstly at the sub-environment level, followed by re-aggregation at the environment level, and finally, at the overall level. This allows for comparison of performance between the 33 provinces (or six regions) at different levels, from the overall competitiveness to specific indicators.

2.2.5 *What-if* Competitiveness Simulation

A competitiveness ranking in itself is like a beauty contest. It identifies who are doing well and who are facing challenges, but stops short of giving more constructive advice on improving the rankings. It is in this context that there is a need to go one step beyond by tackling the "so what" question.

The wealth of data that we have allows us to do an in-depth analysis of the performance of each province according to the different indicators, sub-environments and environments. Hence, we are able to identify not only the rankings *per se*, but also the specific indicators for which the province is doing well or struggling.

The ACI's *what-if* competitiveness simulation is based on the improvement of each province's top 20% weakest indicators by policies, and a re-calculation of the standardised score based on such improvement. To conduct the simulation, we firstly looked at each province and sorted the different indicators for each province from the highest to the lowest score. This allowed us to identify the top 20% weakest indicators of each province. Next, we raised the scores of these 20% weakest indicators moderately to match the average score. This means that the scores of these indicators are raised to zero, if previously negative. If they are already zero or positive, then no changes are made to the scores.

Once these scores were raised, we re-calculated the ranking with the assumption that other provinces remained constant. Therefore, this policy simulation was done one-by-one for each province. Each province would then have a new and improved standardised score. This allowed us to answer the question: if a particular province improves on its weakest indicators while assuming that other provinces remain constant, how would that province's competitiveness ranking improve?

2.3 EMPIRICAL FINDINGS

2.3.1 Review of Ranking and Score

Using the methodology introduced in Section 2.2, the rankings are derived by sorting the scores of each province as shown in Tables 2.2–2.6. For rankings on each of the four environments, their respective sub-environment scores are also provided. Additionally, rankings are illustrated on maps to gain insights on the geographical spread of diverse performances across provinces. The 2015 results are based on 2012 secondary data collected from official sources and 2014 primary data collected from ACI's perception survey.[6]

Review of Ranking and Score: Overall Competitiveness

With persistence economic disparity favouring Java Island, it is not surprising that Java's six provinces dominate the top 10 (Table 2.2). DKI Jakarta as the nation's capital is still considered an outlier, given its extremely high score (3.260) compared to the runner up, East Java (1.951) with a score difference of 1.309. Banten returns to the top 10, achieving ninth rank, after dropping out to 12th position in the 2014 study. Most top performers stay at the top with no or minimal change in ranking. Riau Islands records the highest jump of four positions to seventh,

[6]As of 2016, there are 34 provinces in Indonesia. North Kalimantan, the newly created province carved out of East Kalimantan in 2012, is included not as an individual province, but as part of East Kalimantan, due to lack of disaggregated data. Henceforth, the discussion on East Kalimantan includes North Kalimantan as well.

Table 2.2: 2015 Overall Competitiveness: Ranking and Score

2015 Rank	2014 Rank	Province	Score
1	1	DKI Jakarta	3.260
2	2	East Java	1.951
3	3	East Kalimantan	1.769
4	5	West Java	1.133
5	4	Central Java	1.057
6	6	DI Yogyakarta	0.900
7	11	Riau Islands	0.724
8	8	South Kalimantan	0.422
9	12	Banten	0.411
10	7	South Sulawesi	0.356
11	10	North Sulawesi	0.246
12	14	Bali	0.159
13	15	Central Kalimantan	0.141
14	27	Jambi	–0.048
15	19	North Sumatra	–0.075
16	9	Riau	–0.202
17	16	South Sumatra	–0.256
18	25	West Sulawesi	–0.262
19	18	West Kalimantan	–0.300
20	21	Central Sulawesi	–0.301
21	29	Southeast Sulawesi	–0.336
22	17	West Sumatra	–0.341
23	30	Bengkulu	–0.562
24	13	Aceh	–0.652
25	24	Lampung	–0.707
26	22	West Nusa Tenggara	–0.762
27	28	Gorontalo	–0.819
28	26	West Papua	–0.968
29	23	Maluku	−1.124
30	20	Bangka Belitung Islands	−1.126
31	33	North Maluku	−1.152
32	32	East Nusa Tenggara	−1.162
33	31	Papua	−1.375

Source: Asia Competitiveness Institute.

from its initial rank of 11th. The province's Batam, Bintan, and Karimun Special Economic Zone (SEZ) is a hub for global manufacturing that drives the much needed value-added economic output to spearhead its competitiveness. East Kalimantan (3rd), South Kalimantan (8th) and South Sulawesi (10th) remain in the top 10, steadily positioning their role as the economic engines of eastern part of Indonesia. In total, there are only 13 out of 33 provinces with positive standardised scores.

On the other hand, North Maluku (31st), East Nusa Tenggara (32nd) and Papua (33rd), stay at the bottom three. In fact, Papua's score is substantially lower than its peers (–1.375). Poor maritime connectivity presents a disadvantage for Indonesia's easternmost provinces riddled by lack of hard and soft infrastructure. Steep price disparity for primary commodities is one of the downsides, and remains as a perennial issue to be solved. The maritime outlet pilot project, initiated by Ministry of Trade and Ministry of Transportation, is hoped to tackle the issue by ensuring frequent vessels covering western, central and eastern parts of Indonesia to bring containers of staple food, as part of realisation of central government's sea toll programme (Antara News 2015).

The Overall Competitiveness ranking can also be viewed on a map of Indonesian provinces, as seen in Figure 2.3. On the map, provinces are colour coded based on three groups: top 10 positions (green), bottom 10 positions (red) and middle 13 positions (yellow). More noticeable geographic concentration of high, mediocre, and low competitiveness provinces can be observed. Majority of top provinces are located in Java Island, while the remaining four provinces spread across Sumatra (Riau Islands), Kalimantan (East Kalimantan and South Kalimantan) and Sulawesi (South Sulawesi). Bottom 10 provinces are mostly part of the eastern region, highlighting that disparity between eastern region *vis-à-vis* the rest of Indonesia from 2015 ranking is more pronounced than the one found in 2014 ranking (Tan *et al.* 2015b, 2015c).

Figure 2.3: 2015 Map of Overall Competitiveness Ranking

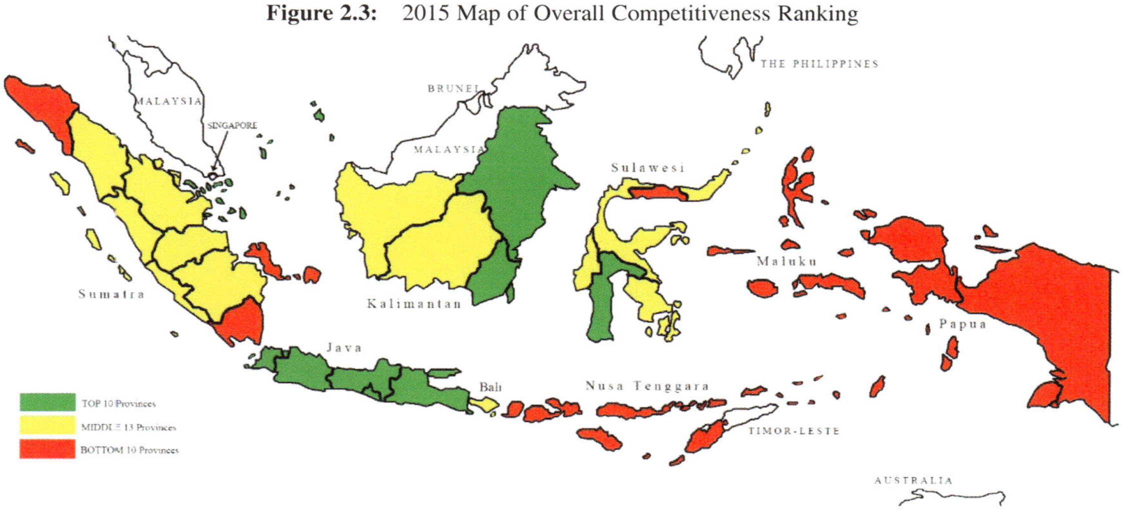

Source: Asia Competitiveness Institute.

The low performing provinces from the western grouping are mostly part of Sumatra Island, namely Aceh (24th), Lampung (25th), and Bangka Belitung Islands (30th). Meanwhile, more than half of provinces from Sumatra Island as well as Sulawesi Island belong to the middle 13 group. Hence, we can infer that for Overall Competitiveness, that (i) provinces in Java tend to be highly competitive; (ii) provinces in Kalimantan are either competitive or mediocre; (iii) mediocre provinces are mostly found in Sumatra and Sulawesi and (iv) provinces in eastern region of Indonesia tend to perform poorly in the competitiveness ranking.

Review of Ranking and Score: Macroeconomic Stability

DKI Jakarta (4.309) tops the Macroeconomic Stability ranking, further strengthening its unwavering position as the epicentre of Indonesia's economic growth (Table 2.3). The score gap with the runner-up, East Java (2.003), is even more profound (2.306). The provinces in the top 10 has a distinct comparative advantage in either fossil fuel resources (East Kalimantan and Riau) or rapid industrialisation (mostly provinces in Java Island except DI Yogyakarta). However, being rich in natural resources is not a determining factor to excel in this environment, as can be seen by the relatively lower rank obtained by Aceh (26th) — rich in natural gas — and Papua (22nd), where copper and gold are abundant.

Most provinces at the top 10 excel in all three sub-environments, though West Java falls short in its Openness to Trade and Services sub-environment. Its provincial government has urged for the development of an international seaport located in West Java to seamlessly send goods directly to the international market, thereby enhancing its openness to trade. The existing heavy reliance on land connectivity has put pressure on roads and congestion is inevitable. Despite cancellation of the long-awaited Cilamaya Port construction project in Karawang that would ease strain on the nation's Tanjung Priok Port, both the central and provincial governments are pushing forward for the project to be relocated further to the east, either in Subang or Indramayu (Antara News 2015).

On the other hand, the bottom 10 provinces tend to underperform in all sub-environments. Bengkulu, Bangka Belitung Islands, North Maluku, Aceh and Lampung score much lower in Attractiveness to Foreign Investors sub-environment. Meanwhile, Maluku and West Nusa Tenggara fall behind in Regional Economic Vibrancy sub-environment. By delving into sub-environment scores, each province can identify the underlying driver behind their performance in Macroeconomic Stability environment.

The map for Macroeconomic Stability (Figure 2.4) shows less apparent geographic clustering among the high, mediocre and low-competitiveness provinces. Although half of the top 10 provinces are from Java Islands, the remaining five provinces are scattered across Sumatra (Riau Islands at 5th; Riau at 9th and North Sumatra at 10th), Kalimantan (East Kalimantan at 4th) and Sulawesi (South Sulawesi at 8th). The middle 13 and bottom 10 provinces are even more spread out across the islands, except that there is no bottom 10 province in Kalimantan Island. We can infer that for Macroeconomic Stability, (i) provinces in Java tend to be highly competitive with the exception of DI Yogyakarta at 20th; (ii) provinces in Kalimantan are either competitive or mediocre performers; (iii) provinces in Sumatra and Sulawesi show mixed

Table 2.3: 2015 Macroeconomic Stability: Ranking and Score

2015 Rank	2014 Rank	Province	2015 Score	Sub–Environment Scores		
				REV	OTS	AFI
1	1	DKI Jakarta	4.309	3.765	4.869	3.040
2	2	East Java	2.003	2.221	0.900	2.305
3	3	West Java	1.403	1.951	–0.414	2.264
4	4	East Kalimantan	0.952	0.750	0.768	1.063
5	5	Riau Islands	0.851	0.569	1.858	–0.123
6	7	Banten	0.461	0.132	–0.026	1.142
7	6	Central Java	0.409	0.905	0.039	0.165
8	11	South Sulawesi	0.191	0.017	–0.388	0.889
9	8	Riau	0.090	0.487	0.026	–0.268
10	9	North Sumatra	0.074	0.419	0.204	–0.424
11	10	South Kalimantan	0.066	–0.506	0.658	0.026
12	12	South Sumatra	0.015	0.120	–0.273	0.193
13	13	North Sulawesi	–0.202	–0.257	–0.411	0.121
14	15	Central Kalimantan	–0.246	–0.536	–0.490	0.361
15	23	Southeast Sulawesi	–0.286	–0.332	–0.360	–0.084
16	16	Central Sulawesi	–0.293	–0.354	–0.507	0.069
17	17	West Sulawesi	–0.373	–0.420	–0.549	–0.042
18	18	Bali	–0.379	–0.342	–0.506	–0.178
19	14	West Papua	–0.393	0.188	–0.256	–0.996
20	22	DI Yogyakarta	–0.399	–0.475	–0.547	–0.060
21	20	Jambi	–0.422	–0.464	–0.396	–0.284
22	24	Papua	–0.439	–0.464	–0.108	–0.618
23	21	West Kalimantan	–0.448	–0.607	–0.375	–0.232
24	26	West Sumatra	–0.452	–0.244	–0.298	–0.681
25	29	Lampung	–0.545	–0.292	–0.201	–0.984
26	28	Aceh	–0.675	–0.192	–0.464	–1.171
27	27	West Nusa Tenggara	–0.678	–1.295	–0.449	–0.092
28	30	Maluku	–0.683	–1.011	–0.325	–0.513
29	32	North Maluku	–0.734	–0.720	–0.224	–1.043
30	25	Gorontalo	–0.756	–0.854	–0.523	–0.672
31	19	Bangka Belitung Islands	–0.773	–0.670	–0.208	–1.216
32	31	Bengkulu	–0.820	–0.588	–0.489	–1.144
33	33	East Nusa Tenggara	–0.831	–0.903	–0.534	–0.813

Note: MS = Macroeconomic Stability; REV = Regional Economic Vibrancy; OTS = Openness to Trade and Services; AFI = Attractiveness to Foreign Investors.
Source: Asia Competitiveness Institute.

Figure 2.4: 2015 Map of Macroeconomic Stability Ranking

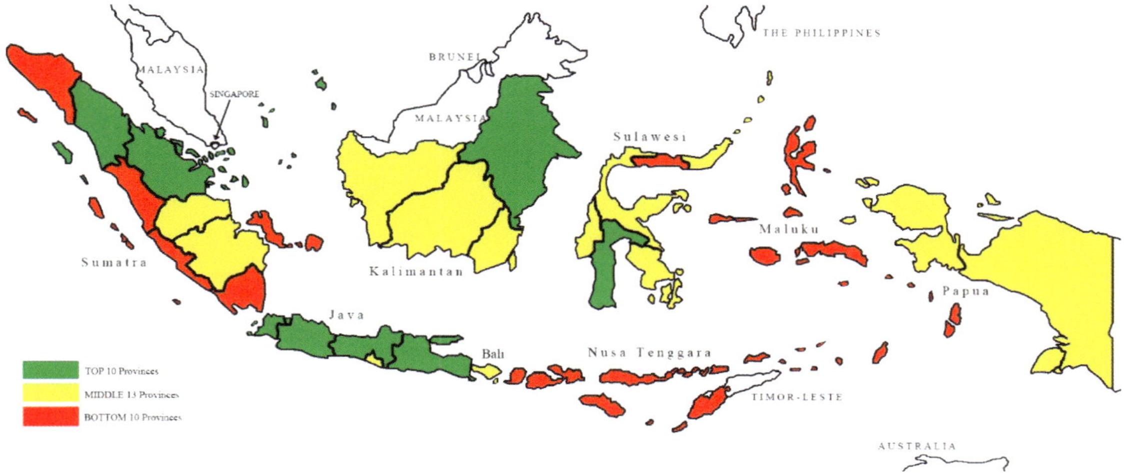

Source: Asia Competitiveness Institute.

performance as they host a range of high, mediocre and low-competitiveness provinces and (iv) provinces in Bali-Nusa Tenggara and Maluku–Papua islands tend to exhibit either low or mediocre performance.

Review of Ranking and Score: Government and Institutional Setting

In Table 2.4 for Government and Institutional Setting environment, the top 10 provinces are relatively more diverse. There are four provinces from Java Island, three from Kalimantan Island and three form Sulawesi Island. East Kalimantan (1.921) emerges as the runner-up, closely trails DKI Jakarta (2.074) with a relatively narrow gap (0.153). The spread of the scores between the top and bottom performing provinces are more symmetrical (DKI Jakarta: 2.074 and North Maluku: –1.755) compared to the other environments (Tables 2.3, 2.5 and 2.6).

Further analysing the performance at the respective sub-environments, only East Kalimantan (2nd), Central Java (4th), East Java (5th) and South Kalimantan (7th) fare equally well in all three sub-environments. DKI Jakarta's strongest boost comes from its stellar Government Policies and Fiscal Sustainability, while the remaining provinces exert their strengths from Institutions, Governance, and Leadership and Competition, Regulatory Standards, and Rule of Law sub-environments.

A similar pattern is also observed in the bottom three provinces where West Papua (31st), Bangka Belitung Islands (32nd) and North Maluku (33rd) perform poorly in all three sub-environments. On the other hand, Aceh and Riau's slides to the bottom 10 aredue to their poor performance in Institutions, Governance, and Leadership as well as Competition, Regulatory Standards and Rule of Law.

Table 2.4: 2015 Government and Institutional Setting: Ranking and Score

2015 Rank	2014 Rank	Province	2015 Score	Sub–Environment Scores		
				GPFS	IGL	CRRL
1	1	DKI Jakarta	2.074	4.647	–0.045	0.112
2	4	East Kalimantan	1.921	0.482	2.128	1.756
3	7	DI Yogyakarta	1.631	–0.197	1.936	1.968
4	2	Central Java	1.382	0.913	0.715	1.514
5	5	East Java	1.310	1.369	0.969	0.640
6	8	North Sulawesi	0.906	–0.387	1.296	1.149
7	11	South Kalimantan	0.688	0.347	0.725	0.493
8	19	Central Kalimantan	0.676	–0.281	0.915	0.903
9	10	West Sulawesi	0.628	–0.759	1.010	1.177
10	22	Southeast Sulawesi	0.611	–0.598	1.176	0.811
11	26	Jambi	0.606	–0.393	0.663	1.109
12	6	West Java	0.591	1.501	–0.495	0.337
13	3	South Sulawesi	0.495	–0.025	1.065	0.086
14	13	West Kalimantan	0.412	–0.273	0.069	1.140
15	12	Central Sulawesi	–0.002	–0.510	0.239	0.266
16	23	Banten	–0.054	0.587	–0.092	–0.618
17	17	South Sumatra	–0.084	–0.044	–0.114	–0.033
18	31	Riau Islands	–0.269	–0.256	–0.886	0.532
19	24	Bali	–0.321	0.086	0.005	–0.822
20	15	West Nusa Tenggara	–0.445	–0.454	–0.054	–0.503
21	32	East Nusa Tenggara	–0.454	–0.636	0.003	–0.400
22	18	Gorontalo	–0.598	–0.705	0.138	–0.793
23	30	Bengkulu	–0.611	–0.549	–0.609	–0.231
24	25	West Sumatra	–0.638	–0.280	–0.557	–0.614
25	28	Papua	–0.693	–0.532	–1.097	0.053
26	20	Maluku	–0.757	–0.687	0.135	–1.167
27	27	North Sumatra	–0.975	0.302	–0.945	–1.574
28	21	Lampung	–0.980	–0.212	–1.222	–0.794
29	9	Aceh	–1.024	–0.117	–0.821	–1.390
30	14	Riau	–1.089	–0.246	–1.132	–1.097
31	29	West Papua	–1.559	–0.754	–1.943	–0.846
32	16	Bangka Belitung Islands	–1.624	–0.496	–1.752	–1.443
33	33	North Maluku	–1.755	–0.843	–1.424	–1.721

Note: GIS = Government and Institutional Setting; GPFS = Government Policies and Fiscal Sustainability; IGL = Institutions, Governance, and Leadership; CRRL = Competition, Regulatory Standards and Rule of Law.
Source: Asia Competitiveness Institute.

Figure 2.5: 2015 Map of Government and Institutional Setting Ranking

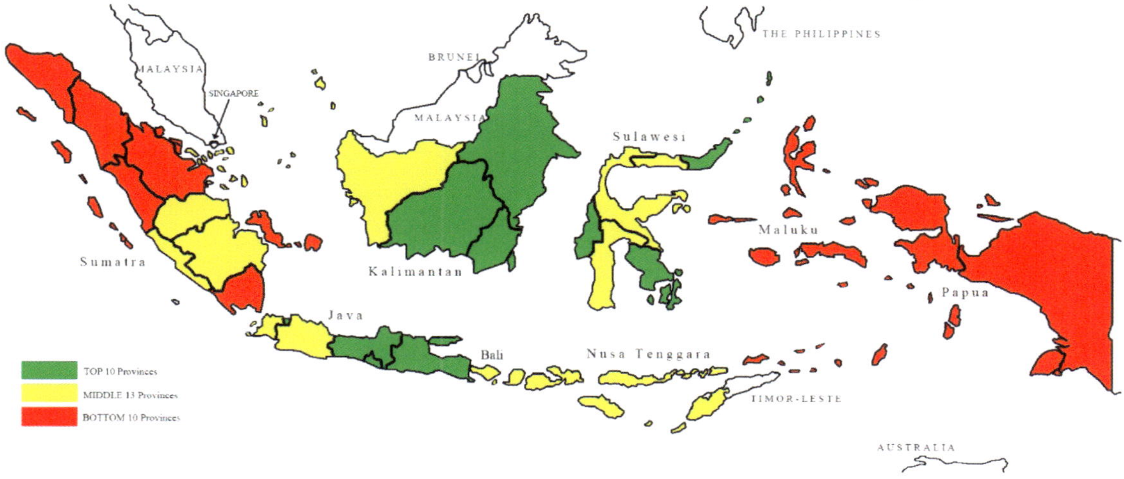

Source: Asia Competitiveness Institute.

Figure 2.5 shows noticeable geographical concentration of high and low-competitiveness provinces. The top 10 provinces tend to be located around Java, Kalimantan and Sulawesi islands. In fact, it is only in this Government and Institutional Setting environment that we can see more representations of non-Java provinces belonging to top 10 where three-fourths of provinces in Kalimantan Island and half of provinces in Sulawesi Island are part of the top 10. On the other hand, concentration of low performing provinces is found in Maluku–Papua cluster and Sumatra Island. The following general conclusions can be made in regard to the geographic spread of this environment, (i) provinces in Java, Sumatra and Kalimantan are either competitive or mediocre; (ii) provinces in Bali-Nusa Tenggara tend to be mediocre; (iii) provinces in Sumatra exhibit either low or mediocre performances; (iv) competitiveness of provinces in Maluku–Papua is relatively low.

Review of Ranking and Score: Financial, Businesses and Manpower Conditions

The top 10 in Financial, Businesses and Manpower Conditions (Table 2.5) largely consists of incumbent provinces with three newcomers — West Papua (7th), Bali (8th) and DI Yogyakarta (9th). It is very encouraging to have one of the easternmost provinces, West Papua, among the top 10 despite lagging performance of its immediate neighbour, Papua (29th). Other easternmost provinces are far behind, with Maluku being the last (33rd). In this environment, we see another example where the standardised score is skewed upwards, where DKI Jakarta's score (3.340) is much higher than that of Maluku (−1.598).

Among the top 10, there is a pattern that provinces located in Java Island tend to excel in their Labour Market Flexibility sub-environment, owing to their large pool of workforce. However,

Table 2.5: 2015 Financial, Businesses and Manpower Conditions: Ranking and Score

2015 Rank	2014 Rank	Province	2015 Score	Sub–Environment Scores		
				FDBE	LMF	PP
1	1	DKI Jakarta	3.340	3.527	−0.138	3.597
2	3	East Java	2.095	1.205	3.253	−0.076
3	2	Central Java	1.591	1.106	2.829	−0.608
4	4	East Kalimantan	1.304	0.601	−0.771	2.899
5	5	West Java	1.244	0.321	2.541	−0.259
6	6	Riau Islands	0.521	−0.342	−0.281	1.713
7	12	West Papua	0.459	0.829	−0.993	1.123
8	17	Bali	0.422	0.514	0.856	−0.487
9	13	DI Yogyakarta	0.320	0.676	0.613	−0.620
10	7	Riau	0.256	−0.040	−0.399	0.974
11	9	Central Kalimantan	0.089	0.481	−0.323	0.028
12	8	West Kalimantan	0.080	0.111	0.195	−0.139
13	21	North Sumatra	0.065	−0.059	0.092	0.103
14	10	South Sulawesi	0.010	0.492	−0.220	−0.251
15	15	South Kalimantan	0.006	0.252	−0.033	−0.207
16	30	West Sulawesi	−0.075	0.669	−0.134	−0.692
17	22	Banten	−0.079	0.330	−0.291	−0.205
18	16	North Sulawesi	−0.176	0.441	−0.802	−0.007
19	24	Bengkulu	−0.281	0.150	−0.101	−0.637
20	28	Jambi	−0.323	−0.174	−0.067	−0.434
21	26	Lampung	−0.416	−0.466	0.170	−0.573
22	27	Central Sulawesi	−0.416	−0.235	−0.402	−0.233
23	31	North Maluku	−0.455	0.415	−0.528	−0.839
24	19	West Sumatra	−0.512	−0.479	−0.575	−0.016
25	18	South Sumatra	−0.566	−1.100	−0.025	−0.058
26	25	Aceh	−0.740	−0.309	−1.132	−0.107
27	33	Gorontalo	−0.941	−0.373	−0.702	−0.893
28	14	Bangka Belitung Islands	−0.954	−1.400	−0.566	−0.030
29	11	Papua	−0.994	−1.569	−0.403	−0.108
30	32	Southeast Sulawesi	−1.046	−1.533	−0.180	−0.475
31	29	East Nusa Tenggara	−1.099	−0.994	−0.435	−0.869
32	20	West Nusa Tenggara	−1.130	−1.406	−0.195	−0.762
33	23	Maluku	−1.598	−1.639	−0.852	−0.851

Note: FBMC = Financial, Businesses and Manpower Conditions; FDBE = Financial Deepening and Business Efficiency; LMF = Labour Market Flexibility; PP = Productivity Performance.
Source: Asia Competitiveness Institute.

DKI Jakarta is rather behind in this aspect as its unemployment rate and minimum wage per month are among the highest in the country. Other provinces with heavy reliance on labour-intensive sectors tend to perform poorly in their Productivity Performance sub-environment, which is mostly determined by the ratio of value-added per worker.

For the bottom 10 provinces, they are mostly mediocre performers in one or two sub-environment(s) and laggards in the remaining sub-environment(s). East Nusa Tenggara's poor performance is not surprising as the province struggled with underutilisation of labour force (Tan *et al.* 2015c, 152–159). It is indeed imperative for the province to address this issue in order to improve its Productivity Performance sub-environment, currently the second lowest in the country.

According to Figure 2.6, the top 10 provinces are still dominated by those based in Java Island. Performance across provinces from the Maluku–Papua region is relatively varied with representations of top, mediocre and low performing provinces. Such variation is also observed in the case of Sumatra, with two provinces belonging to top 10 (Riau Islands at 6th and Riau at 10th), four provinces belonging to middle 13 (North Sumatra at 13th, Bengkulu at 19th, Jambi at 20th and Lampung at 21st), and four provinces belonging to bottom 10 (West Sumatra at 24th, South Sumatra at 25th, Aceh at 26th and Bangka Belitung Islands at 28th). Meanwhile, most provinces in Kalimantan and Sulawesi islands are mediocre performers.

Therefore, in general, we observe that (i) provinces in Java tend to be highly competitive; (ii) provinces in Sumatra and Maluku–Papua islands show mixed performance; (iii) provinces in Kalimantan Island show mediocre performance, except East Kalimantan which belongs to the top 10; (iv) provinces in Sulawesi Island are mostly mediocre performers, except Gorontalo and Southeast Sulawesi which belong to the bottom 10 group and (v) provinces in Nusa Tenggara tend to be low performers.

Figure 2.6: 2015 Map of Financial, Businesses and Manpower Conditions Ranking

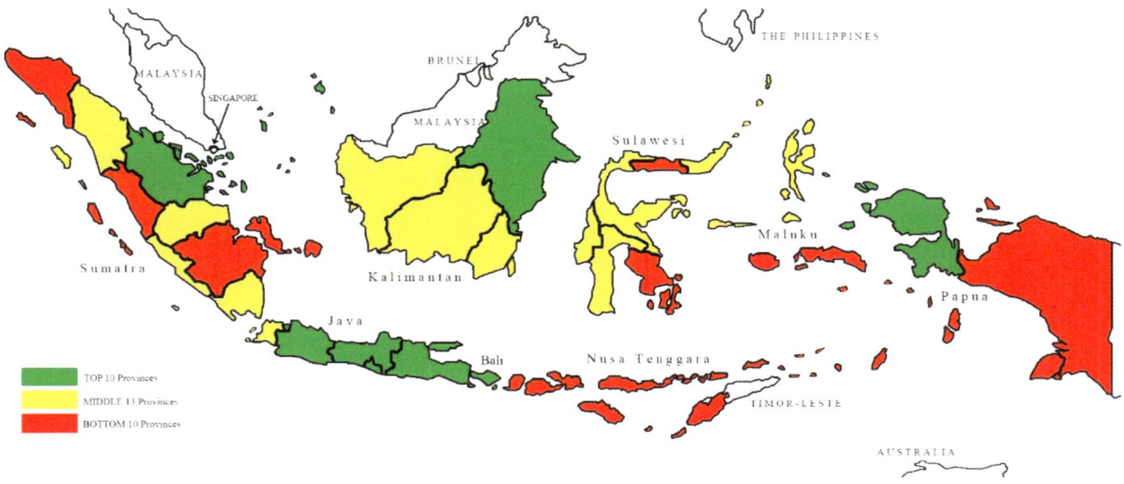

Source: Asia Competitiveness Institute.

Review of Ranking and Score: Quality of Life and Infrastructure Development

In Table 2.6, there is no significant change in terms of composition of provinces occupying the top 10, middle 13 and bottom 10, compared to the previous year. Such trend can indicate that it takes time to observe the impacts of policy reforms related to Quality of Life and Infrastructure Development environment. East Kalimantan tops the ranking, replacing DI Yogyakarta which now holds the runner-up position. In general, the scores of different provinces are distributed in a rather sequential pattern, with a significant gap observed between the scores of West Papua (−1.823) at 32nd and Papua (−2.584) at 33rd. This is proof that for this environment, the scores are skewed downwards towards, Papua, unlike the situation found in previous environments (Tables 2.3, 2.4 and 2.5) with strikingly high scores for the top performing province, DKI Jakarta.

The highly populated provinces in Java Island tend to report sub-standard performance in Standard of Living, Education and Social Stability sub-environment. Only East Java is the exception as the province is consistently acquiring high scores in all three respective sub-environments. There is plenty of opportunities to learn from one another for cross fertilisation of ideas to improve the provision of public services, especially those related to education and health services.

Papua's position as the least performing province for two consecutive years with its very low score is worrying. Particularly, Papua is far behind the rest of Indonesia's provinces in terms of Standard of Living, Education, and Social Stability sub-environment (−3.500). Although the Special Autonomy Law No. 21/2001[7] provided significant funding for Papua to catch up in terms of improving its people's living standards *vis-à-vis* other provinces, the progress has been less than expected. Systematic and continuous policy reforms to gradually enhance the physical connectivity across Papua's challenging landscape and improve capability of its human resources are required for Papua to move upwards in the competitiveness ranking.

The geographical concentration of low performing provinces is even more apparent in Figure 2.7. All provinces from easternmost region of Indonesia, including East Nusa Tenggara (31st), are part of the bottom 10 group. The remaining provinces are spread across Sumatra (Lampung at 24th and Bangka Belitung Islands at 25th), Kalimantan (West Kalimantan at 29th), and Sulawesi (Gorontalo at 26th and West Sulawesi at 30th). Provinces belonging to middle 13 group are even more spread out, dominated by those from Sumatra (six provinces), Kalimantan (one province), Sulawesi (four provinces), Java (one province) and Nusa Tenggara (one province). Hence, in general, (i) provinces in Java are highly competitive, (ii) provinces in Sumatra, Kalimantan, Sulawesi and Bali-Nusa Tenggara islands show mixed performance and (iii) provinces in Maluku–Papua tend to be low performers.

[7]Special Autonomy Law 21/2001 stipulated that natural resource revenues from Papua region are mostly to be returned to the provinces of Papua and West Papua, to be utilised under greater provincial autonomy.

Table 2.6: 2015 Quality of Life and Infrastructure Development: Ranking and Score

2015 Rank	2014 Rank	Province	2015 Score	Sub–Environment Scores		
				PI	TI	SLES
1	2	East Kalimantan	1.882	1.496	1.492	1.266
2	1	DI Yogyakarta	1.530	−0.257	1.704	2.012
3	3	DKI Jakarta	1.442	−0.212	3.571	−0.099
4	5	Riau Islands	1.378	0.608	1.939	0.568
5	4	East Java	1.276	2.239	0.148	0.498
6	7	Banten	1.079	2.427	0.989	−0.977
7	8	Bali	0.821	0.596	0.637	0.624
8	6	South Kalimantan	0.687	1.895	0.217	−0.558
9	15	West Java	0.644	1.197	0.414	−0.156
10	14	North Sumatra	0.578	0.839	−0.172	0.640
11	9	South Sulawesi	0.524	0.346	0.216	0.622
12	11	West Sumatra	0.434	−0.221	0.088	1.114
13	12	North Sulawesi	0.317	−0.245	0.049	0.911
14	13	Central Java	0.237	1.367	0.130	−0.960
15	10	Aceh	0.204	−0.168	−0.461	1.091
16	16	Riau	0.052	−0.358	0.034	0.441
17	19	Jambi	−0.028	−0.189	−0.282	0.408
18	17	Central Kalimantan	−0.036	−0.387	−0.269	0.576
19	21	Bengkulu	−0.213	−0.948	−0.206	0.673
20	18	South Sumatra	−0.241	−0.292	−0.248	−0.005
21	20	Central Sulawesi	−0.320	−0.189	−0.620	0.087
22	26	West Nusa Tenggara	−0.357	−0.222	−0.786	0.201
23	24	Southeast Sulawesi	−0.429	−0.470	−0.583	0.083
24	22	Lampung	−0.479	−0.754	−0.533	0.205
25	25	Bangka Belitung Islands	−0.507	−0.669	−0.257	−0.220
26	27	Gorontalo	−0.509	−0.649	−0.454	−0.048
27	23	Maluku	−0.812	−0.694	−0.884	−0.259
28	31	North Maluku	−1.004	−0.546	−1.335	−0.388
29	30	West Kalimantan	−1.072	−1.187	−0.371	−0.865
30	29	West Sulawesi	−1.076	−0.480	−1.067	−0.886
31	32	East Nusa Tenggara	−1.596	−0.818	−1.196	−1.594
32	28	West Papua	−1.823	−1.965	−0.648	−1.507
33	33	Papua	−2.584	−1.087	−1.255	−3.500

Note: QLID = Quality of Life and Infrastructure Development; PI = Physical Infrastructure; TI = Technological Infrastructure; SLES = Standard of Living, Education and Social Stability.
Source: Asia Competitiveness Institute.

Figure 2.7: 2015 Map of Quality of Life and Infrastructure Development Ranking

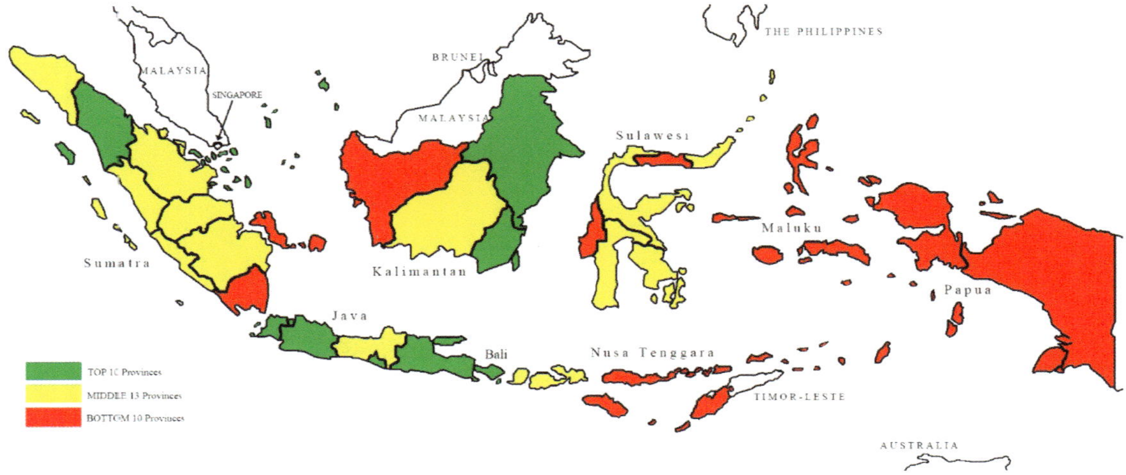

Source: Asia Competitiveness Institute.

2.3.2 Review of *What-if* Competitiveness Simulation

The details for *what-if* competitiveness simulation have been explained in Section 2.2.5. The results will be shown in Tables 2.7–2.11, comparing the ranking and score for each province before and after simulation. The simulation hopes to assist the provinces in prioritising key areas which will increase their competitiveness significantly.

Review of What-if *Competitiveness Simulation: Overall Competitiveness*

For Overall Competitiveness (Table 2.7), we have seen the pattern that significant changes in ranking are less likely to occur among the top 10 as the competition is already intense to begin with. Nevertheless, after policy simulation, their standardised scores increase, alerting that even low-hanging fruits exist for the top performers. Some provinces end up sharing the same ranking as the *what-if* competitiveness simulation assumes *ceteris paribus* (when simulation is conducted for one province, other provinces are held as constant). For instance, there are four provinces which eventually sit at 23rd position after the simulation, namely, Maluku, North Maluku, East Nusa Tenggara and Papua.

Some provinces emerge with much better ranking, demonstrating their potential to improve competitiveness. Bangka Belitung Islands' ranking increases by 14 positions with its standardised score improving from –1.126 to –0.207, the highest increment among all provinces. Such a leapfrog is also observed in West Papua which increases its ranking by 12 positions. Other provinces whose rankings increase by 10 positions are Papua, West Nusa Tenggara, Lampung and Aceh. By identifying their top 20% weakest indicators and lifting them to the average values, they have transformed from the bottom 10 provinces to the middle 13 provinces.

Table 2.7: 2015 *What-if* Competitiveness Simulation on Overall Competitiveness

	Rank		Score	
Economy	**Before**	**After**	**Before**	**After**
Aceh	24	14	−0.652	0.055
Bali	12	8	0.159	0.597
Bangka Belitung Islands	30	16	−1.126	−0.207
Banten	9	7	0.411	0.835
Bengkulu	23	16	−0.562	−0.097
Central Java	5	4	1.057	1.452
Central Kalimantan	13	8	0.141	0.432
Central Sulawesi	20	14	−0.301	0.030
DI Yogyakarta	6	4	0.900	1.238
DKI Jakarta	1	1	3.260	3.727
East Java	2	2	1.951	2.194
East Kalimantan	3	2	1.769	1.998
East Nusa Tenggara	32	23	−1.162	−0.576
Gorontalo	27	19	−0.819	−0.312
Jambi	14	12	−0.048	0.224
Lampung	25	15	−0.707	−0.079
Maluku	29	23	−1.124	−0.447
North Maluku	31	23	−1.152	−0.422
North Sulawesi	11	8	0.246	0.540
North Sumatra	15	8	−0.075	0.431
Papua	33	23	−1.375	−0.451
Riau	16	11	−0.202	0.294
Riau Islands	7	5	0.724	1.092
South Kalimantan	8	8	0.422	0.651
South Sulawesi	10	8	0.356	0.659
South Sumatra	17	14	−0.256	0.081
Southeast Sulawesi	21	12	−0.336	0.169
West Java	4	4	1.133	1.551
West Kalimantan	19	14	−0.300	0.086
West Nusa Tenggara	26	16	−0.762	−0.175
West Papua	28	16	−0.968	−0.117
West Sulawesi	18	14	−0.262	0.123
West Sumatra	22	14	−0.341	0.056

Source: Asia Competitiveness Institute.

Review of What-if *Competitiveness Simulation: Four Environments*

The *what-if* competitiveness simulation is not only performed for Overall Competitiveness, but also for each of the four environments. The scenario for each simulation is to raise each province's top 20% weakest indicators in a particular environment to attain the average score. Afterwards, the standardised score is re-calculated based on such an improvement, one at a time.

In Table 2.8, substantial changes in ranking are less common, highlighting that most of the provinces' top 20% weakness indicators are not dominated by those from Macroeconomic Stability environment. The biggest improvement is mostly found among the bottom 10 provinces, such as West Sumatra and Bengkulu, with their rankings increase by 11 and 10 positions, respectively. Despite their rise to middle 13 positions, their scores are still negative.

Table 2.9 shows plenty of opportunities for provinces to increase its competitiveness by prioritising reforms in governance aspect. Several provinces show potential to jump by more than 10 positions. Bangka Belitung Islands moves up by 14 positions; North Maluku and Lampung by 13 positions; Riau and North Sumatra by 12 positions; West Papua, Maluku and Aceh by 11 positions. Their improvement in scores is also considered the highest, ranging from an increase by 0.814 to 1.459. Among them, only Lampung, Maluku and North Sumatra which not only graduate to middle 13 group but also obtain positive scores, signifying an above average performance.

Table 2.10 presents the simulation findings for Financial, Businesses and Manpower Conditions. In this environment, we see the biggest improvement in ranking with Papua as a case in point. After increasing the score of its top 20% weakest indicators to the average value, Papua's ranking leapfrogs from 29th to 11th, only one spot behind to join the top 10. Its standardised score also improves significantly from –0.994 to 0.064. Aceh is another province emulating Papua's trajectory, with its ranking improves by 15 positions from 26th (–0.740) to 11th (0.174).

Other provinces with proclivity to move up the rankings post-simulation are Bangka Belitung Islands (by 14 positions), West Nusa Tenggara (by 12 positions), South Sumatra (11 positions) and Southeast Sulawesi (10 positions). Nevertheless, their scores do not yet reach positive values, highlighting the need to increase the top 20% weakest indicators beyond the average.

In Table 2.11, we see more movements in the ranking before and after simulation. This indicates that for many provinces, their top 20% weakest indicators generally come from Quality of Life and Infrastructure Development environment. This is the only environment where it is feasible to have three provinces (East Kalimantan, DI Yogyakarta and DKI Jakarta) achieve the first rank, post-simulation. Had DKI Jakarta addressed its shortcomings in this environment, it would have been able to acquire not only the first position but also achieve the highest score, ahead of East Kalimantan and DI Yogyakarta.

Post-simulation, most of the bottom 10 provinces improve its ranking to join the middle 13 group, except Papua (33rd to 28th rank). This is consistent with the earlier finding in Table 2.6 that highlights how far back Papua is compared to other provinces in Indonesia. For Papua to thrive in this environment, significant efforts to rectify its top 20% weakest indicators beyond achieving the average values are required. On the other hand, West Sulawesi and West Kalimantan register the biggest leap, with an increase of 13 and 10 positions, respectively.

Table 2.8: 2015 *What-if* Competitiveness Simulation on Macroeconomic Stability

	Rank		Score	
Economy	**Before**	**After**	**Before**	**After**
Aceh	26	21	–0.675	–0.423
Bali	18	13	–0.379	–0.197
Bangka Belitung Islands	31	22	–0.773	–0.438
Banten	6	6	0.461	0.484
Bengkulu	32	22	–0.82	–0.455
Central Java	7	6	0.409	0.490
Central Kalimantan	14	13	–0.246	–0.044
Central Sulawesi	16	13	–0.293	–0.172
DI Yogyakarta	20	13	–0.399	–0.050
DKI Jakarta	1	1	4.309	4.326
East Java	2	2	2.003	2.013
East Kalimantan	4	4	0.952	1.050
East Nusa Tenggara	33	31	–0.831	–0.775
Gorontalo	30	26	–0.756	–0.577
Jambi	21	14	–0.422	–0.226
Lampung	25	17	–0.545	–0.351
Maluku	28	25	–0.683	–0.525
North Maluku	29	25	–0.734	–0.515
North Sulawesi	13	13	–0.202	–0.066
North Sumatra	10	9	0.074	0.183
Papua	22	17	–0.439	–0.336
Riau	9	9	0.090	0.147
Riau Islands	5	5	0.851	0.882
South Kalimantan	11	8	0.066	0.222
South Sulawesi	8	8	0.191	0.320
South Sumatra	12	12	0.015	0.015
Southeast Sulawesi	15	13	–0.286	–0.171
West Java	3	3	1.403	1.454
West Kalimantan	23	18	–0.448	–0.376
West Nusa Tenggara	27	19	–0.678	–0.389
West Papua	19	14	–0.393	–0.213
West Sulawesi	17	17	–0.373	–0.310
West Sumatra	24	13	–0.452	–0.208

Source: Asia Competitiveness Institute.

Table 2.9: 2015 *What-if* Competitiveness Simulation on Government and Institutional Setting

	Rank		Score	
Economy	**Before**	**After**	**Before**	**After**
Aceh	29	18	−1.024	−0.123
Bali	19	15	−0.321	0.206
Bangka Belitung Islands	32	18	−1.624	−0.165
Banten	16	15	−0.054	0.339
Bengkulu	23	18	−0.611	−0.238
Central Java	4	4	1.382	1.455
Central Kalimantan	8	7	0.676	0.712
Central Sulawesi	15	15	−0.002	0.331
DI Yogyakarta	3	3	1.631	1.750
DKI Jakarta	1	1	2.074	2.187
East Java	5	5	1.310	1.310
East Kalimantan	2	2	1.921	1.980
East Nusa Tenggara	21	18	−0.454	−0.094
Gorontalo	22	18	−0.598	−0.162
Jambi	11	7	0.606	0.708
Lampung	28	15	−0.980	0.066
Maluku	26	15	−0.757	0.057
North Maluku	33	20	−1.755	−0.433
North Sulawesi	6	6	0.906	1.065
North Sumatra	27	15	−0.975	0.086
Papua	25	18	−0.693	−0.223
Riau	30	18	−1.089	−0.127
Riau Islands	18	15	−0.269	0.139
South Kalimantan	7	7	0.688	0.688
South Sulawesi	13	7	0.495	0.732
South Sumatra	17	15	−0.084	0.164
Southeast Sulawesi	10	6	0.611	0.982
West Java	12	6	0.591	1.046
West Kalimantan	14	14	0.412	0.458
West Nusa Tenggara	20	18	−0.445	−0.133
West Papua	31	20	−1.559	−0.465
West Sulawesi	9	7	0.628	0.744
West Sumatra	24	18	−0.638	−0.204

Source: Asia Competitiveness Institute.

Table 2.10: 2015 *What-if* Competitiveness Simulation on Financial, Businesses and Manpower Conditions

	Rank		Score	
Economy	**Before**	**After**	**Before**	**After**
Aceh	26	11	−0.740	0.174
Bali	8	6	0.422	0.628
Bangka Belitung Islands	28	14	−0.954	−0.011
Banten	17	9	−0.079	0.367
Bengkulu	19	11	−0.281	0.111
Central Java	3	3	1.591	1.985
Central Kalimantan	11	7	0.089	0.445
Central Sulawesi	22	18	−0.416	−0.131
DI Yogyakarta	9	6	0.320	0.646
DKI Jakarta	1	1	3.340	3.880
East Java	2	2	2.095	2.448
East Kalimantan	4	3	1.304	1.735
East Nusa Tenggara	31	26	−1.099	−0.699
Gorontalo	27	18	−0.941	−0.154
Jambi	20	11	−0.323	0.110
Lampung	21	16	−0.416	−0.084
Maluku	33	26	−1.598	−0.732
North Maluku	23	19	−0.455	−0.207
North Sulawesi	18	11	−0.176	0.132
North Sumatra	13	9	0.065	0.386
Papua	29	11	−0.994	0.064
Riau	10	7	0.256	0.508
Riau Islands	6	6	0.521	1.001
South Kalimantan	15	10	0.006	0.253
South Sulawesi	14	9	0.010	0.386
South Sumatra	25	14	−0.566	−0.003
Southeast Sulawesi	30	20	−1.046	−0.297
West Java	5	3	1.244	1.771
West Kalimantan	12	9	0.080	0.324
West Nusa Tenggara	32	20	−1.130	−0.322
West Papua	7	6	0.459	0.679
West Sulawesi	16	16	−0.075	−0.014
West Sumatra	24	16	−0.512	−0.068

Source: Asia Competitiveness Institute.

Table 2.11: 2015 *What-if* Competitiveness Simulation on Quality of Life and Infrastructure Development

	Rank		Score	
Economy	**Before**	**After**	**Before**	**After**
Aceh	15	11	0.204	0.562
Bali	7	3	0.821	1.405
Bangka Belitung Islands	25	19	−0.507	−0.091
Banten	6	2	1.079	1.670
Bengkulu	19	14	−0.213	0.250
Central Java	14	6	0.237	1.055
Central Kalimantan	18	13	−0.036	0.371
Central Sulawesi	21	16	−0.320	0.076
DI Yogyakarta	2	1	1.530	1.911
DKI Jakarta	3	1	1.442	2.693
East Java	5	2	1.276	1.775
East Kalimantan	1	1	1.882	2.105
East Nusa Tenggara	31	23	−1.596	−0.400
Gorontalo	26	19	−0.509	−0.174
Jambi	17	16	−0.028	0.177
Lampung	24	16	−0.479	0.099
Maluku	27	21	−0.812	−0.323
North Maluku	28	21	−1.004	−0.287
North Sulawesi	13	8	0.317	0.723
North Sumatra	10	7	0.578	0.827
Papua	33	28	−2.584	−1.038
Riau	16	12	0.052	0.480
Riau Islands	4	2	1.378	1.730
South Kalimantan	8	6	0.687	1.069
South Sulawesi	11	7	0.524	0.824
South Sumatra	20	16	−0.241	0.101
Southeast Sulawesi	23	16	−0.429	0.064
West Java	9	6	0.644	1.066
West Kalimantan	29	19	−1.072	−0.109
West Nusa Tenggara	22	14	−0.357	0.245
West Papua	32	23	−1.823	−0.405
West Sulawesi	30	17	−1.076	0.003
West Sumatra	12	9	0.434	0.670

Source: Asia Competitiveness Institute.

2.3.3 Analysis of Median and Maximum Competitiveness Webs

To better understand each province's relative strengths and weaknesses, it is useful to compare and contrast its attainment against the median and maximum scores of Indonesia's 33 provinces for the 12 sub-environments that make up the four environments.

The median competitiveness web analysis in Figure 2.8 plots the attained scores across the 12 sub-environments for DKI Jakarta (ranked first) and Papua (ranked last), along with the median scores for the 33 provinces of Indonesia. By scrutinising their performances at the sub-environment level, we can gather detailed insights regarding factors that drive or hamper their competitiveness.

DKI Jakarta certainly leads in all three sub-environments under Macroeconomic Stability. However, its performance is not equally distributed for the rest of sub-environments belonging to the remaining three environments. For instance, among sub-environments under Quality of Life and Infrastructure Development, DKI Jakarta's score is higher than the median only in Technological Infrastructure, alerting that the province should take heed not to be complacent. Besides Physical Infrastructure and Standard of Living, Education and Social Stability, DKI Jakarta also scores lower than the median in Institutions, Governance and Leadership.

For Papua, most of its sub-environment scores are below the median. Exceptions are found in Openness to Trade and Services; Productivity Performance; and Competition, Regulatory Standards, and Rule of Law, albeit very marginal difference. As a low performing province starting at the low base, even small improvement would tend to get the desired results for confidence building.

Not only are the scores for DKI Jakarta and Papua mapped against the median score, in Figure 2.9, their scores are also plotted along with the maximum scores for the 33 provinces of

Figure 2.8: 2015 Median Competitiveness Web Analysis: Top and Bottom Performing Provinces

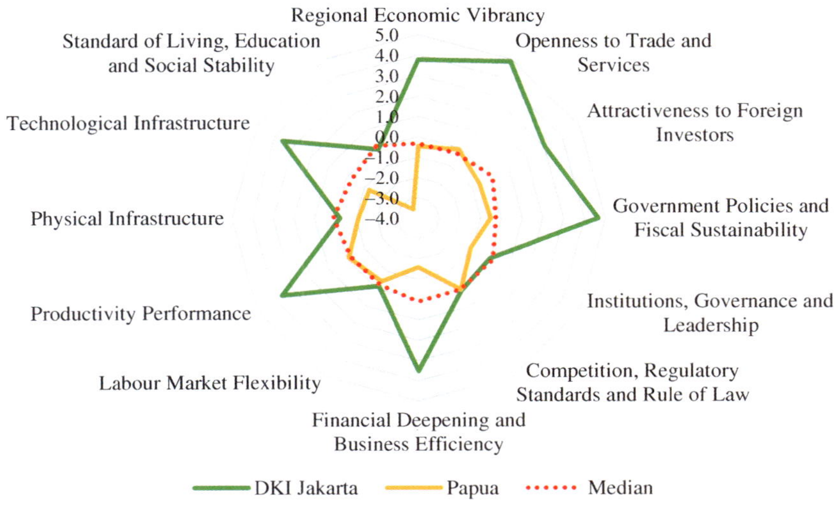

Source: Asia Competitiveness Institute.

Figure 2.9: 2015 Maximum Competitiveness Web Analysis: Top and Bottom Performing Province

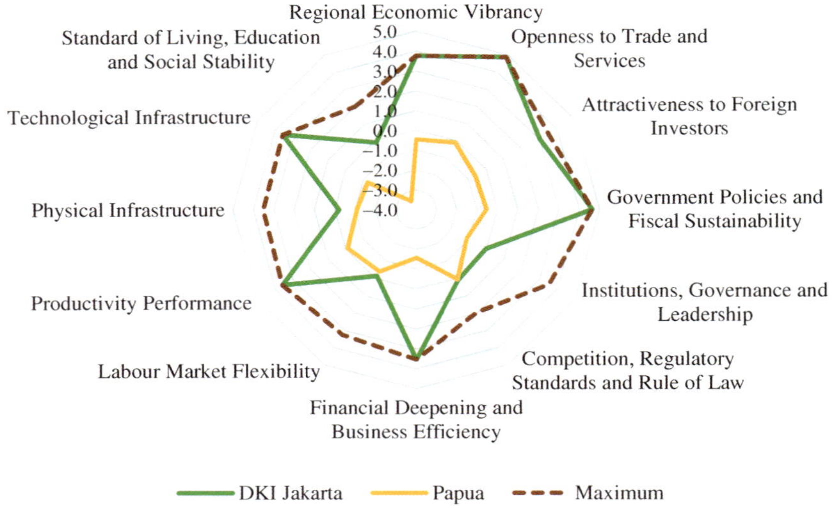

Source: Asia Competitiveness Institute.

Indonesia. As the number one province, DKI Jakarta achieves maximum scores in six out of 12 sub-environments. The province becomes a national's benchmark in Regional Economic Vibrancy; Openness to Trade and Services; Government Policies and Fiscal Sustainability; Financial Deepening and Business Efficiency; Productivity Performance; and Technological Infrastructure.

In contrast, Papua's scores seem very distant from the maximum scores. The widest gaps are found in Standard of Living, Education and Social Stability; Government Policies and Fiscal Sustainability; and Financial Deepening and Business Efficiency.

2.4 CONCLUSION AND POLICY IMPLICATIONS

In general, the results from our 2015 competitiveness analysis still highlight the high competitiveness of six provinces in Java Island as they all occupy the top 10 group. DKI Jakarta tops in most environments, though the province still struggles to perform equally well in ensuring the continuous improvement in the quality of life of its people. East Java, Central Java and West Java also perform consistently well across four environments, unlike DI Yogyakarta which slips to the 20th position in Macroeconomic Stability and Banten which moderately holds 16th and 17th position in Government and Institutional Setting; and Financial, Businesses and Manpower Conditions, respectively. With a highly centralised system adopted during the New Order era, Java (especially Jakarta) was favoured over other regions in Indonesia, creating regional disparity that still persists even until today. Compared to other islands, Java's road connectivity is the most advanced, making it possible for growth spillover from DKI Jakarta to neighbouring provinces, further advancing the pivotal role of provinces in Java as manufacturing and service hubs.

Additionally, we also observe varying performance among provinces endowed with rich natural resources. East Kalimantan becomes an exemplar of a province which performs well in translating its wealth of revenue into high competitiveness, joining the top four in all environments and even tops in Quality of Life and Infrastructure Development. East Kalimantan also leads in governance, being the only province from outside Java to win the 2012 Citra Bhakti Abdi Negara for excellent public service delivery.

Its neighbouring province, South Kalimantan which is also rich in coal, joins East Kalimantan in the top 10, although its performance in Financial, Businesses and Manpower Conditions is relatively moderate. Other provinces endowed with extensive natural resources, especially those that are located in Sumatra such as Aceh, South Sumatra and North Sumatra are relatively further behind. Proper management of resources is key to make sure that sustainability is taken into account and wealth is well distributed to the benefit of people. There is plenty of opportunities for peer learning to identify the areas that can be adopted from the experience of high performing province.

Last but not least, our finding still captures the disparity between the easternmost provinces and the rest of Indonesian provinces. Papua, East Nusa Tenggara and North Maluku are the bottom three provinces in Overall Competitiveness. Papua's lagging performance in Quality of Life and Infrastructure Development is particularly worrying due to its very low standardised score, rendering it as an outlier. Despite its abundant natural resources and generous fund allocation from the central government owing to Special Autonomy Law, Papua's competitiveness remains far behind.

Most provinces in the eastern part of Indonesia which are defined as 'archipelagic' provinces also perform poorly, as in the case of East Nusa Tenggara, North Maluku, Maluku and West Nusa Tenggara. This underlines distinct challenges that they face to connect their sparse and remote islands to main economic centres of the province. Further efforts to strengthen maritime connectivity not only within the province but also across provinces are the way forward to revitalise Indonesia's competitiveness as a whole.

While infrastructure development has been a priority of central government for years, it is yet to seamlessly connect Indonesia's vast archipelago from Sabang in its westernmost point to Merauke in its easternmost. For such ambition, maritime infrastructure plays a key role. A number of projects related to port construction and upgrading in various locations all over Indonesia are in the pipeline, with varying degrees of progress. At the same time, the idea of maritime highway project is being implemented step by step, firstly by the launch of the above mentioned maritime outlet project to ensure availability of regular vessels traveling between western and eastern parts of Indonesia. Building connectivity is hard work, but it is not an impossible task. To make it feasible, strong and long-term commitment is required.

All in all, the ACI's competitiveness analysis provides ample insights into the competitiveness profile of each province. Such mapping of potential, strengths and weaknesses can provide a roadmap for the central and provincial government officials to review their past policies, fine-tune their ongoing policies, and plan their future policies in advance. The competitiveness analysis should not be viewed as merely 'competing' with one another but seen as a platform to track each province's performance and offer fresh perspective to learn from one another's success story.

REFERENCES

Antara News. 2015. "Indonesia Launches Maritime Outlets to Reduce Price Disparity." June 16. http://www.lexisnexis.com/us/lnacademic/ (accessed June 30, 2015).

Antara News. 2015. "Kalla Confirms Plan to Cancel Cilamaya Location for New Port." April 3. http://www.lexisnexis.com/us/lnacademic/ (accessed June 30, 2015).

Bank Indonesia. 2015. *Indonesian Financial Statistics (SEKI)*. Jakarta: Bank Indonesia. http://www.bi.go.id/en/statistik/seki/terkini/moneter/Contents/Default.aspx/.

Bristow, Gillian. 2010. *Critical Reflections on Regional Competitiveness: Theory, Policy, and Practice*. New York: Routledge.

Camagni, Roberto. 2002. "On the Concept of Territorial Competitiveness: Sound or Misleading?" *Urban Studies* 39(13): 2395–2411.

Kitson, Michael, Ronald Leonard Martin and Peter, Tyler. 2004. "Regional Competitiveness: An Elusive yet Key Concept?" *Regional Studies* 38(9): 991–999.

Parlina, Ina. 2014. "Jokowi Aims for 7 Percent Annual Growth." *The Jakarta Post*, December 24. http://www.thejakartapost.com/news/2014/12/24/jokowi-aims-7-percent-annual-growth.html (accessed June 30, 2015).

Porter, Michael. *Competitive Strategy*. New York: Free Press.

Sato, Yuri and Arie Damayanti. 2015. "Survey of Recent Developments." *Bulletin of Indonesian Economic Studies* 51(2): 165–188.

Susanto, Slamet. 2015. "Jokowi Launches Mega Power Plant Projects." *The Jakarta Post*, May 5. http://www.thejakartapost.com/news/2015/05/05/jokowi-launches-mega-power-plant-projects.html/ (accessed June 30, 2015).

Tan, Khee Giap, Linda Low, Kartik Rao and Tan Kong Yam. 2015a. *2014 Regional Competitiveness Analysis and a Master Plan on Regional Development Strategies for India.* Singapore: World Scientific.

Tan, Khee Giap, Nurina Merdikawati, Mulya Amri and Blake Harley Berger. 2015b. *2014 Annual Competitiveness Analysis and Development Strategies for Indonesian Provinces.* Singapore: World Scientific

Tan, Khee Giap, Nurina Merdikawati, Mulya Amri and Tan Kong Yam. 2015c. *2014 Provincial and Inaugural Regional Competitiveness Analysis: Safeguarding Indonesia's Growth Momentum.* Singapore: World Scientific.

Tan, Khee Giap, Sangiita Yoong Wei Cher, Sasidaran Gopalan and Nguyen Le Phuong Anh. 2015d. *2014 Annual Competitiveness Ranking and Simulation Study for ASEAN-10 and Development Strategies to Enhance Asia Economic Connectivity*. Singapore: World Scientific.

Tan, Khee Giap, Yuan Randong and Sangiita Yoong Wei Cher. 2015. 2015. *2014 Annual Provincial and Regional Competitiveness Analysis for Greater China Economies: Development Strategies under the New Normal*. Singapore: World Scientific.

Chapter 3

2015 Regional Competitiveness Ranking and Analysis for Indonesia: An Annual Update

3.1 BALANCING REGIONAL GROWTH AND DEVELOPMENT OF INDONESIA: AN OVERVIEW

Geographically, Indonesia is a vast archipelagic country spanning 5,150 kilometres east to west consisting of five big islands, namely Sumatra, Java, Kalimantan, Sulawesi and Papua. Historically, Java has been the epicentre of Indonesia's growth, even long before Indonesia's independence in 1945. During Dutch colonisation, Jakarta (then Batavia) was the heart of Dutch East India Company's (VOC) Asian operation, monopolising spice trading in the 16th and 17th centuries. Post-independence, Java continues to play a strategic role with Jakarta named as the capital city and eventually developed into not only the centre of government but also the centre of economic activities. As early as in 1975, Java contributed to 50% of Indonesia's gross domestic product (GDP) and was home to 63% of Indonesia's population. Following the pivot to industrialisation in 1980s after the fall in oil prices, Java continued to assume more dominant role in Indonesia's economy as most labour-intensive manufacturing sites were first developed in the island and by 1993, its contribution to Indonesia's GDP went up to 59% (Garcia and Soelistianingsih 1998).

Such disparity persisted with Java's contribution to Indonesia's GDP still hovering around 60% in 2012 (Figure 3.1). Java's long standing advancement in generating economic output attracted substantial investment, as seen from its three year average of foreign domestic investment (FDI) in 2010–2012 which reached 65.48% of Indonesia's total FDI. Despite earlier efforts to redistribute Indonesia's population through government-led transmigration programme, Java was still home to 57.19% of Indonesia's population in 2012. Java's supremacy is in contrast to its relatively small size, with its land size only accounted for 6.77% of total land in Indonesia, that is, high in density.

The issue of regional disparity also takes place in other countries, emerging and developed countries alike. China's initial strategy to open up the country focused on development of eastern coastal area as shown by establishment of the first four special economic zones (SEZs) in Shenzhen, Zhuhai, Shantou and Xiamen. Hence, its coastal areas with seaport and accessibility are far more developed than the rest of the country (Tan, Yuan and Yoong 2015). For the case of Germany, even after reunification between East and West German territories in 1989, the regional disparity remains, with the former West German territories chart higher per capita income and worker productivity (Matthews 2014).

Figure 3.1: Regional Share of GDP, FDI, Population and Land Area

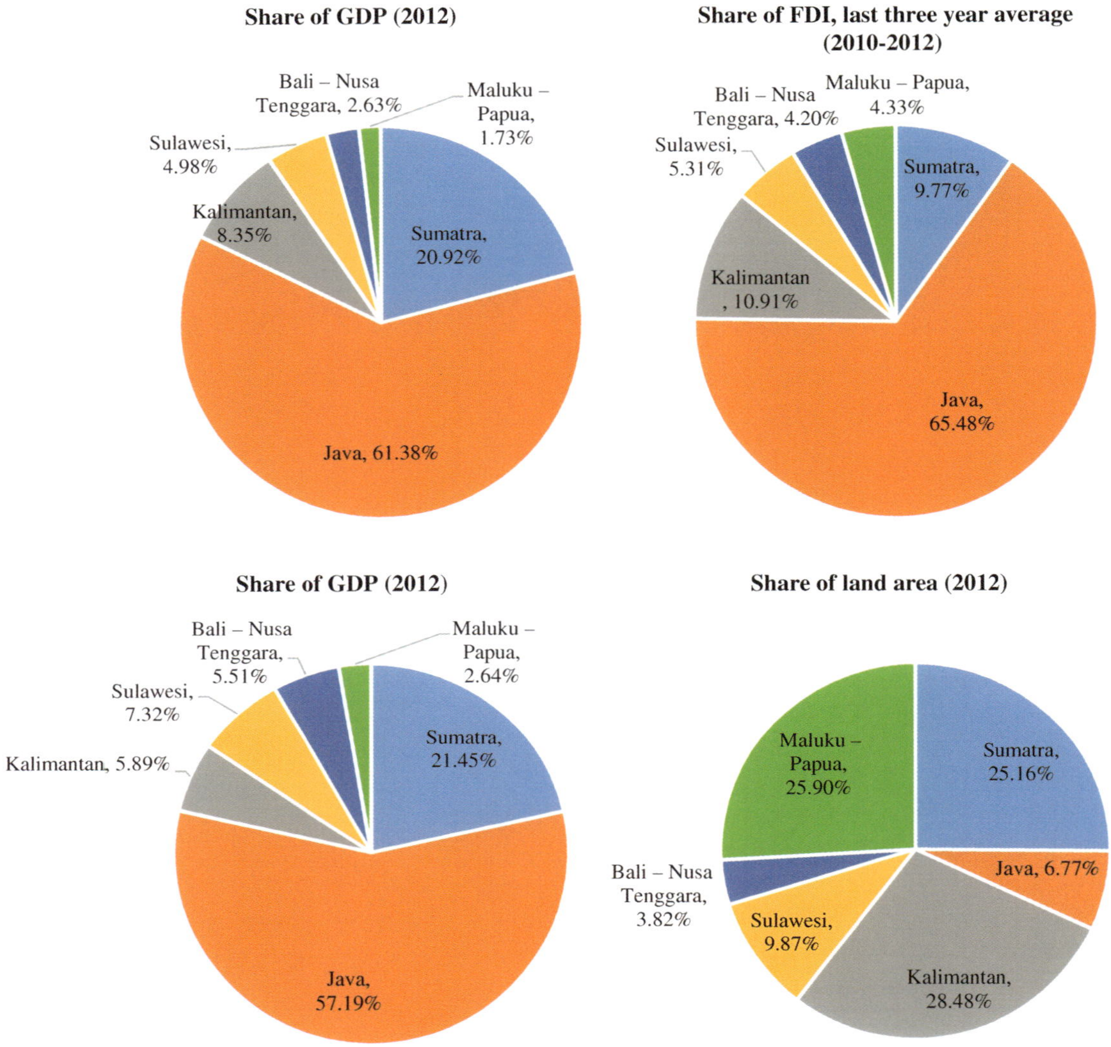

Source: Asia Competitiveness Institute based on data from Indonesia's Central Statistical Agency (BPS).

The OECD (2010) summed up three categories of policy responses to address the regional disparity. The first category is ensuring that the main policy focus is on regional disparities. The second category is giving support to the lagging regions though this is not the main policy focus. The third category is prioritising on 'national' economic growth despite the disparities within the country. In the case of Indonesia, in highly centralised system under the leadership of President Soeharto during the New Order era in 1966–1998, policies were geared towards the third category, to spur 'national' economic growth which relied heavily on development in Java, at the expense of regional disparity.

Political turmoil following the downfall of repressive New Order regime gave birth to decentralisation,[1] which delegated substantial powers and resources to district and city level, instead of provincial level to pre-empt emergence of large administrative unit disintegrating from the country (Mietzner 2013). Such devolution of power also eased and mitigated growing discontent among locals regarding natural resources taken out from their areas to fund the central government with little return for the locals. Decentralisation has its own merits that it broadens and spreads growth, providing incentives for the local officials to attract investment to spur economic growth in their respective localities.[2]

Papua, which consists of Papua and West Papua province, is granted a special autonomy status based on Law No. 21/2001, providing the region with greater revenue streams that can be used to finance their local development.[3] Additionally, the region also received special revenues amounting to 2% of the ceiling of general allocation fund (DAU) intended to finance education and health and another additional funding from the central government for infrastructure development. More policies considered to be part of the second category to support the lagging region were reflected in President Susilo Bambang Yudhoyono's term (2004–2014) aiming to address wide-ranging issues in Papua related to poverty, education, and health. In 2011, the unit for acceleration of development in Papua and West Papua (UP4PB) was launched to build a basis for sustainable development, aligned with the local aspirations.

Consistent with the shift in regional policies found among OECD countries from top–down interventions targeted at providing aid to lagging regions towards broader aim to enhance regional competitiveness (OECD 2010), the central government created Masterplan for Acceleration and Expansion of Indonesia's Economic Development 2011–2025 (MP3EI). The MP3EI intended to be all region-focus to tap underutilised regional potential and integrate development projects with wider policy area coverage, by identifying six economic corridors (Figure 3.2) and their corresponding themes for their role in national economic development (Coordinating Ministry of Economic Affairs 2011).

The aim to spread growth centres across Indonesia is a step in a right direction as heavy reliance on Java that only accounts for 6.77% of land area in Indonesia but attracting 57.19% of people gave rise to pollution and traffic congestion. Exodus of able young generation from outside Java to Java further aggravates the situation and leaves lagging regions without adequate capable human resources to drive their economic development. While the MP3EI puts more emphasis on infrastructure development, investments in education and healthcare are equally important to reduce the regional imbalance. Garcia and Soelistianingsih (1998) found that lagging regions reaped the most benefits from improvement in education and healthcare that allowed them to catch up with other regions.

---

[1]Based on Law No. 22/1999 on local government and Law No. 25/1999 on intergovernmental fiscal relationship.

[2]For more details on how decentralisation and governing institutions shape economic development in Indonesia, please refer to Chapter 4.

[3]The special autonomy law granted higher provincial share of natural resource revenues; 70% of gas oil and revenues and 80% of forestry, fishery and mining revenues are allocated to the province.

Figure 3.2: Map of Six Economic Corridors

Source: Asia Competitiveness Institute (ACI) based on regional classification adopted in the MP3EI.

Spreading of growth in other regions can also take place as a result of invisible hand of the market economy as in the case of China (Tan, Yuan and Yoong 2015). With rising wages in eastern coastal area, more labour-intensive manufacturing was shifted to western China. Such spillover was made possible due to well-developed infrastructure connecting the two regions. This phenomenon did take place in Indonesia but only limited to Java Island, deconcentrating from Jakarta to its nearby provinces (Banten and West Java) and further to Central Java and East Java where minimum wage is the lowest nationally. Indonesia's archipelago landscape provides a distinct challenge compared to China as a landmass. For growth to organically spillover to other regions, a seamless connectivity across regions is a must.

Under President Joko Widodo's leadership, maritime infrastructure emerged as the main policy focus which can play a significant role for spreading the growth across Indonesia. This is to avoid a situation that Java became more self-sufficient and less involved in interregional trade (Sonis *et al.* 1997); and regions outside Java and Sumatra were losing out as a result of any economic growth in the western part of Indonesia (Nazara, Sonis and Hewings 2000). Ideally, regional development policies should not be a zero sum game but more on maximising growth for each region which eventually maximising national growth. All regions have potential to engage in extensive exchange in production inputs or activities, instead of limited exchange in consumption goods. Much anecdotal evidence reveals how eastern provinces such as Papua and West Papua merely become consumers of goods shipped from Java, but the cargos are left behind empty and stacked in their ports with no return goods bound to Java. If Merauke Integrated Food and Energy Estate (MIFEE) delineated in the MP3EI came to realisation, more goods will be shipped out of Papua Region that will incentivise more frequent shipment and trade between western and eastern part of Indonesia.

Given such dynamics evolution of regional development policies in Indonesia, it is timely for us to evaluate regional competitiveness in Indonesia by adopting regional classification based on the MP3EI. Our competitiveness methodology allows us to cover more indicators,[4] not only focusing on economics related indicators such as GRDP. Our study contributes to the literature by shedding light in terms of regional disparity from competitiveness perspective. This builds up from our forte to track competitiveness of Indonesia over time.[5] The results and analysis spur further intellectual debates among key stakeholders to lift competitiveness of Indonesia as a whole.

The structure of the chapter is as follows. Section 3.1 provides a snapshot of regional disparity and efforts to balance regional growth and development in Indonesia. Section 3.2 lays out research methodology for data aggregation. Section 3.3 gives details on the empirical findings, including rankings and scores for six regions based on Overall Competitiveness and four environments. Discussions on sub-environment spread as well as median and maximum competitiveness webs analysis are also provided. Section 3.4 concludes.

3.2 RESEARCH METHODOLOGY

The construction of the competitiveness ranking by region follows the same methodology used for the provincial competitiveness ranking mentioned in Chapter 2, once the appropriate dataset for indicators at regional level is ready.[6] For 2015 results, the data are based on 2012 for secondary data collected from official sources and 2014 for primary data collected from ACI's perception survey.

As each region consists of a few provinces, the main problem to be solved in order to extend the ranking analysis from provincial to regional level is data aggregation. Many of the indicators used for the provincial ranking can be directly aggregated to obtain the indicator values for a region by summing across all the constituent provinces in that region, as long as those indicators are based on absolute quantities, such as 1.1.01 Gross Regional Domestic Product (GRDP) and 4.1.01 Population.

For those indicators that are defined as ratios, they can be computed according to their definition by firstly aggregating the absolute quantities upon which they are defined (e.g. aggregating the denominator and numerator first). As an illustration, below are three examples for data aggregation to derive the regional indicator values. The first example is for indicator 1.1.01 GRDP. Since it is based on absolute quantity, the regional value can be obtained by summing across all the provinces within this region. The second example is for 2.1.03 Tax Revenue/Government Revenue. According to its definition, it is calculated as the ratio between tax revenue and government revenue for a particular region. Since both the numerator and denominator are absolute quantities, they are firstly aggregated across all the provinces within the region to obtain the regional values. The ratio is then computed from these obtained values, hence, arriving at the

---

[4]More details on the competitiveness methodology can be found in Chapter 2 while full the list of indicators is available in Appendix 1.

[5]Please see previous ACI's publication on Indonesia's competitiveness in Tan *et al.* (2013, 2015a, 2015b).

[6]For the provincial analysis, the ACI uses a total of 103 indicators that cover 33 provinces. North Kalimantan, the newly created province being carved out of East Kalimantan in 2012, is not yet included pending availability of data.

regional value for indicator 2.1.03 Tax Revenue/Government Revenue. The third example is when the calculation is average-weighted at the regional level by population of the province. This applies to indicators collected from ACI survey and also from indicators that are calculated as percentage of households at original source, as provided in the following example for 4.2.01 Telephone Ownership.

Approach 1: 1.1.01 GRDP; Unit: Million Rupiahs, 2000 Constant Prices

For Region A with n provinces at time t,

$$\text{GRDP}_{A,t} = \sum_{i=1}^{n} \text{Real GRDP}_{i,t}.$$

Approach 2: 2.1.03 Tax Revenue/Government Revenue; Unit: Ratio of Tax Revenue to Government Revenue

For Region A with n provinces at time t,

$$\text{Tax Revenue/Government Revenue}_{A,t} = \frac{\sum_{i=1}^{n} \text{Tax Revenue}_{i,t}}{\sum_{i=1}^{n} \text{Government Revenue}_{i,t}}.$$

Approach 3: 4.2.01 Telephone Ownership; Unit: Percentage of Households

For Region A with n provinces at time t,

$$\text{Telephone Ownership}_{A,t} = \sum_{i=1}^{n} \left(\text{Telephone Ownership}_{i,t} \times \frac{\text{Population}_{i,t}}{\sum_{i=1}^{n} \text{Population}_{i,t}} \right).$$

For a complete list of indicators used for the regional competitiveness analysis, please refer to Appendix 1. For algorithm to compute the competitiveness ranking, please refer to Appendix 2. For explanatory notes on how to derive regional indicator data from provincial data, please refer to Appendix 3. Once the data aggregation is completed for all relevant indicators, the competitiveness ranking analysis is performed by following the computational procedure.

3.3 EMPIRICAL FINDINGS

3.3.1 Review of Ranking and Score

Using data aggregation methodology in Section 3.2 and adopting competitiveness methodology described in Chapter 2, the following section will show the results of regional ranking for Overall Competitiveness and each of the four environments. Additional tables are included to outline the top and bottom performing provinces in each region to give an insight on disparity within the region. The discussion on the relative performance of each region at the sub-environment level will also be provided. The results are based on 2012 data from official sources and 2014 data from ACI's perception survey, collated and analysed in 2015.[7]

Review of Ranking and Score: Overall Competitiveness

Table 3.1 shows the Overall Competitiveness ranking and score for the six regions in Indonesia. Consistent with the results from provincial competitiveness analysis in Chapter 2, Java Region attains the top position with a score of 1.691 while Maluku–Papua Region is ranked last with a score of −1.407. The difference in score between the top performing region and bottom performing region is 3.098, as compared to 4.635 for the difference in score between the first and bottom ranked province (DKI Jakarta and Papua, respectively). This indicates that DKI Jakarta's score is, in fact, an outlier in the provincial competitiveness ranking. When DKI Jakarta is grouped with the remaining five provinces to form a region, the score for Java Region is not too high, as compared to the subsequent regions.

Despite Sumatra Region's proximity to Java Region as the engine of Indonesia's growth, its competitiveness is rather behind, occupying the fourth position in the past two years. Nevertheless, its score difference with Sulawesi Region is rather narrow (0.134). Inter-regional friendly rivalry can be a catalyst to strengthen the Overall Competitiveness of Indonesia as a whole.

Table 3.2 provides a list of top and bottom performing provinces in each region in terms of its Overall Competitiveness ranking. The numbers in brackets refer to their respective provincial ranking which can be found in greater details in Chapter 2. Within region, the performance across provinces can be quite diverse. In Sumatra Region, Riau Islands as an industrialised province relying on high value added sector is ranked seventh in the Overall Competitiveness, while Bangka Belitung Islands is at 30th. The latter is at the transition to shift its reliance from extractive tin industry to unleash the full potential of its budding tourism sector. Such disparity

Table 3.1: 2015 Overall Competitiveness: Ranking and Score

2015 Rank	2014 Rank	Region	Score
1	1	Java	1.691
2	2	Kalimantan	0.690
3	3	Sulawesi	−0.013
4	4	Sumatra	−0.147
5	5	Bali–Nusa Tenggara	−0.814
6	6	Maluku–Papua	−1.407

Source: Asia Competitiveness Institute.

[7]As of 2016, there are 34 provinces in Indonesia. North Kalimantan, the newly created province being carved out of East Kalimantan in 2012, is not yet included pending availability of data.

Table 3.2: 2015 Overall Competitiveness: Top and Bottom Provinces in Each Region

	Region					
	Sumatra	**Java**	**Kalimantan**	**Sulawesi**	**Bali–Nusa Tenggara**	**Maluku–Papua**
Top Province	Riau Islands (7)	DKI Jakarta (1)	East Kalimantan (3)	South Sulawesi (10)	Bali (12)	West Papua (28)
Bottom Province	Bangka Belitung Islands (30)	Banten (9)	West Kalimantan (19)	Gorontalo (27)	East Nusa Tenggara (32)	Papua (33)

Source: Asia Competitiveness Institute.

Figure 3.3: 2015 Overall Competitiveness: Geographical Spread

Source: Asia Competitiveness Institute.

is also observed in Bali–Nusa Tenggara Region where Bali is ranked 12th while East Nusa Tenggara is at 32nd. This is not surprising as Bali is long well known for its thriving tourism industry that attracts significant number of foreign and domestic tourists. On the other hand, East Nusa Tenggara still has to struggle with inadequate infrastructure that becomes a stumbling block to generate growth in the province.

Figure 3.3 illustrates the geographical spread of Overall Competitiveness rankings in six regions in Indonesia. The regions are colour coded according to their competitiveness performance, with darker shade for more competitive regions and lighter shade for least competitive regions. Less competitive regions are mostly found to the east of Java Region, where Bali–Nusa Tenggara and Maluku–Papua Region are at the bottom of Overall Competitiveness ranking.

Review of Ranking and Score: Macroeconomic Stability

For Macroeconomic Stability, there is no change between 2014 and 2015 rank among the six regions (Table 3.3). Java and Sumatra are the top performing regions, illustrating the dichotomy

Table 3.3: 2015 Macroeconomic Stability: Ranking and Score

2015 Rank	2014 Rank	Region	Score
1	1	Java	2.046
2	2	Sumatra	0.075
3	3	Kalimantan	0.032
4	4	Sulawesi	–0.328
5	5	Maluku–Papua	–0.784
6	6	Bali–Nusa Tenggara	–1.041

Source: Asia Competitiveness Institute.

Table 3.4: 2015 Macroeconomic Stability: Top and Bottom Provinces in Each Region

	Region					
	Sumatra	Java	Kalimantan	Sulawesi	Bali–Nusa Tenggara	Maluku–Papua
Top Province	Riau Islands (5)	DKI Jakarta (1)	East Kalimantan (4)	South Sulawesi (8)	Bali (18)	West Papua (19)
Bottom Province	Bengkulu (32)	DI Yogyakarta (20)	West Kalimantan (23)	Gorontalo (30)	East Nusa Tenggara (33)	North Maluku (29)

Source: Asia Competitiveness Institute.

between the western and eastern part of Indonesia in terms of macroeconomic prowess. Although the difference between the top and bottom performing regions in Macroeconomic Stability (3.087) is comparable to the finding from Overall Competitiveness (3.098), more significant gap is found between Java and Sumatra regions (1.971). This is not unusual as Java contributed to more than 60% of Indonesia's GDP in 2012.

The smallest difference in score is found between Sumatra and Kalimantan (0.044), underlining more intense competition between the two regions. However, in terms of GRDP size, share of Indonesia's GDP from Sumatra Region was 20.9%, more than twice that from Kalimantan Region (8.4%) in 2012. Kalimantan Region is able to punch above its weight to get closer to the top as the region consists of only high and mediocre performing provinces (East Kalimantan at fourth; South Kalimantan at 11th; Central Kalimantan at 14th; and West Kalimantan at 23rd), and no low performing provinces. On the other hand, Sumatra Region faces more diverse competitiveness performance among its provinces, ranging from Riau Islands at fifth to Bangka Bengkulu at 32nd.

While Java Region is ranked first in Macroeconomic Stability environment, one of its respective provinces, DI Yogyakarta, slips to 20th (Table 3.4). Unlike its peers, industrialisation does not take off in DI Yogyakarta as the province puts more emphasis on its tertiary sector to drive its economy. With its rich culture and history, DI Yogyakarta has its own charm to attract tourists from all over Indonesia and the world to come and visit their heritage sites. On top of that, DI

Figure 3.4: 2015 Macroeconomic Stability: Sub-Environment Spread

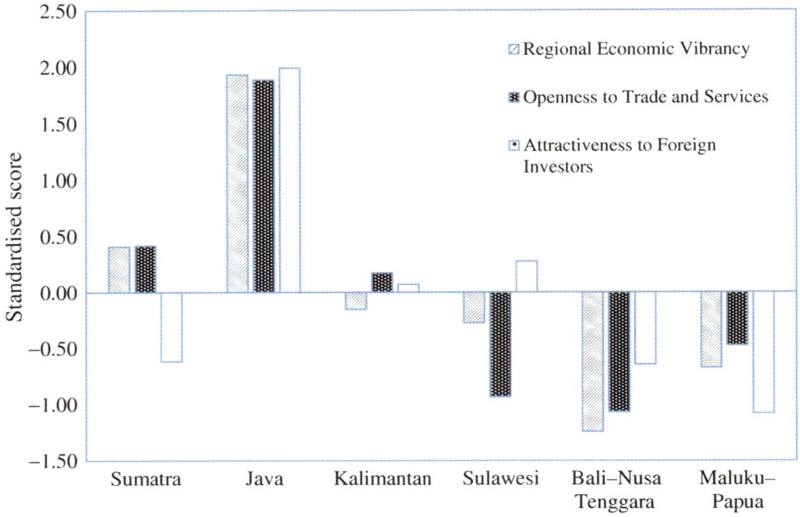

Source: Asia Competitiveness Institute.

Yogyakarta is also home to more than 100 higher education institutions, earning the province a nickname *Kota Pelajar* (The City of Students).

For Kalimantan Region, the stark difference in terms of the ranking of its top and bottom provinces can be traced to their natural resource endowment. East Kalimantan has richer oil, gas, and mining endowment than the remaining provinces in Kalimantan. A number of big multinational companies (MNCs) have set up their operations in East Kalimantan, namely Pertamina, Total and Chevron. In Sulawesi Region, the more established provinces such as South Sulawesi and North Sulawesi perform much better in Macroeconomic Stability environment as compared to newly created provinces such as Gorontalo and West Sulawesi. However, in Maluku–Papua Region, the relatively young province, West Papua, earns higher ranking at 19th as compared to Papua (22nd) and Maluku (28th).

Every region has varying performance in each of the sub-environments that makes up the Macroeconomic Stability environment, as illustrated in Figure 3.4. Java is the only region performing consistently well in all three sub-environments while Sumatra lags behind in Attractiveness to Foreign Investors with a standardised score that resembles Bali–Nusa Tenggara's. This highlights the need for Sumatra to strategise its policies towards creating a conducive business environment for investment to thrive, taking cues from Java and Sulawesi which succeed in making their regions as attractive investment destinations. Again, inter-provincial friendly rivalry is a good first step for a big and diverse Indonesia.

Review of Ranking and Score: Government and Institutional Setting

Table 3.5 shows a relatively symmetrical distribution for the standardised scores of all six regions in Government and Institutional Setting. Java Region's score at the top is 1.326 while

Table 3.5: 2015 Government and Institutional Setting: Ranking and Score

2015 Rank	2014 Rank	Region	Score
1	1	Java	1.326
2	3	Kalimantan	1.053
3	2	Sulawesi	0.417
4	5	Bali–Nusa Tenggara	–0.484
5	4	Sumatra	–0.996
6	6	Maluku–Papua	–1.316

Source: Asia Competitiveness Institute.

Table 3.6. 2015 Government and Institutional Setting: Top and Bottom Provinces in Each Region

	Region					
	Sumatra	**Java**	**Kalimantan**	**Sulawesi**	**Bali–Nusa Tenggara**	**Maluku–Papua**
Top Province	Jambi (11)	DKI Jakarta (1)	East Kalimantan (2)	South Sulawesi (6)	Bali (19)	Papua (25)
Bottom Province	Bangka Belitung Islands (32)	Banten (16)	West Kalimantan (14)	Gorontalo (22)	East Nusa Tenggara (21)	North Maluku (33)

Source: Asia Competitiveness Institute.

Maluku–Papua Region's score at the bottom is −1.316, with a score difference of 2.643, much narrow compared to other environments (Tables 3.3, 3.7 and 3.9). The biggest gap (0.901) is found between Sulawesi Region's above average score (0.417) and Bali–Nusa Tenggara's below average score (–0.484). Sumatra Region's declining performance enables Bali–Nusa Tenggara to climb to fourth position. The findings from provincial competitiveness ranking in Chapter 2 echo the fact that all provinces from Bali–Nusa Tenggara are in the middle 13 while six out of 10 provinces from Sumatra end up in the bottom 10.

Based on Table 3.6, it is only in Government and Institutional Setting environment that Riau Islands is no longer holding the top position among provinces located in Sumatra Region. Jambi sets the example for the remaining provinces in Sumatra by occupying 11th rank. This is consistent with Indonesia Governance Index[8] that ranks Jambi at fourth, only behind DI Yogyakarta, East Java and DKI Jakarta. A string of corruption cases further holds back Banten's achievement in this environment, though its ranking improves from 23rd to 16th.[9] Meanwhile, its peers in Java Region belong to top five, except West Java at 12th.

[8]The index is based on four governance area comprising government, bureaucracy, civil society and economic society. For more information on the index, please refer to http://www.kemitraan.or.id/igi/.

[9]Refer to Chapter 2 for full list of 2015 and 2014 rank.

Figure 3.5: 2015 Government and Institutional Setting: Sub-Environment Spread

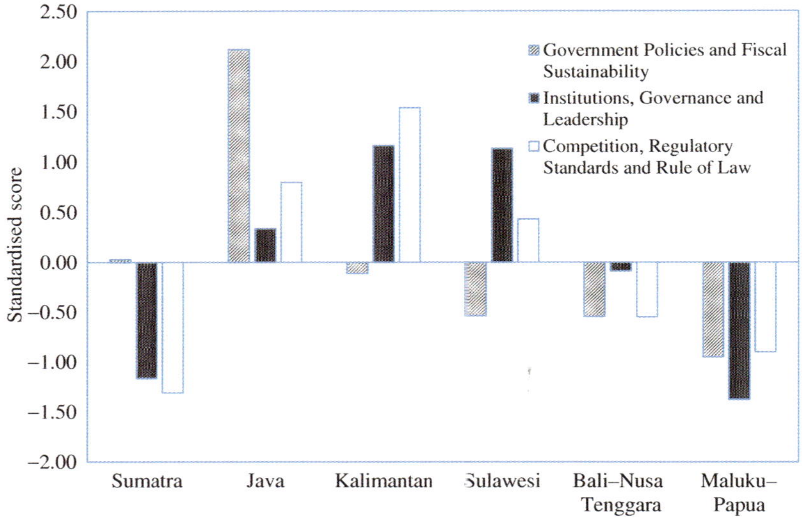

Source: Asia Competitiveness Institute.

The performance of provinces in Bali–Nusa Tenggara Region for this environment is relatively homogenous, with Bali at 19th, West Nusa Tenggara at 20th and East Nusa Tenggara at 21st. East Nusa Tenggara is no longer falling behind while North Maluku retains the bottom position at 33rd for two consecutive years. In Maluku–Papua Region, more resources should be directed to build the governance capacity and capability of the young provinces of West Papua and North Maluku, which are lagging in Government and Institutional Setting environment.

Analysing the scores from each sub-environment allows us to pinpoint the driver for each region's performance in Government and Institutional Setting environment. Based on Figure 3.5, Java becomes the only region with favourable Government Policies and Fiscal Sustainability given its sizeable government's financial resources. On the other hand, Kalimantan and Sulawesi regions compete head-to-head to lead in Institutions, Governance and Leadership. Both regions also perform well in Competition, Regulatory Standards and Rule of Law, with Kalimantan Region as the frontrunner, scoring 1.535.

Among the bottom performing regions, Sumatra is ranked last in terms of Competition, Regulatory Standards and Rule of Law while Maluku–Papua scores the lowest in Institutions, Governance and Leadership. It is obvious that both Sumatra and Maluku–Papua regions have plenty to catch-up to be on par with the quality of governance in the remaining regions.

Review of Ranking and Score: Financial, Businesses and Manpower Conditions

For regions which excel in macroeconomic indicators as captured in Table 3.3, they also perform equally well in the microeconomic indicators as reflected in their Financial, Businesses and Manpower Conditions ranking in Table 3.7. Java Region still leads as the most competitive

Table 3.7: 2015 Financial, Businesses and Manpower Conditions: Ranking and Score

2015 Rank	2014 Rank	Region	Score
1	1	Java	1.688
2	2	Kalimantan	0.854
3	4	Sumatra	–0.022
4	5	Sulawesi	–0.391
5	6	Bali–Nusa Tenggara	–1.054
6	3	Maluku–Papua	–1.075

Source: Asia Competitiveness Institute.

Table 3.8: 2015 Financial, Businesses and Manpower Conditions: Top and Bottom Provinces in Each Region

	Region					
	Sumatra	Java	Kalimantan	Sulawesi	Bali–Nusa Tenggara	Maluku–Papua
Top Province	Riau Islands (6)	DKI Jakarta (1)	East Kalimantan (4)	South Sulawesi (6)	Bali (8)	West Papua (7)
Bottom Province	Bangka Belitung Islands (28)	Banten (17)	South Kalimantan (14)	Southeast Sulawesi (30)	East Nusa Tenggara (32)	Maluku (33)

Source: Asia Competitiveness Institute.

region while Maluku–Papua sits at the bottom with a score difference of 2.764. Such drastic shift from its previous position at third is triggered by its deteriorating performance in Financial Deepening and Business Efficiency. Meanwhile, Sumatra's rise to third position is due to its improved performance in Financial Deepening and Business Efficiency, whose score was the lowest in 2014 rank. This is a case in point for the region which takes heed on its weaknesses and prioritises policy improvement in those areas.

Disparity within region is more striking in the case of Maluku–Papua Region where West Papua as the top province is at seventh while Maluku as the bottom province sits at 33rd (Table 3.8). West Papua can be a role model for its peers to boost their performance in Financial, Businesses and Manpower Conditions environment. The province is particularly doing well in Financial Deepening and Business Efficiency, and Productivity Performance sub-environments. Other striking gaps can also be observed in Bali–Nusa Tenggara Region (Bali at 8th; West Nusa Tenggara at 32nd) and Sumatra Region (Riau Islands at 6th; Bangka Belitung Islands at 28th). For Java Region, Banten is the only province out of the top 10. This signals that the business perceptions[10] towards Financial, Businesses and Manpower Conditions in Banten remain weak, albeit slight improvement from its 2014 ranking at 22nd.

[10]More than one-fourth of indicators (8 out of 27) in Financial, Businesses and Manpower Conditions environment come from ACI's business perception survey administered in collaboration with Indonesian Employers' Association (APINDO).

Figure 3.6: 2015 Financial, Businesses and Manpower Conditions: Sub-Environment Spread

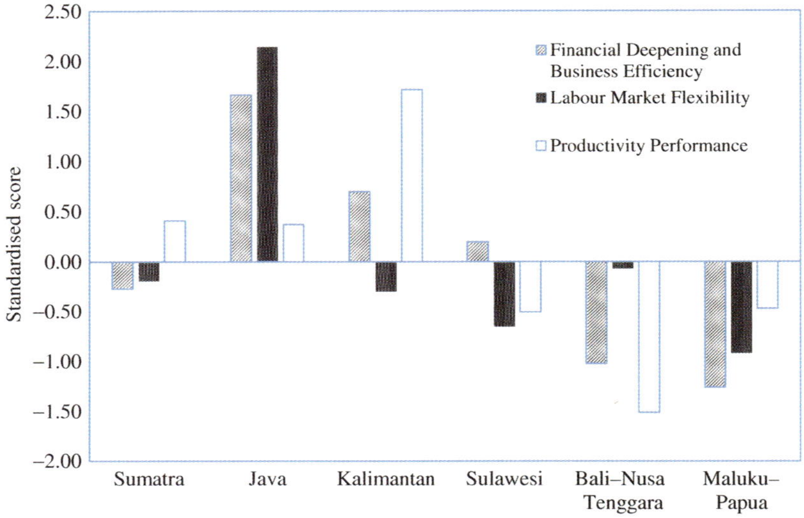

Source: Asia Competitiveness Institute.

To get more detailed picture of each region's performance in Financial, Businesses and Manpower Conditions, Figure 3.6 presents the score breakdown for each sub-environment. Java at the top becomes the only region which consistently scores above average in all three sub-environments. In fact, it is the only region scoring positive value in Labour Market Flexibility, given its abundant pool of manpower. Despite the nation-wide trend of rising minimum wages, East Java, Central Java and West Java still emerged as the provinces with the lowest minimum wage in 2012. Kalimantan Region's runner-up position is mostly driven by its Productive Performance, scoring higher than Java Island. Kalimantan's economic structure that relies on oil and gas extraction and its related processing activities is relatively more capital intensive, hence, driving its score in this sub-environment.

In contrast, the bottom two regions are riddled with below average score performance in the three sub-environments. Nonetheless, Bali–Nusa Tenggara Region's score in Labour Market Flexibility is hovering around zero, with Bali's stellar performance at fourth providing strong leverage to increase the regional score. In contrast, its score in Productivity Performance is the lowest among all six regions. In spite of less developed and extensive manufacturing sector, the region can boast higher competitiveness by adopting information, communications and technology (ICT) to increase value add from its core sector, such as tourism and other services.

Review of Ranking and Score: Quality of Life and Infrastructure Development

For Quality of Life and Infrastructure Development, four out of six regions obtain positive scores, reflecting their above average performance (Table 3.9). Though Java Region at the top scores almost twice that of Kalimantan Region, the score differences between Kalimantan and Sumatra

Table 3.9: 2015 Quality of Life and Infrastructure Development: Ranking and Score

2015 Rank	2014 Rank	Region	Score
1	1	Java	1.144
2	2	Kalimantan	0.594
3	3	Sumatra	0.402
4	4	Sulawesi	0.255
5	5	Bali–Nusa Tenggara	–0.409
6	6	Maluku–Papua	–1.986

Source: Asia Competitiveness Institute.

Table 3.10: 2015 Quality of Life and Infrastructure Development: Top and Bottom Provinces in Each Region

	Region					
	Sumatra	**Java**	**Kalimantan**	**Sulawesi**	**Bali–Nusa Tenggara**	**Maluku–Papua**
Top Province	Riau Islands (4)	DI Yogyakarta (2)	East Kalimantan (1)	South Sulawesi (11)	Bali (7)	Maluku (27)
Bottom Province	Bangka Belitung Islands (25)	Central Java (14)	West Kalimantan (29)	West Sulawesi (30)	East Nusa Tenggara (31)	Papua (33)

Source: Asia Competitiveness Institute.

(0.192) and Sumatra and Sulawesi (0.147) are relatively narrow, underlining tight competition among the regions occupying second to fourth position. Unfortunately, wide gap still exists, as Maluku–Papua Region's score is significantly below average (–1.986). Its score difference with Bali–Nusa Tenggara Region at fifth is quite stark (1.577), let alone its score difference with Java Region at the top (3.130). At the provincial level, Papua (–2.584) and West Papua (–1.823) are the bottom two, while Maluku (–0.812) and North Maluku (–1.004) sit at 27th and 28th, respectively.

In Kalimantan Region, performance among provinces in Quality of Life and Infrastructure Development varies widely, as can be seen from East Kalimantan's position at the top while West Kalimantan ends up near to the bottom (Table 3.10). The bottleneck for the latter seems to come from Physical Infrastructure, and Standard of Living, Education, and Social Stability sub-environments. Newly created provinces in Sumatra and Sulawesi regions tend to lag behind as in the case of Bangka Belitung Islands at 25th, Gorontalo at 26th and West Sulawesi at 30th. Nevertheless, Riau Islands is an exception as soft and hard infrastructure has been developed significantly to support its Batam, Bintan and Karimun Special Economic Zone (SEZ). As mentioned above, all provinces in Maluku–Papua Region are in the bottom 10, with the highest ranking of 27th (Maluku) and the lowest is 33rd (Papua). East Nusa Tenggara's position at 31st is also relatively further behind its immediate neighbour's position, West Nusa Tenggara at 22nd.

Figure 3.7: 2015 Quality of Life and Infrastructure Development: Sub-Environment Spread

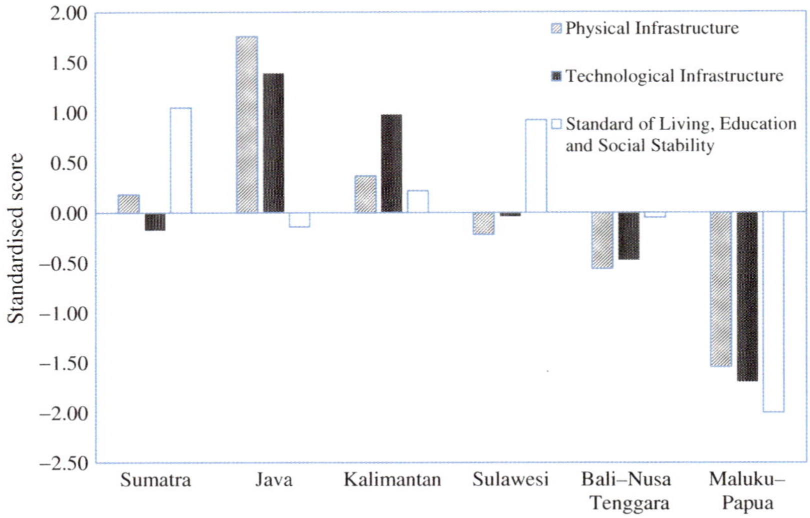

Source: Asia Competitiveness Institute.

Even among the top four regions, each region performs differently in each sub-environment, as illustrated in Figure 3.7. For instance, Java Region sets to become a benchmark and attains the highest scores in Physical Infrastructure and Technological Infrastructure sub-environments. Nonetheless, Java's below average score in Standard of Living, Education and Social Stability is way behind Sumatra, Sulawesi and Kalimantan regions. Much can be achieved from adopting best practices from the high performing region. On the other hand, the scores for the bottom two regions are below average for all three sub-environments. Maluku–Papua Region faces tough challenges to catch-up with the rest of Indonesia to improve not only its hard infrastructure, but also its soft infrastructure in equipping its human capital with necessary skills to unlock the region's potential.

3.3.2 Analysis of Median and Maximum Competitiveness Webs

From the sub-environment spreads illustrated in Figures 3.4–3.7, we can pinpoint the source of each region's performance in each environment. Other charts, median and maximum competitiveness webs, will allow us to compare and contrast attainment of each region, not only in three sub-environments under their respective environment, but in all 12 sub-environments. Figure 3.8 provides a snapshot for comparison between the top and bottom performing regions against the median score while Figure 3.9 provides comparison with the maximum score.

As a top performing region, Java Region attains higher scores than the median scores in all sub-environments, except Standard of Living, Education and Social Stability. Consequently, Java leads in eight out of 12 sub-environments. Kalimantan achieves the maximum score in Institutions, Governance and Leadership; Competition, Regulatory and Rule of Law; and Productivity Performance while Sumatra tops the Standard of Living, Education, and Social

Figure 3.8: 2015 Median Competitiveness Web Analysis: Top and Bottom Performing Regions

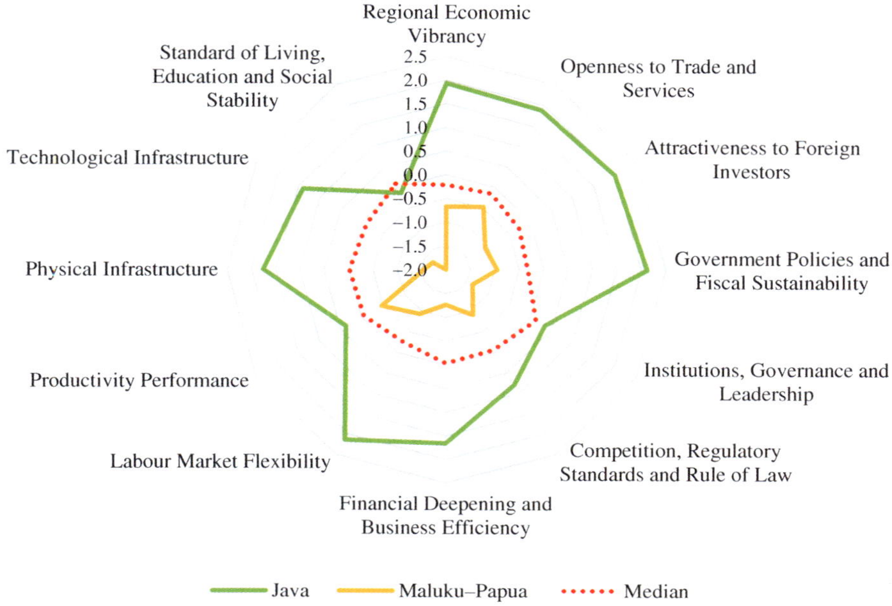

Source: Asia Competitiveness Institute.

Figure 3.9: 2015 Maximum Competitiveness Web Analysis: Top and Bottom Performing Regions

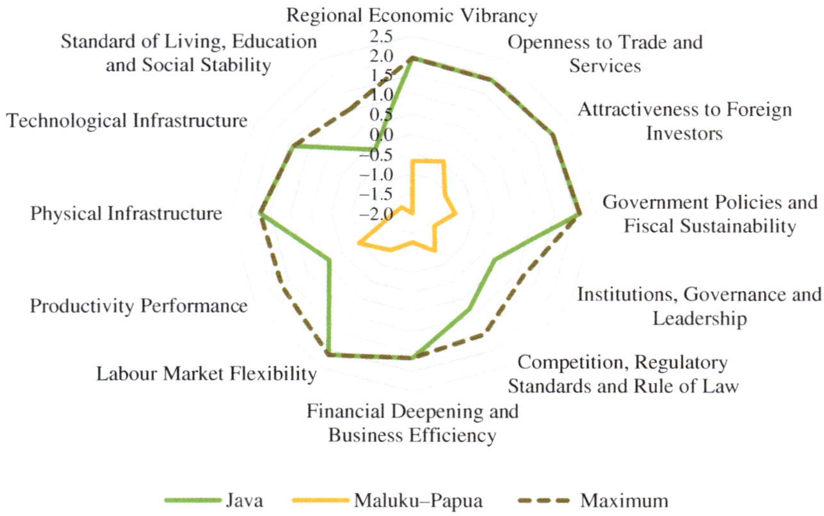

Source: Asia Competitiveness Institute.

Stability. For Maluku–Papua Region, its scores in all 12 sub-environments are certainly below the median and maximum scores. The widest gap between each sub-environment's score and the respective median score is found in Standard of Living, Education and Social Stability.

Despite challenges for public services to reach out to sparse population across mountainous Papua or small islands in Maluku, more innovative initiatives can provide ingenious solution to this perennial problem. Ensuring good quality teachers in the less developed areas is an arduous task, in spite of 'special area' allowance granted to those teach in remote locations. Breakthrough initiatives from civil society such as *Indonesia Mengajar* (Teach for Indonesia) that deploys young graduates to teach in isolated areas to promote a spirit that everyone has a role to make changes they want to see, one child at a time. For every selected primary school in each district, the programme will run for five years and focus on behavioural changes not only at the school level but also all stakeholders in the community.[11] More of these initiatives will do Indonesia good, encouraging collaboration, partnership, and supports from all sectors — public, private and civil society, comprising non-governmental organisations (NGOs).

3.4 CONCLUSION AND POLICY IMPLICATIONS

Aligning with a paradigm shift in regional policy from providing subsidies to lagging regions to unleashing competitiveness of each region, the central government of Indonesia launched the MP3EI in 2011. For growth to be spread out, six economic corridors have been identified, together with their development themes. By adopting such regional classification, our research found that Java Region is still lauded as the most competitiveness region, leading in all four environments.

The dichotomy between western and eastern part of Indonesia is less profound as Sumatra Region which is often coined as Java's peer in western domination stays at fourth position, below Kalimantan and Sulawesi regions. The sub-environment spread allows us to dig deeper into factors enhancing or impending each region's competitiveness. For instance, despite Sumatra's runner-up position in Macroeconomic Stability, the region suffers from below average Attractiveness to Foreign Investors. Given ACI's strength to drill deeper into provincial level, more direct impact and tangible policy-making can be done. The results also help us to infer which region can be a benchmark for best practice policies as in the case of Kalimantan and Sulawesi regions for Institutions, Governance and Leadership. All in all, this provides abundant learning opportunities from interregional friendly rivalry to unleash the potential of each region that eventually improve national competitiveness.

Disparity within region is also prevalent in some instances. For example, in Sumatra Region, Riau Islands often leads in the top 10 while its peers which are less industrialised and relying on extractive industries fall behind in the bottom 10. Such differences also persist between oil rich province and not so well endowed province as in the case of East Kalimantan which holds first position in terms of Quality of Life and Infrastructure Development while its neighbour, West Kalimantan, ranks 29th. This signals that even the gaps between soft and hard infrastructure within region still exist, while such gaps across the regions remain a perennial challenge.

The performance of most eastern region, Maluku–Papua, continues to fall behind, particularly in Quality of Life and Infrastructure Development environment with extremely low standardised

---

[11] More information on *Indonesia Mengajar* can be found in https://indonesiamengajar.org/.

score. As the least developed region, Maluku–Papua stands to benefit the most, especially from improvement in education and health outcomes. Improvement in human resources is key for the region to achieve higher competitiveness. The existing national agenda for Indonesia to enhance its maritime infrastructure gives a promising outlook for Maluku–Papua Region to be more involved in the interregional trade that may increase complementarity among Indonesia's regions. Committed government, both at central and local level, is an important aspect to strengthen the impetus for higher competitiveness for Indonesia as a whole. Starting from a low base, getting result as quickly also boost confidence to tackle other less low-lying fruits.

REFERENCES

Coordinating Ministry for Economic Affairs. 2011. *Master Plan for Acceleration and Expansion of Indonesia's Economic Development 2011–2025 (MP3EI)*. Jakarta: Coordinating Ministry for Economic Affairs.

Garcia, Jorge and Lana Soelistianingsih. 1998. "Why Do Differences in Provincial Incomes Persist in Indonesia?" *Bulletin of Indonesian Economic Studies* 34(1): 95–120.

Matthews, Chris. 2014. "Poor Germany: Why the East Will Never Catch Up to the West." *Fortune*, November 9. http://fortune.com/2014/11/09/germany-east-west-economy/(accessed July 28, 2015).

Mietzner, Marcus. 2013. "Indonesia's Decentralisation: The Rise of Local Identities and the Survival of the Nation-State." Paper presented at the Indonesia Update Conference 2013, Canberra, Australia, September 20.

Nazara, Suahasil, Michael, Sonis and Geoffrey J.D. Hewings. 2000. "Interregional Competition and Complementarity in Indonesia." *The Regional Economics Applications Laboratory (REAL) Discussion Paper REAL 01-T-2*: 1–22.

OECD. 2010. *Regional Development Policy Trends in OECD Member Countries*. Paris: OECD Publishing.

Sonis, Michael, Geoffrey J.D. Hewings, Jiemin, Guo and Edison, Hulu. 1997. "Interpreting Spatial Economic Structure: Feedback Loops in the Indonesian Interregional Economy, 1980, 1985." *Regional Science and Urban Economics* 27: 325–342.

Tan, Khee Giap, Mulya Amri, Linda, Low and Tan, Kong Yam. 2013. *Competitiveness Analysis and Development Strategies for 33 Indonesian Provinces*. Singapore: World Scientific.

Tan, Khee Giap, Nurina Merdikawati, Mulya, Amri and Blake, Harley Berger. 2015a. *2014 Annual Competitiveness Analysis and Development Strategies for Indonesian Provinces*. Singapore: World Scientific.

Tan, Khee Giap, Nurina Merdikawati, Mulya, Amri and Tan, Kong Yam. 2015b. *2014 Provincial and Inaugural Regional Competitiveness Analysis: Safeguarding Indonesia's Growth Momentum*. Singapore: World Scientific.

Tan, Khee Giap, Yuan, Randong and Sangiita Yoong, Wei Cher. 2015. *2014 Annual Provincial and Regional Competitiveness Analysis for Greater China Economies: Development Strategies under the New Normal*. Singapore: World Scientific.

Discussant Notes: 2015 Provincial and Regional Competitiveness Ranking and Simulation for Indonesia: An Annual Update

Ir Alma Karma, MEM

Director of Regional Potential Development
Investment Coordinating Board (BKPM), Indonesia

As a consequence of the regional autonomy implementation in Indonesia, the local government moved to work and unleash its potential, with the aim to increase revenue, develop regional economy and reduce its dependence from central government. One of the main efforts in developing the region's potential is to attract investors by improving regional competitiveness.

The ability to promote its potentials is an important factor to improve the welfare of regions. The ability to promote should also be supported by conducives business and investment climate in the regions such as security and legal certainty for investment. Local governments should be able to enact regulations that spur economic growth by seizing domestic and foreign investors as well as empowering local investors.

Aside from macroeconomic, political stability and adequate infrastructure, Indonesian government realises that a conducive business climate is the key to attract investment. Therefore, the government has a strong committment to improve business climate, including improving BKPM services to investors. Let us take a look at BKPM action in implementing One Stop Service (OSS/PTSP):

- Earlier this year, President Jokowi has inaugurated OSS/PTSP Center at BKPM. Twenty-two ministries and institutions have assigned their officers to become Liaison Officers (LOs) at BKPM to provide consultation and license services to investors. All investment permits at national level are now obtained at BKPM.
- Together with ministries and other institutions, BKPM also established OSS/PTSP at the local level with the system in the BKPM. Currently, 90% of the 561 districts in Indonesia have formed OSS/PTSP. There are 61% of regions that have implemented an electronic licensing system to be integrated with the central government. The OSS/PTSP system is targeted to cover all regions in Indonesia by the end of 2016.
- The next stage is to simplify the licensing both at the central and regional level and strengthening institutional and services of Investment Board and One Stop Services (BPMPTSP) in the region because most licensing and non-licensing related to investments are under the authority of regions.

Since 2012, although Indonesia has been maintaining its economic growth above 5% per year, the growth has been slowing down. In the first quarter of 2015, Indonesia's economy only grew at 4.7%. However, the investment realisation has always been increasing. Between January and March 2015, BKPM booked almost 125 trillion Rupiahs of investment realisation, an increase of 16.9% compared to the same period last year. This has created 315,000 job opportunities so that in the last two quarters, direct investment has employed 785,000 direct labors in Indonesia.

With increasing contribution to the GDP, direct investment is expected to be the major source of economic growth, aside from government spending for infrastructure. To support the average economic growth of 7% per year between 2014 and 2019, total direct investment is targeted to increase by 15.1% per year in average for the next five years.

For example, there are six manufacturing companies constructing investment projects worth 46 trillion Rupiahs (3.5 billion Dollars), which in turn absorbs more than 10,500 direct labours, not including another 40,000 indirect labours. Those investment projects will also contribute to 800 million Dollars of export value and substitute 810 million Dollars of import. They will also generate 986 megawatt (MW) of power, 67% of which are sold to public through state-owned electricity company (PT PLN).

Growth is not only seen in the investment realisation, but also in the number of projects. In the first quarter of 2015, BKPM approved project plans worth 320 trillion Rupiahs, a 13.9% increase compared to last year. In Sragen, Central Java, the trend is also positive. In 2013, the local government issued investment permits worth 650 billion Rupiahs. The year after, the value jumped 130% to 1.5 trillion Rupiahs. From January until early June 2015, 1.2 trillion Rupiahs of investment plan has been approved.

In accordance to the national medium term development plan (RPJMN) from 2015 to 2019, the national economic growth projection is between 5 to 8% with a target of 15% growth in realised investment each year so that the projected total investment realisation from 2015 until 2019 is 3,518 trillion Rupiahs with domestic investment ratio of 39% in 2019. Investment growth is extremely important to support the national economic growth target of 8% in 2019. The growth and improvement in the investment is the result of the service and investment climate improvement at the national and regional level on an ongoing basis, both in terms of improvement of legislation, simplification of licensing and non-licensing services and the provision of investment incentives.

The focus of investment in 2015 per region is expected to achieve 282.6 trillion Rupiahs in Java, 75.2 trillion Rupiahs in Sumatra, 74.5 trillion Rupiahs in Kalimantan, 27.8 trillion Rupiahs in Sulawesi, 19 trillion Rupiahs in Bali and Nusa Tenggara, 7.3 trillion Rupiahs in Maluku and 33.2 trillion Rupiahs in Papua and West Papua. In Java, the focus is on high-tech industries, service and trade. While in outside Java, the focus is to increase the value-add in industrial activities, including labour-intensive industries and downstream industries in agricultural, fisheries, and mining sector. Particularly for Papua and West Papua, the focus is to encourage economic equality through the development of processing industries from agricultural, fisheries and mining sector, as well as chemical industry.

In the era of regional autonomy and fiscal decentralisation, local governments have great discretion in determining the regional development policy. Local governments allocate its resources based on their identified priorities. Facing the competition ahead, the local government can take initiatives by directing resources in an effort to increase competitiveness. The initial step that is required is how to map the capabilities in the possessed area (input factor) and what goals to be achieved (output factor). Prioritisation will be the next step considering the limited resources. Furthermore, implementation process and its evaluation and monitoring are very important.

The importance of competitiveness itself relates to three important priorities of the nine vision, mission, and programme of President Jokowi, known as *Nawacita*. Three priorities related to competitiveness are (1) improving the quality of human life; (2) increasing people's productivity and competitiveness in the international market; and (3) realising economic independence by moving the strategic sectors of the domestic economy.

The Law No. 23/2014 regarding regional government, which revoked the previous Law, is more rigid in dividing the concurrent matters or authority of central, provincial and municipal governments. Moreover, several sectors have been overrided from municipal to provincial authority such as mining and fishery due to the evaluation of their implementation after several years. The Law simply gives more authority to the Governor as a representative of central government. For example, they can evaluate the district/city regulations and also can give rewards and sanctions to their mayors or regents related with the regional governance.

In order to face the era of globalisation, free market, middle income trap and also economic slowdown, improving competitiveness among regions is very important in order to seize potential investors, both domestic and foreign investors. Regional readiness especially human resource managers, infrastructure availability and service excellence, will be crucial to capture the investors to invest in the region. Competition between regions must be developed in an atmosphere of fair, positive and healthy competition.

Chapter 4

Decentralisation, Governing Institutions and Economic Development in Indonesia

Li Hui and Yee Wai-Hang[1]

4.1 INTRODUCTORY REMARKS

Decentralisation reform in Indonesia was introduced to better public services and benefit economic growth. However, one major challenge in the reform is that sub-national governments may fail to achieve desirable governing institutions that are crucial in linking decentralisation and economic development. This chapter investigates the governing institutions of Indonesian provinces under decentralisation reform and their relations with economic development. While decentralisation may influence the development of desirable governing institutions, this study examines more closely on how these governing institutions influence business investment in provinces which contributes directly to economic growth.

The decentralisation reform in Indonesia was introduced after the fall of the Suharto regime in the late 1990s. The resignation of President Suharto in the aftermath of the Asian Financial Crisis brought Indonesia under the threat of political instability. Against the backdrop of possible declaration of independence by certain provinces (given particularly the large size of the population) and thus the potential divide of the country, a "big bang" decentralisation governmental reform was introduced. The passage of two Laws — Law No. 22/1999 on Regional Government and Law No. 25/1999 on Fiscal Balance between Central and Regional Governments have often been cited as the mark of the beginning of the decentralisation reform (see e.g. Holtzappel 2009). As a result, all major government responsibilities are decentralised except foreign affairs, defence, justice, finance, religion, management of natural resources and state administration to the district level. The implementation of the two Laws, drafted in the aftermath of a political and economic turmoil, encountered huge setbacks and they were replaced by Law No. 32/2004 and Law No. 33/2004. The new laws maintain the "spirit" of decentralisation as conceived in 1999, but with more measures to keep local governments in check. For example, the head of individual

[1]The authors are Assistant Professors at the Lee Kuan Yew School of Public Policy (LKYSPP), and Research Fellows at the Asia Competitiveness Institute, LKYSPP, National University of Singapore.

regional government is now held accountable to its people through direct election and to the central government through budget provision, which accounted for a majority of the regional government's financial source (92.6%) (World Bank 2003; UNDP 2009).[2]

A growing literature is trying to evaluate this major reform. Hadiz (2003), for example, argues that decentralisation helps Indonesia balance competing interests in policy making under its weak institutional settings. Ray (2009) traced the change in local regulatory process and observed dramatic increase in regulatory fees and heavy reliance on local levies in regional governments. A notable policy paper from the UNDP proposes that good governance (GG) at the provincial level is the "missing link" to Indonesia's decentralisation. Provinces, it argues, should strengthen the role of supervising and coordinating districts and cities, harmonising the discharge of their responsibilities (UNDP 2009).

Though many empirical investigations do seek to evaluate the reform through tracing influence of governing institutions, their inference are largely based on limited evidence from small samples of provinces and regional governments. In this study, we look into the "political-institutional complex" behind decentralisation reform by comparing the quality of governing institutions and the extent of economic activities among all Indonesian provinces. In particular, we seek to understand how the quality of various governing institutions are linked with investment decisions of businesses among these provinces.

4.2 RESEARCH DESIGN, DATA AND METHODOLOGY

Business investments contribute directly to economic growth. Their decisions to hire more staff for expansion, upgrading their equipment, renewing their production methods or engaging in research and development (R&D) directly affect local economic performance. These decisions, however, vary in terms of their respective length of time for returning on investment and are often affected by whether local political and institutional conditions are conducive to economic activities or whether local governments are facilitative to busines operations. In a sense, they may be seen as the micro foundation linking the quality of governing institutions and economic performance. While the former formulates the investment environment of businesses, the latter contributes directly to local economic performance.

In general, one may expect that the longer the period of the return on investment, the more likely a more conducive political and institutional environment is required for businesses to engage in such decisions. New institutional economics literature suggests that governing institutions such as the rule of law (Murrell 2001), public order and security (O&S) (North, Wallis and Weingast 2009), stable and sound property and regulatory regime (Coase 1960; Levy and Spiller 1994), clean and transparent government are often considered as crucial to a country's social and economic development (see North 1990; Shirley 2005).

The existence of both *inclusive* economic institutions, which allow for mass participation in the economy, and *inclusive* political institutions which are sufficiently centralised and pluralistic,

---

[2]Indonesia's parliament passed a bill in September 2014 to end direct elections for regional leaders but that legislation was reversed in January 2015 due to a huge popular uproar.

is essential to sustainable economic growth and prosperity (Acemoglu and Robinson 2012, 70–95). These institutional arrangements, if rightly designed, can lower costs in economic transactions and provide incentives for increasing investment and productivity of individuals and organisations, which thus improves economic performance (North 1990).

Meanwhile, business entrepreneurs do not always make decisions based on simply the existence or the strength of one single condition, "holding all others constant". Some concerns are more foundational than others and the presence of these conditions are necessary for their investment decisions. In other words, a set-oriented logic (Ragin 2008) is governing their decisions. If individual entrepreneur, for example, feels that the local political condition is uncertain, even if other production function factors are independently favourable, they will probably decide to withhold their investment or make investment that yields faster return. They will probably invest less heavily into the future, restraining from expanding their business or engaging in long term R&D.

On the other hand, there may also be alternative causal paths that lead to such investments. One common feature in developing economies is the heavy reliance on informal social network. In any case, these considerations render the relations between conditions and asymmetric outcomes. The necessity and sufficiency of conditions, as well as their combinatorial effects are not readily discoverable by traditional statistical methods. A more cautious set-oriented approach is warranted.

Our study proposes to measure the perceived quality of various governing institutions from the business perspective and also the planned and actual investment in various aspects of business operations of all provinces in Indonesia. The Asia Competitiveness Institute (ACI) (Tan *et al.* 2013) has been tracking the change in governing institutions and economic performance of 33 Indonesian provinces under the theme of competitiveness (see Porter 1990a, 1990b).[3] This study looks into the empirical findings collected from a survey that ACI conducted with Indonesian business owners and operators in 2013.

Respondents were invited through individual chapters of the Indonesian Employers' Association (APINDO) in each of the 33 Provinces. The survey was conducted using an electronic response system. Questions were presented onto a computer-linked projector and respondents were expected to key in their respective answers using electronic keypads (or "clickers"). Facilitators from ACI were present in each survey to read out the questions and give clarifications when needed. In the rare case that an electronic survey could not be conducted, respondents were given paper-based survey forms to fill in. A total of 725 respondents participated in the survey, equivalent to around 22 per province on average, as reported in Table 4.1. The number of respondents from each province ranges from 10 to 43.

A nine-point Likert scale was adopted for all questions unless otherwise specified, with "strongly disagree" and "strongly agree" on both ends, and "neutral" in the middle.[4] For each

[3]The ACI defines competitiveness through four different environments: Macroeconomic Stability; Government and Institutional Setting; Financial, Businesses and Manpower Conditions; and Quality of Life and Infrastructure Development.

[4]For the questions about quality of infrastructure, "very poor" and "excellent" are on the two ends with "neutral" in the middle.

Table 4.1: Number of Respondents from Each Province

No.	Province	Participants	No.	Province	Participants
1	Aceh	19	18	West Nusa Tenggara	30
2	North Sumatra	10	19	East Nusa Tenggara	19
3	West Sumatra	13	20	West Kalimantan	21
4	Riau	30	21	Central Kalimantan	20
5	Riau Islands	13	22	South Kalimantan	25
6	Jambi	16	23	East Kalimantan	19
7	South Sumatra	25	24	North Sulawesi	31
8	Bangka Belitung Islands	22	25	Gorontalo	21
9	Bengkulu	21	26	Central Sulawesi	23
10	Lampung	32	27	South Sulawesi	43
11	DKI Jakarta	28	28	Sulawesi West	22
12	West Java	21	29	Southeast Sulawesi	16
13	Banten	15	30	Maluku	23
14	Central Java	36	31	North Maluku	12
15	DI Yogyakarta	18	32	Papua	24
16	East Java	13	33	West Papua	28
17	Bali	16		Total	725

Source: Asia Competitiveness Institute.

questionnaire item, the mean values of all responses from a particular province were calculated to represent the "score" of the province on that item.

Principle component analysis was adopted on 12 related items on governing institutions to understand how businesses in Indonesia categorised these items. Table 4.2 reported three extracted dimensions, namely *administrative efficiency* (AE), GG and O&S.

AE measured the cost businesses incurred in dealing with the administrative process, which included the time needed for applying for public permits and documents and the extent of associated corruption. In particular, the items loaded on this dimension included (1) time needed for applying for public permits and documents, (2) administrative requirement to deal with permits and other public documents and (3) corruption is not a severe problem. It is interesting to observe that extent of corruption was loaded on this dimension, rather than on GG. It seemed that the businesses surveyed considered corruption as a more specific operational issue than a general governance issue.

GG measured the perception whether there was a guarantee that major governmental powers were used non-arbitrarily. It involved business assessment on judiciary independence, as well as whether government contracts were rewarded based on merit and whether the government was willing to listen to voices of the citizens and businessmen. In particular, the component included the following six items: (1) in this province, the government regulators follow closely the laws

Table 4.2: Dimensions of Governing Institutions

	Loadings		
	GG	**AE**	**O&S**
In this province, the government regulators follow closely the laws and regulations in their enforcement.	**0.860**	0.194	0.228
In the province, judiciary services are readily accessible.	**0.833**	0.343	0.074
In this province, the government carefully considers the voice of businesses and citizens in making their policy decisions.	**0.772**	0.206	0.307
In the province, judiciary bodies are independent and fair.	**0.766**	0.279	0.274
In this province, public contracts are generally awarded based on meritocracy (not on favouritism or kickbacks).	**0.727**	0.177	0.165
In the province, contracts are respected and enforced.	**0.641**	0.242	0.337
Time to deal with permits and other public documents or matters is not burdensome.	0.330	**0.893**	0.058
Administrative requirement to deal with permits and other public documents or matters is not burdensome.	0.314	**0.869**	−0.041
Corruption is not a severe problem.	0.168	**0.617**	0.310
Control of crimes and violence in the province is effective.	0.258	0.326	**0.830**
The political condition (including ethnic and religious relations) in the province is stable.	0.205	−0.165	**0.799**
Businesses and citizens do not have to worry about their property rights.	0.414	0.362	**0.613**

Note: Dimensions were derived using principal component analysis with varimax rotation; Kaiser–Meyer–Olkin index = 0.769; Bartlett's test of Sphericity is significant at 0.001 level. Boldface items in each column are those used for the same dimension.
Source: Asia Competitiveness Institute.

and regulations in their enforcement, (2) in the province, judiciary services are readily accessible, (3) in this province, the government carefully considers the voice of businesses and citizens in making their policy decisions, (4) in the province, judiciary bodies are independent and fair, (5) in this province, public contracts are generally awarded based on meritocracy (not on favouritism or kickbacks) and (6) in the province, contracts are respected and enforced.

The last one, O&S, measured the security and political conditions in the province, including three items: (1) control of crimes and violence in the province is effective, (2) the political condition (including ethnic and religious relations) in the province is stable and (3) businesses and citizens do not have to worry about their property rights. As can be seen from the analysis, concern about property right was loaded on this dimension, which suggested that concern about property right to our business respondents was not a transactional but a security one.

In addition, whether local governments within provinces, such as districts and cities, were well coordinated was reported as one major institutional issue in the Indonesian decentralisation reform (Abidin 2009; UNDP 2009). Hence, we also adopted the questions that assessed whether laws and regulations across different local governments in the province were harmonised and

Table 4.3: Causal Conditions and Measures

Conditions	Measures
AE	— Time to deal with permits and other public documents or matters is not burdensome. — Administrative requirement to deal with permits and other public documents or matters is not burdensome. — Corruption is not a severe problem.
GG	— In this province, the government regulators follow closely the laws and regulations in their enforcement. — In the province, judiciary services are readily accessible. — In this province, the government carefully considers the voice of businesses and citizens in making their policy decisions. — In the province, judiciary bodies are independent and fair. — In this province, public contracts are generally awarded based on meritocracy (not on favouritism or kickbacks). — In the province, contracts are respected and enforced.
O&S	— Control of crimes and violence in the province is effective. — The political condition (including ethnic and religious relations) in the province is stable. — Businesses and citizens do not have to worry about their property rights.
LGC	— Laws and regulations across different local governments in the province were harmonised. — There is good collaboration and coordination among local governments within the province.
BI	— Quality of power supply. — Quality of water supply. — Quality of roads. — Access/coverage of internet.

Source: Asia Competitiveness Institute.

whether there was good collaboration and coordination among local governments within the province. We termed this condition as *local government coordination* (LGC). All causal conditions and measures were reported in Table 4.3.

Finally, we also measured how satisfied our respondents were with the quality of *basic infrastructure* (BI) in the province. Only basic infrastructural facilities, such as water and electricity supplies, quality of roads and access to internet, were measured, as they could be found commonly among all provinces and were less likely to be affected by existing level of business investment (as compared to, for example, quality of airport and seaport).

With the above *five* causal conditions developed from averaging the constituted items, we further identified a cut-off point of 4.5. If the value was smaller than 4.5 (worse than neutral, i.e. "dissatisfactory"), we coded that condition as zero (0), indicating the absence of such condition. Otherwise, they were coded as one (1) to indicate its existence.

For the dependent outcomes, we adopted questionnaire items that asked whether the respondent's company *would* invest in various dimensions of business operations and whether they *had* already made investment that would take a relatively longer time to materialise. These questions included (1) "Your firm will invest in upgrading its equipment over the next five years;" (2) "Your firm has applied many innovative methods in production process over the past three years;" and (3) "Your firm spends substantially on Research and Development." For the dependent outcomes, a slightly higher cut-off point of six was used to indicate positive (i.e. larger than neutral) investment decisions. If the value was smaller than six, we coded it as zero (0), indicating the absence of such outcome. They were coded as one (1) otherwise to indicate existence. Finally, we termed these investment outcomes as *equipment upgrade*, *new methods* and *R&D*, respectively.

Respondents were also asked about whether they would increase their growth of staff. A five-point scale was adopted (1 = decrease by more than 10%; 2 = decrease by 0–10%; 3 = increase by 0–10%; 4 = increase by 10–25%; 5 = increase by more than 25%). The mean values of all responses from a particular province in 2013 were compared with the same figure which recorded their anticipation for 2014. If the latter is larger than the former, we coded the outcome for such province as 1 to indicate increase in growth. Otherwise, such outcome was coded as 0. This outcome was termed as *staff hiring*.

4.3 RESEARCH FINDINGS

Table 4.4 reports descriptive statistics of the conditions and outcomes. For the five causal conditions measured, the ascending order of their mean values is AE (3.39), LGC (4.27), BI (4.49), GG (4.54) and O&S (5.85), with three of them below the cut-off point of 4.5 (3.39, 4.27 and 4.49, respectively). The mean value of AE (3.39) is much lower than the other causal conditions, suggesting that low AE is a common issue across provinces. Business respondents believe that both the time and administrative requirements to deal with permits and other public documents are quite burdensome and corruption is a severe problem (the mean values of the three items are 3.95, 3.47 and 2.76, respectively).

The high correlation between them (demonstrated by the high loadings of the three items in Table 4.2) confirms the general observation in Indonesian studies that the long and winding road in the Indonesia business license processing is a major source of corruption and viewed by

Table 4.4: Descriptive Statistics

	N	Min	Max	Mean
Staff Hiring	33	0.00	1.00	0.6970
Equipment Upgrade — Your firm will invest in upgrading its equipment over the next five years	33	5.88	8.88	7.0815
New Methods — Your firm has applied many innovative methods in production process over the past three years	33	4.40	7.53	5.9999
R&D — Your firm spends substantially on R&D	33	3.14	6.45	4.9065
Administrative Efficiency (AE)	33	1.80	5.72	3.3943
Local Government Coordination (LGC)	33	1.21	6.46	4.2708
Good Governance (GG)	33	2.36	5.72	4.5422
Order and Security (O&S)	33	3.39	7.28	5.8476
Basic Infrastructure (BI)	33	2.15	7.07	4.4862

Source: Asia Competitiveness Institute.

businesses as the most severe problem in doing businesses in Indonesia.[5] The low mean value of LGC is not surprising either, which has been regarded as the missing link during Indonesia's decentralisation process (Abidin 2009; UNDP 2009); whereas the high mean value of O&S (5.85) indicates respondents' overall satisfaction with the security and political conditions in their provinces.

For the dependent outcome of *staff hiring*, the mean value of 0.70 indicates that most respondents anticipated staff growth for 2014. For the other three dependent outcomes, the ascending order of their means is *R&D* (4.91), *new methods* (6.00) and *equipment upgrade* (7.08). From the analysis, respondents are more willing to invest in *equipment upgrade* than *R&D* and *new*

Table 4.5: Governing Conditions and Investment Outcomes

Province	AE	LGC	BI	GG	OS	Hire Staff	Up Equip	New Method	R&D
Riau Islands	0	0	0	0	0	1	1	0	0
North Maluka	0	0	0	0	0	1	1	0	0
West Papua	0	0	0	0	0	1	1	1	0
Lampung	0	0	0	1	0	1	1	0	0
Bali	0	0	0	0	1	0	0	0	0
Bengkulu	0	0	0	0	1	1	1	1	0
Central Kalimantan	0	0	0	0	1	1	1	1	1
East Nusa Tenggara	0	0	0	0	1	0	1	0	0
North Sumatra	0	0	0	0	1	0	1	0	0
West Sumatra	0	0	0	0	1	0	1	0	0
South Sumatra	0	0	0	0	1	1	1	0	0
South Kalimantan	0	0	1	0	1	1	1	0	0
Maluku	0	1	1	0	1	1	1	1	0
Bangka Belitung Islands	0	0	0	1	1	0	1	1	0
Jambi	0	0	0	1	1	0	1	0	0
North Sulawesi	0	0	0	1	1	1	1	0	0
East Kalimantan	0	1	0	1	1	1	1	1	0
Southeast Sulawesi	0	1	0	1	1	1	1	0	0
West Kalimantan	1	1	0	1	1	0	1	1	0
Banten	0	0	1	1	1	0	1	1	0
West Java	0	0	1	1	1	1	1	0	0
East Java	0	0	1	1	1	0	1	0	0
Papua	0	0	1	1	1	1	1	0	0
Riau	0	0	1	1	1	1	1	1	0
Yogyakarta	0	0	1	1	1	0	1	1	0
Gorontalo	0	1	1	1	1	1	1	1	0
Jakarta	0	1	1	1	1	1	1	0	0
Central Java	0	1	1	1	1	1	1	1	0
West Nusa Tenggara	0	1	1	1	1	1	1	1	1
South Sulawesi	0	1	1	1	1	1	1	1	0
Aceh	1	1	1	1	1	1	1	1	0
West Sulawesi	1	1	1	1	1	1	1	0	0
Central Sulawesi	1	1	1	1	1	1	1	0	0

Source: Asia Competitiveness Institute.

[5]For example, accordingly to World Economic Forum (2012), 15.4% of all companies interviewed considered corruption as the most severe problem affecting the business environment in Indonesia. Moreover, according to World Bank (2009), nearly 15% of the companies reported being expected to pay bribes to public officials to "get things done".

methods. The mean value for *R&D* is lowest, probably because that *R&D* investment is costly and takes longer to get return from investment.

Table 4.5 reports the coding values of both conditions and outcomes. Using 4.5 as the cut-off point for all the five causal conditions, we found that AE is generally *dissatisfactory* among all but four provinces (88%). The only four provinces where AE is deemed satisfactory are Aceh, West Kalimantan, West Sulawesi and Central Sulawesi. In terms of O&S, however, the result is generally *satisfactory* among all but four provinces (88%). The only four provinces where O&S is perceived to be dissatisfactory were Riau Islands, Lampung, North Maluku and West Papua. For the condition of LGC, 12 out of 33 (36%) provinces reported satisfaction and for BI and GG, 16 out of 33 (48%) and 21 out of 33 (64%), respectively.

Our results also showed an interesting pattern among the causal conditions, which indicated that O&S was a precondition for GG, which was in turn a precondition for either BI or LGC. All but one province reported as possessing GG (20 in total) were contained in the set of provinces with satisfactory O&S (33 in total). Thus, O&S could be seen as a precondition for GG. Within the set of GG, there seemed to be two distinctive paths of development — one subset contained satisfactory BI but dissatisfactory LGC (seven provinces: Banten, West Java, East Java, DI Yogyakarta, Riau, South Kalimantan and Papua), while the other subset contained satisfactory LGC but dissatisfactory BI (three provinces: East Kalimantan, West Kalimantan and Southeast Sulawesi).

There was also *another* major subset of provinces in which respondents were satisfied with all of the above four governing conditions (eight provinces: DKI Jakarta, Central Java, Aceh, West Nusa Tenggara, Gorontalo, South Sulawesi, West Sulawesi and Central Sulawesi). GG, thus, could also be seen as a precondition for satisfactory BI or LGC conditions. For AE, three out of the total four provinces (Aceh, West Sulawesi and Central Sulawesi) were found in the set of provinces with four other governing conditions. The remaining one province (West Kalimantan) was found in the set with LGC (and GG and O&S) but without BI. From the data, satisfaction with AE was always found coexisting with LGC (though not the other way round). LGC thus seemed to be a precondition for AE.

For the dependent outcomes coded using the cut-off point of 6, only two provinces (West Nusa Tenggara and Central Kalimantan) showed positive investment decision of *R&D* (6%). The possible explanation for the fairly low presence of *R&D* is that the period of return on R&D investment is long. For investment in *new methods* of production, 15 out of 33 provinces (45%) showed satisfactory investment outcome and for *staff hiring*, 23 out of 33 provinces (70%) reported staff growth. For *equipment upgrade*, all but one provinces (97%) showed positive investment decisions, the highest of the four investment outcomes.

Concerning the relations between various causal conditions and investment outcomes, only one significant correlation was found in our correlation test in Table 4.6. However, by analysing Table 4.5 directly here, we found different results. First, we found that the eight provinces which recorded satisfactory results for the combination of four key governing conditions (namely, LGC, BI, GG and O&S) would all (eight out of eight) have annual staff growth (100%). Second, for provinces which recorded satisfactory results for three out of the above four governing conditions, seven out of ten provinces showed the presence of staff growth (70%). Third, for provinces possessing two or less of the above four governing conditions, there were only 10 (out of a total of 15) showing the presence of staff growth (and equipment upgrade) (67%). The decreasing percentage of the results suggested the importance of satisfactory governing institutions in inducing staff expansion.

Table 4.6: Correlations

	AE	LGC	BI	GG	O&S	Staff Hiring	Equipment Upgrade	New Methods
AE								
LGC	0.716**							
BI	0.424*	0.543**						
GG	0.589**	0.826**	0.667**					
O&S	0.391*	0.538**	0.629**	0.613**				
Staff Hiring	0.181	0.330	0.214	0.203	−0.072			
Equipment Upgrade	−0.024	−0.020	0.136	−0.013	0.187	0.101		
New Methods	0.102	0.127	0.289	0.173	0.153	0.222	0.271	
R&D	0.040	−0.167	−0.073	−0.176	−0.158	0.015	0.198	0.556**

Note: **Correlation is significant at the 0.01 level (two-tailed); *Correlation is significant at the 0.05 level (two-tailed). AE: Administrative Efficiency; LGC: Local Government Coordination; BI: Basic Infrastructure; GG: Good Governance; O&S: Order and Security.
Source: Asia Competitiveness Institute.

Note that however, although for provinces with two satisfactory governing conditions, only half of them showed the presence of staff growth (50%), six out of eight provinces (75%) with only one satisfactory governing condition and all the three provinces with zero conditions (100%) still recorded increase in staff growth. It suggested that there were alternative causal paths for staff growth. In addition, three out of four provinces with satisfactory AE showed presence of staff growth (75%), compared with 20 out of 29 provinces with dissatisfactory AE (69%). It suggests that AE helps although relatively it is a minor condition compared with the other four conditions. However, explanation should be given with caution since satisfactory AE condition is only present in four provinces. With one single governing institution broadly absent almost everywhere in Indonesia, businesses with the "set-orientated logic" will still make investment decisions considering the presence of other important conditions, especially in the case of domestic investors (our primary respondents in this study) who are expected to be less sensitive to this issue than foreign investors.

Investment on *equipment upgrade* was found to be *unrelated* to satisfaction on various governing conditions. On the other hand, all but one province recorded investment on *equipment upgrade* irrespective of governing conditions. Only two provinces which recorded investment in *R&D*, one possessed four governing conditions (i.e. LGC, BI, GG and O&S) and the other did not possess any governing condition measured, so we cannot infer any relationship from those two provinces. But overall, 31 out of 33 provinces did not report positive tendencies to R&D. This deserves further research.

For investment in *new methods*, there were six out of nine provinces with four or more governing conditions which displayed positive outcome (67%), whereas five out of 11 provinces possessing three satisfactory governing conditions showed such investment (45%). Further, of the 15 provinces with two or less satisfactory governing conditions, only four showed positive outcome (27%). Furthermore, among the 15 provinces with positive investment in *new methods*, 10 provinces were recorded to have three or more satisfactory governing conditions (67%). The findings suggested the importance of satisfactory governing institutions to inducing investment in *new methods*. In addition, two out of four provinces with satisfactory AE showed presence of new methods (50%), compared with 13 out of 29 provinces with dissatisfactory AE (45%), suggesting that AE helps attract more investment in *new methods*.

In summary, our results showed that despite the uniform decentralisation reform introduced in Indonesia in the last decade, there was variety among individual provinces in terms of their quality of governing institutions and investment decisions. Moreover, our results demonstrated the important effect of governing institutions in mediating the effect of decentralisation on inducing the level of business activities in various provinces. That said, not all kinds of investment decisions were found to be related with governing institutions in the analysis. In particular, investment decisions on *staff hiring* and *new methods* were found related, whereas those on *equipment upgrade* and *R&D* were not.

In addition, analysis of various governing institutions as causal conditions for investment outcomes also shed light on the governance situation of local provinces. First, principal component analysis grouped corruption practice with costs in dealing with administrative process. This showed that from the business perspective, their perception about government corruption was associated with the local administrative process through which public permits and documents were obtained from the local units of government within the province. Second, the data showed that there seemed to be two distinctive paths of development for provinces, with one focusing on producing better BI and another improving LGC. Third, our data also showed an interesting pattern among the causal conditions: O&S was a precondition for GG, which was in turn a precondition for either BI or LGC and AE which were in turn preconditioned by satisfactory LGC. It corresponded with our fieldwork findings that one of the most difficult tasks for the provincial investment coordination board was to smoothen and streamline the business registration processes created by various local government units which were reported to be largely competing and uncooperative with provincial government initiatives.

Finally, our analysis of the results showed the *combinatorial* effects of governing conditions on business investment decisions. In addition to the nested nature and influence of governing institutions, with some more fundamental than the others, they exerted their most influence when they were combined into four or at least three coexisting conditions. In fact, our results suggested that as far as conditions of governing institutions were concerned, the combination of four key satisfactory governing conditions (i.e. LGC, BI, GG and O&S) was sufficient to induce increase in *staff hiring* and produce a high likelihood in investment in *new methods*. Yet investment outcomes did not always require the *coexistence* of those four governing conditions and that only four out of 33 provinces reported satisfactory AE suggested the existence of alternative paths for development.

The four provinces that scored unsatisfactory for O&S (Riau Islands, Lampung, North Maluku and West Papua) still gained positive marks for staff hiring and upgrading of equipment. Looking closer within these provinces, we suspect that the vibrancy of Riau Islands' and Lampung's economies are related to their geographic positions which are close to, respectively, Singapore and the Jakarta metropolitan area. As for West Papua, natural resources may be seen as one main driver behind its growing economy that triggered investment decisions. All in all, alternative factors such as economic structure as well as geography seem to complement account of governance for inducing business investment. Further, empirical research is warranted to look into such alternative paths for development.

4.4 POLICY IMPLICATIONS

How may provinces and their local governments attract business investment? The results of our analysis indicated several fundamental governing conditions. First, one fundamental condition involves the fostering of a secured environment and a stable political order such that businesses will find it safe to operate in the area.

Second, to enhance the trust of businesses, governments may further adopt various institutional measures to signal to investors that political power will not be used arbitrarily and thus a fair, open and competitive market environment may be guaranteed. Common values under the general rubric of GG (e.g. meritocracy, judiciary independence and accountability) serves well in this purpose.

Third, under the specific influence of decentralisation which all sub-national governments in Indonesia are experiencing, a major consideration that can significantly affect business investment decisions is whether provincial and local governments are able to create a conducive operational environment. On this regard our findings suggest two alternative development strategies that provincial and local governments may work on. One is to ensure the satisfactory provision of basic physical infrastructure such as water and electricity supplies, roads and access to internet. This strategy has been adopted by most of the Java provinces, as well as South Kalimantan and Riau and is likely an appropriate strategy especially for provinces which score low on the physical infrastructure sub-environment, namely West Kalimantan, East Nusa Tenggara, Bengkulu and West Papua.[6]

The other strategy is to maintain a well-functioning governmental system such that districts and cities within the provinces are well coordinated. This strategy has been applied by East Kalimantan, West Kalimantan and Southeast Sulawesi and is apt for provinces which score low on Coordination of Local Governments, such as North Maluku, Riau Islands and Papua. Either of these strategies give confidence for businesses to engage in longer-term investment. At the central level, President Joko Widodo has also taken a series of initiative measures to make massive investment in infrastructure and strengthen interministerial and intergovernmental policy coordination in order to accelerate regional economic development.

Fourth, a related but relatively minor consideration involves whether the administrative process is efficient. Although the combination of the four key governing institutions of O&S, GG, BI and LGC are sufficient to induce increase in *staff hiring* and *new methods*, our findings suggest that provinces with satisfactory AE achieved better investment outcomes, which is consistent with other studies on the effect of AE (Levi and Spiller 1994). It definitely helps if local

---

[6]Refer to Chapter 1 in Tan *et al.* (2015) for full list of findings from ACI's 2014 provincial competitiveness analysis.

businesses do not need to spend extra time, money and effort to apply for public permits and documents or in dealing with government officials on various operational issues in general. Apparently, the dissatisfactory condition of AE in most provinces makes it the most potential area for most provinces to work on to attract business investment.

The President Joko Widodo's administration is acutely aware of the dissatisfactory condition of AE and has started to implement the president's plan to reform the bureaucracy and restructure ministries. President Joko Widodo has also asked that the government's permit process be streamlined by combining ministry licenses into a one stop service (OSS), eradicating the need for multiple applications at different agencies for the same activity. At the local level, provinces are expected to implement those initiatives and they will risk losing regional grants from the national budget if they fail to comply.

Overall, the combinatorial effect of fundamental governing institutions suggests a set-oriented consideration from the investor's perspective. It implies that provincial and local governments and also the central government, may have to take a combination of improvements in order to secure strong business investment, especially for longer-term investments such as *R&D*. It also implies that some factors are preconditions for other factors — for instance, O&S is a precondition for GG, GG is a precondition for satisfactory BI or LGC and LGC is a precondition for AE — which suggests a potential multi-phase reform agenda for business environment improvement in different provinces. A single-phase holistic governance reform is not a prerequisite for sustainable business growth. It would be more practical for provincial and local governments to start with the easier and more "preconditioning" reforms before proceeding to the more difficult but less "preconditioning" ones.

REFERENCES

Abidin, Adi. 2009. "When the Burden is Shouldered Alone: Experiences in Autonomy at Districts and Cities." In *Decentralisation and Regional Autonomy in Indonesia: Implementation and Challenges*, edited by Coen J. G. Holtzappel and Martin Ramstedt, 59–74. Singapore: Chung Printing.

Acemoglu, Daron and James A. Robinson. 2012. *Why Nations Fail: The Origins of Power, Prosperity and Poverty*. London: Profile Books.

Akai, Nobuo and Masayo Sakata. 2002. "Fiscal Decentralisation Contributes to Economic Growth: Evidence from State-Level Cross-Section Data for the United States." *Journal of Urban Economics* 52(1): 93–108.

Azis, Iwan Jaya. 2003. "Concepts and Practice of Decentralisation: Some Notes on the Case of Indonesia." Paper presented at the Policy Dialogue on Empowering Women in Autonomy and Decentralisation Processes, New York, May 29.

Bardhan, Pranab. 2002. "Decentralisation of Governance and Development." *The Journal of Economic Perspectives* 16(4): 185–205.

Blanchard, Olivier and Andrei Shleifer. 2001. "Federalism With and Without Political Centralisation: China Versus Russia." *IMF Staff Papers* 48(4): 171–179.

Casson, Mark C., Marina Della Giusta and Uma S. Kambhampati. 2010. "Formal and Informal Institutions and Development." *World Development* 38(2): 137–141.

Coase R.H. 1960. "The Problem of Social Cost." *Journal of Law & Economics* 3: 1–69.

Davoodi, Hamid and Heng-fu Zou. 1998. "Fiscal Decentralisation and Economic Growth: A Cross Country Study." *Journal of Urban Economics* 43: 244–257.

Faguet, Jean Paul. 2014. "Decentralisation and Governance." *World Development* 53: 2–13.

Hadiz,Vedi R. 2003. "Power and Politics in North Sumatra: The Uncompleted Reformasi." In *Local Power and Politics in Indonesia: Democratisation and Decentralisation*, edited by Edward Aspinall and Greg Fealy, 119–31. Singapore: Institute of Southeast Asian Studies

Hayek, Friedrich A. 1945. "The Use of Knowledge in Society." *American Economic Review* 35: 519–30.

Hayek, Friedrich A. 1948. *Individualism and Economic Order*. Chicago: University of Chicago Press.

Holtzappel, Coen J. G. 2009. "Introduction: The Regional Governance Reform in Indonesia, 1999–2004." In *Decentralisation and Regional Autonomy in Indonesia: Implementation and Challenges*, edited by Coen J. G. Holtzappel and Martin Ramstedt, 1–56. Singapore: Chung Printing.

Levy, Brian and Pablo T. Spiller. 1994. "The Institutional Foundation of Regulatory Commitment: A Comparative Analysis of Telecommunications Regulation." *Journal of Law, Economics, & Organization* 10(2): 201–246.

Lin, Justin Yifu and Zhiqiang Liu. 2000. "Fiscal Decentralisation and Economic Growth in China." *Economic Development and Cultural Change* 49(1): 1–22.

Murrell, Peter, eds. 2001. *Assessing the Value of Law in Transition Economies*. USA: University of Michigan Press.

Neyapti, Bilin. 2005. "Fiscal Decentralisation and Socio-Economic Outcomes in Turkey: An Empirical Investigation." *METU Studies in Development* 32: 433–465.

North, Douglass C. 1990. *Institutions, Institutional Change and Economic Performance*. Cambridge: Cambridge University Press.

North, Douglass C., John Joseph Wallis and Barry R. Weingast. 2009. *Violence and Social Orders: A conceptual Framework for Interpreting Recorded Human History*. New York: Cambridge University Press.

Porter, Michael E. 1990a. The Competitive Advantage of Nations. *Harvard Business Review*, March–April, 73–91.

Porter, Michael E. 1990b. *The Competitive Advantage of Nations*. New York: The Free Press.

Qian, Yingyi and Barry R. Weingast. 1997. "Federalism as a Commitment to Preserving Market Incentives." *Journal of Economic Perspectives* 11(4): 83–92.

Ragin, Charles C. 2008. *Redesigning Social Inquiry: Fuzzy Sets and Beyond.* Chicago and London: University of Chicago Press.

Ray, David. 2009. "Decentralisation, Regulatory Reform, and the Business Climate." In *Decentralisation and Regional Autonomy in Indonesia: Implementation and Challenges*, edited by Coen J.G. Holtzappel and Martin Ramstedt, 150–182. Singapore: Chung Printing.

Shirley, Mary M. 2005. "Institutions and Development." In *Handbook of New Institutional Economics*, edited by Claude Menard and Mary M. Shirley, 611–638. The Netherlands: Springer.

Stansel, Dean. 2005. "Local Decentralisation and Local Economic Growth: A Cross- Sectional Examination of US Metropolitan Areas." *Journal of Urban Economics* 57: 55–72.

Tan, Khee Giap, Mulya Amri, Linda Low and Tan Kong Yam. 2013. *Competitiveness Analysis and Development Strategies for 33 Indonesian Provinces*. Singapore: World Scientific.

Tan, Khee Giap, Nurina. Merdikawati, Mulya Amri and Tan Kong Yam. 2015. *2014 Provincial and Inaugural Regional Competitiveness Analysis: Safeguarding Indonesia's Growth Momentum.* Singapore: World Scientific.

Tiebout, Charles M. 1956. "A Pure Theory of Local Expenditures." *Journal of Political Economy* 64(5): 416–424.

Tosun Mehmet Serkan and Serdar Yilmaz. 2008. "Decentralisation, Economic Development, and Growth in Turkish Provinces." *The World Bank*, Policy Research Working Paper 4725.

UNDP. 2009. *The Missing Link: The Province and its Role in Indonesia's Decentralisation.* Jakarta: UNDP Indonesia.

Weingast, Barry R. 2014. "Second Generation Fiscal Federalism: Political Aspects of Decentralisation and Economic Development." *World Development* 54: 14–25.

World Bank. 2003. *Decentralising Indonesia: A regional public expenditure review report.* Public expenditure review (PER). Washington, DC: World Bank. http://documents.worldbank.org/curated/en/2003/06/2461573/decentralizing-indonesia-regional-public-expenditure-review-overview-report.

World Bank. 2009. *Enterprise Surveys.* Washington, DC: World Bank.

World Economic Forum. 2012. *The Global Competitiveness Report 2011–2012.* Geneva: World Economic Forum. http://www3.weforum.org/docs/WEF_GCR_Report_2011-12.pdf.

Zhang, Tao and Heng-fu Zou. 1998. "Fiscal Decentralisation, Public Spending, and Economic Growth in China." *Journal of Public Economics* 67: 221–240.

Discussant Notes 1: Decentralisation, Governing Institution and Economic Development: Layers of Government in Indonesia

Agung Wicaksono

Assistant Professor, School of Business and Management — Institut Teknologi Bandung and Special Assistant to Head of President's Delivery Unit for Development Monitoring and Oversight (UKP4) 2009–2014, Indonesia

1. INTRODUCTION

Indonesia has undergone a simultaneous process of democratisation and decentralisation since the end of Soeharto's era with *reformasi* in 1998. With the recent election in 2014, Indonesia has the world's record in democracy by having the largest amount of direct mandate on a presidential election. It also has another world's record in decentralisation, since it has the largest amount of autonomous governments in a country.

Indonesia comprises 512 autonomous governments, 414 districts and 98 city governments. As a comparison, China has fewer numbers of autonomous governments, as the autonomy is located at provincial level, which is much lower compared to the amount of districts and cities of Indonesia. India as Asia's largest democracy has its autonomous governments at the state level. Therefore, it is relevant to look at Indonesia when the issue of decentralisation and multiple layers of government is put under scrutiny. The paper by Asia Competitiveness Institute (ACI) on the topic of decentralisation, governing institutions, and economic development has done well in its analysis on the relationship between government institutions and economic development. However, it has not touched on the impact of decentralisation toward governing institution.

2. DECENTRALISED LEADERSHIP AND GOVERNING INSTITUTIONS

It has to be acknowledged that decentralisation brings a blessing to Indonesia. Through decentralisation, a new generation of competent local leaders in Indonesia has been born, as visualised in Figure 1. Jokowi, the nickname of Joko Widodo, the president elect, was a Mayor in Solo, a small town in Central Java. After consecutively winning two periods of direct elections with a margin above 90% in the second period, he rose to be the Governor of Jakarta through another direct election. Now, he is the President of Indonesia. This is clearly one success story of how democracy and decentralisation in Indonesia has given the birth to the seventh president of the country.

Figure 1: New Generation of Indonesian Leaders Born from Decentralisation

Source: Wicaksono (2014).

Another example is in the city of Bandung. Ridwan Kamil, a US trained architect and university professor at Institut Teknologi Bandung (ITB), is now leading Bandung as a Mayor without being a member of any political party. He was an independent, but endorsed as a candidate by political parties which saw strong potential in him. Another result from a big city is in Surabaya, shown by Tri Rismaharini as its Mayor. Nicknamed Risma, she is a female politician with no connection with political families or business elites. Last but not least, is the story of Basuki Tjahaja Purnama. With the nick name of Ahok, the Chinese minority figure, who was elected as Head of District of East Belitung, and is now leading Jakarta. The fruit of decentralisation in Indonesia is clear from the fact that it has given birth to leaders who also represent the spirit of "Bhinneka Tunggal Ika" (unity in diversity). They are leaders with diverse backgrounds, from different gender, ethnicity, and socioeconomic, but have similarities by being popular leaders as products of people's choice.

The ACI's paper has identified three independent variables; Administrative Efficiency, Rule of Law and Order and Security. The anecdotal evidence shows how these variables have been practiced by the local leaders. These are crucial to both build investor's confidence and people's trust for the long term.

In Surabaya, Risma has transformed a number of things starting from city parks to make the city more livable and green so as to increase the happiness index, up to fighting to clean up prostitution in the city. She also transformed the e-government at the city level, which would help to improve investors' confidence. She shows how to be an efficient leader by applying a "no-nonsense" attitude. This is evidence on the importance of Administrative Efficiency as a parameter for governing institution.

Jokowi's major strength was his willingness and ability to address one of the issues in Rule of Law by listening to the voice of businesses and citizens in decision making. When leading the city of Solo, this was showcased by the way he convinced street vendors to move from the city centers to designated area for the market. It was done neither by force nor oppression, but by negotiations and persuasions. Story has it that he conducted 54 lunch meetings to negotiate with the street vendors until they were finally willing to be relocated in order to provide a cleaner and more orderly city center. Jokowi even held a carnival when vendors moved to their new place. Rule of Law is important, but an inclusive decision making process involving the voice of businesses and citizens is more important.

Ahok started by creating a Youtube broadcast of the budget meeting discussing big budget cut in his effort to streamline bureaucracy and prevent corruption in Jakarta. This created the sense of transparency and effective rule with strong control of the big city. He also moved on further by enforcing impromptu inspection visits to areas of public service delivery which are rampant from corruption. Order and Security is the kind of situation he would like to create by this leadership style.

The UKP4 also worked with these local leaders by entrusting them with the tools called LAPOR (*Layanan Aspirasi dan Pengaduan Online Rakyat*), an online complaint holding system. As depicted in Figure 2, LAPOR uses crowdsourcing mechanism allowing people to report on public service delivery by using short message service (SMS) or online platform which connects to social media such as Facebook or Twitter. The complaint would then be forwarded to the head

Figure 2: LAPOR! — Social Media Application on Development Monitoring

Source: President's Delivery Unit for Development Monitoring and Oversight (2009–2014).

Figure 3: Head of UKP4, Professor Kuntoro Mangkusubroto, Signing Memorandum of Understanding (MOU) on LAPOR! with Vice Governor of DKI Jakarta and Mayor of Bandung

Source: President's Delivery Unit for Development Monitoring and Oversight (2009–2014).

of the office in charge of the service. The head of local/central government can check the performance of his office by checking the progress of how the public complaint being handled by his staff.

DKI Jakarta is the first provincial government utilising LAPOR to evaluate the performance of the head of offices (Figure 3). Ahok said that "*LAPOR is an indicator for me to fire and hire head of offices.*" Bandung became the first city government utilising LAPOR. Ridwan Kamil, a media-savvy politician, utilises LAPOR to check the progress of the programme being executed by his staff. His satisfaction with the system has led him to say that "*LAPOR is an effective tool*" for his effort to combine social media and bureaucracy reform.

3. MULTIPLE LAYERS OF GOVERNMENT, MULTIPLE CHALLENGES

However, decentralisation does not only bring good news. It also brings a massive challenge for this country of 250 million people with 512 autonomous governments. That means for every half a million people, there is one autonomous government. Even Singapore has just one government for its five million people. And these autonomous governments are placed in multiple layers with at least three levels, shown in Figure 4, namely, national, provincial and city/district.

It is important to understand the complexity of the Indonesian decentralised system. The 34 provincial governors are elected directly by the people in the provinces. However, so do the

Figure 4: Multiple Layers in Indonesian Government Structure

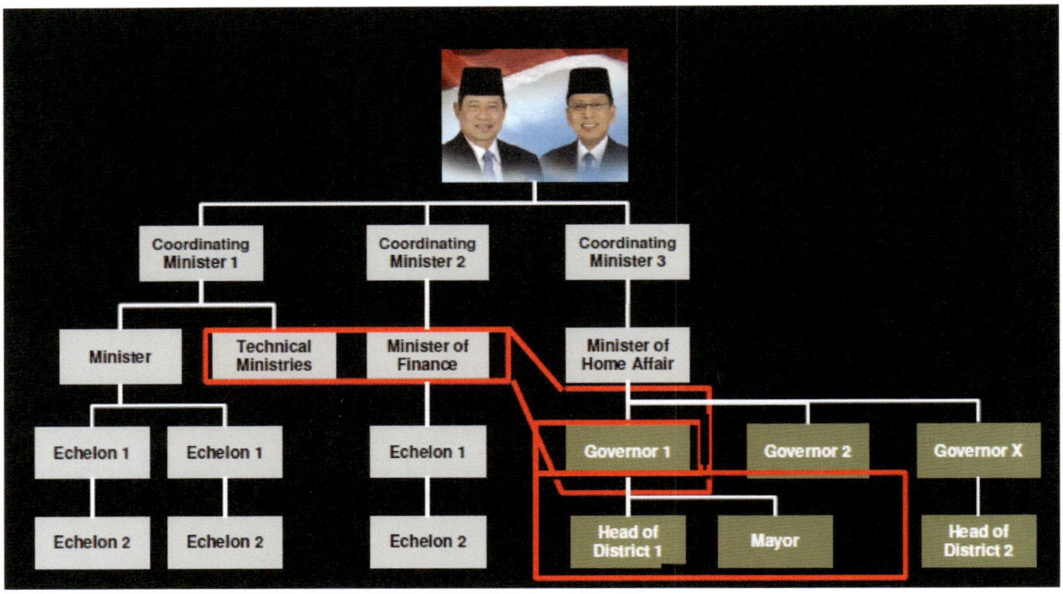

Source: President's Delivery Unit for Development Monitoring and Oversight (2009–2014).

mayors and *bupati* (head of districts). Therefore, it is very difficult to say that they are accountable and responsible to the layer of government above them, which is the central government for the governors and the provincial governments for mayors/*bupatis*. This "three different layers of governments" is not something easy to manage. The irony of this constellation could lead to the situation of a country with no hierarchy.

A case in point was when a *bupati* of an oil and gas rich district but with poor socioeconomic situation decided to issue a local regulation obliging that the local contents for an oil and gas project must come from his own district. Local content was translated as locally from his district and not from Republic of Indonesia in general. The head of district could not think of national interest when the local regulation was designed, since the interests of his local own people were so strong. The local politics and layers of government forced him to do so. Therefore, the central government practically has little power to control the local government.

Looking back at the history when the law on local autonomy was drafted in the early years of *reformasi*, the decision to decentralise was done partly due to pressures from the various regions. There was strong fear that calls for independence could come from various provinces. Therefore, the decision to decentralise to district/city level, instead of provincial level, was done partly in order to avoid the separatist threat. The decision was necessary to keep the country from falling apart, but not creating effective governance at the local level. In the word of a political analyst who was part of the discussion in the late 1990s, it was a "decentralisation under distrust" which

Figure 5: Transfer to Region in Indonesia's State Budget

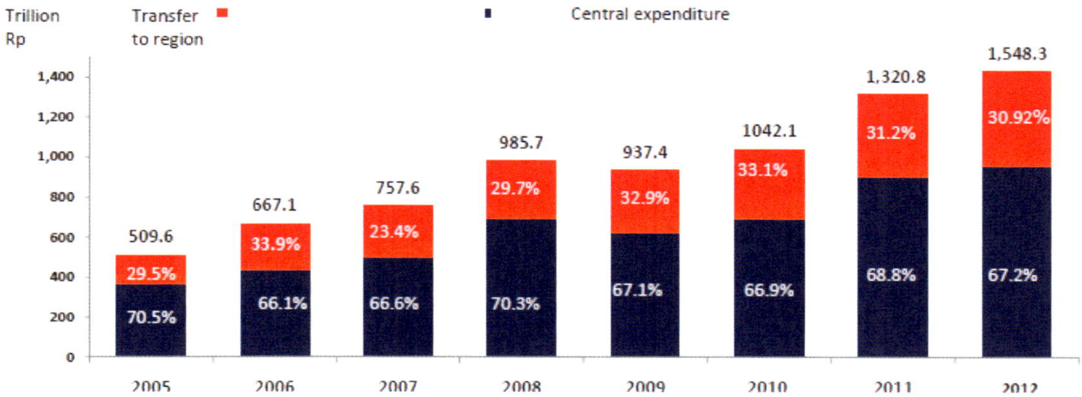

Source: Brodjonegoro (2012).

Indonesia had.[1] However, it created the side-effect of reduced effectiveness of governance, since the number of regions wanting to have its own district status keep growing, while the local apparatus ability to govern was still insufficient. Studies by Regional Autonomy Watch (KPPOD) as well as Ministry of Home Affairs have shown that the performances of newly created autonomous districts are still low.

The increasing trends on the amount of state budget transferred to regions as shown in Figure 5 is an alarming situation if no measure is being taken to improve the governance of multiple layers of governments. About 30% of state budget (APBN) is transferred to the region.

We can see that on average, state expenditures increased by 17 % during the period of 2005 to 2012. However, the proportion of central government expenditures during the period tends to decrease, from 70.5% in 2005 to 67.2% in 2012. At the same time, transfer to the region increases from 29.5% in 2005 to 30.9% in 2012. The pendulum has swung from authoritarianism to democracy and from centralised control to decentralised autonomy. But the effectiveness of local governance is still in question. It was a situation of "democracy first, good governance later."[2] Democracy is unarguably in place in Indonesia. It is now time to see what measures there are for good governance under a democratic and decentralised Indonesia.

4. FISCAL DECENTRALISATION AS TOOLS FOR CENTRAL-LOCAL ALIGNMENT

During the presidential debates, Jokowi, the president-elect, addressed the issues of decentralisation and the need for "budget politics." Budget politics was mentioned by Jokowi as the way for

[1] This was discussed during Cross-Country Roundtable and Policy Dialogue held by UKP4 and Human Development Capability Association on 4th September 2012.

[2] See Ramage (2007).

Figure 6: Proportion of Special Allocation Funds (DAK) in Indonesia's State Budget

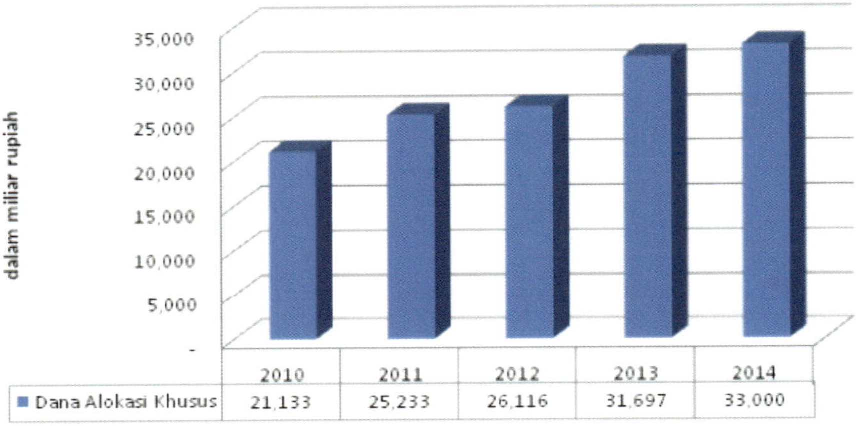

Source: Directorate General for Fiscal Balance, Ministry of Finance.

central government to manage the behavior of local government through budget control. With 85% of the local government budget coming from the central government, he saw that as an opportunity for the central government to utilise the budget transfer as a means to control the local government by exercising punishment and reward.

For example, reward and punishment can be utilised through the exercise of the special allocation fund (DAK) disbursement to the regions. DAK is disbursed to the regions with the main objective to reduce interregional inequalities in public services. The three largest recipients of DAK are education, health, and road infrastructure. Central government authority on the disbursement of DAK by Ministry of Finance can be applied as a control mechanism to align local governments. This is especially since the amount of DAK keeps increasing, amounting to 33 trillion Rupiahs (around three billion US dollars) in 2014, as shown in Figure 6.

The proposal for DAK's control would spark debate as this might not be well accepted by local government. This is because DAK funds actually goes to sectors that affect people's livelihood such as health care, education and infrastructure. This created the impression that if the local government is punished by DAK's cut when it fails to meet certain procedure, it would also punish the people in the districts who should be the beneficiaries of programmes funded by DAK. This is an area worth further exploring as the new government seems to be determined that this is the way to align local government actions with central government's national priority (Figure 7). Policy actions to be developed are procedures that will allow for the alignment between the central and local government's interest which would ensure that national priority is achieved while at the same time keeping the country united.

The Ministry of Finance is currently looking at possibilities to improve the role of monitoring of DAK's disbursement.[3] The current procedure as per Ministry of Finance's decree PMK No. 183/PMK.07/2013 is that the first phase of disbursement is 30% of the earmarked funds, fol-

[3]See Ministry of Finance (2014).

Figure 7: Jokowi and His "Budget Politics"

Source: Wicaksono (2014).

lowed by 45% in the second phase and the remaining 25% in the last phase. This three-staged disbursement is meant as a control mechanism contingent on submission of report by local government before the next phase of disbursement. The effectiveness of this mechanism needs to be examined, as well as possibilities for other measures of monitoring.

5. CONCLUSION AND IMPLICATION ON THE CURRENT ISSUES: NEW VILLAGE LAW AND LOCAL GOVERNMENT ELECTION (*PILKADA*) LAW

To conclude, Indonesia needs to find the solution to align multiple layers of government in achieving national objectives as a united country. This is becoming even more urgent now with the emergence of another layer of government, which is at village level. The newly passed Law No. 6 in 2014 on Village, which among others would allocate budget of 1.4 billion Rupiahs (100,000 US dollars) for every village per year, is clearly an indication that another autonomous layer is starting to pile up the multiple layers of Indonesian government. Budget politics as stated by Jokowi needs to be translated into monitoring and evaluation of fiscal decentralisation.

At last, controlling local government performance through fiscal decentralisation is a better controlling mechanism, rather than changing local government election method from direct election by the people to election by local parliaments (DPRD). The series of political events on changing the Local Government Law and Local Government Election Law at the end of the year 2014, which culminated at the beginning of 2015 will be noted down in the history of Indonesian democracy as part of a swinging pendulum. A swinging pendulum that is on the move to find an equilibrium between democracy by the people's voice and good governance for the people's benefits.

REFERENCES

Brodjonegoro, Bambang. 2012. "Fiscal Decentralisation in Indonesia." Paper presented at Cross-Country Roundtable and Policy Dialogue on Revisiting Indonesian Development Policies, September 4.

Ministry of Finance. 2014. *Kajian peningkatan kinerja DAK melalui perbaikan kualitas penyaluran DAK* [Study to improve the performance of Special Allocation Funds through better disbursement]. Jakarta: Ministry of Finance.

Ramage, Douglas. 2007. "Indonesia in 2006: Democracy First, Good Governance Later." In *Southeast Asian Affairs 2007*, edited by Daljit Singh and Lorraine C. Salazar, 135–157. Singapore: Institute of Southeast Asian Studies.

Wicaksono, Agung. 2014. "Managing Decentralisation in Indonesia: Layers of Government and Politics of Budget." Paper presented at ACI's Review Seminar on Safeguarding Indonesia's Growth Momentum: Enhancing Regional Competitiveness, Increasing Productivity and Improving Layers of Government, Singapore, August 4.

Discussant Notes 2: Governing Institution and Business Climate: The Province's Role and Local Government Coordination

Robert Na Endi Jaweng, MAP
Executive Director of Regional Autonomy Watch (KPPOD), Indonesia

1. INTRODUCTION

This review paper is written to respond to the main paper prepared by the Asia Competitiveness Institute's (ACI) research team in highlighting governing institutions in the era of economic decentralisation and development in Indonesia. Institutions and governance are believed to play a crucial role in linking decentralisation with the creation of a business environment which in turn contributes directly to economic growth. Looking at it from a business perspective, ACI has examined five causal conditions: administrative efficiency, good governance, order and security, local government coordination, basic infrastructure.

In this review paper, my attention is drawn on one causal condition as a crucial issue in the institutional development agenda for regional competitiveness building, namely, local government coordination and the role of the province in influencing the effectiveness of economic decentralisation and the establishment of investment climate.[1] The discussion on provincial role is of significant value in the ACI's study because of the principal finding of two distinctive paths of development for provinces, with one focusing on producing better basic infrastructure and another on improving local government coordination. A well-functioning governmental system is essential in creating a conducive environment to provide confidence in engaging long-term investment and business in the regions.

2. THE PROVINCE IN THE DECENTRALISATION ERA

Decentralisation and regional autonomy in Indonesia are now entering a new phase as well as a crucial momentum. The birth of Law No. 23/2014 on Local Government marks a new round of autonomy policy and relationship between central and local governments at this time.

[1]The discussion on the role of provinces in local government coordination does not mean that there is only one main causal condition in governing institutions' influence to the economic development in Indonesia. The ACI's study shows a number of other factors of no less significance, such as administrative efficiency, basic infrastructure, good governance, order and security. Even for the establishment of sustainable business growth, not a single-phase but a multiphase reform agenda must be adopted by each region.

Rearrangement of affairs and strengthening of provincial governments (and governor's position) are some examples that can be cited as evidence of change. Of course, various changes bring, more or less, a new dynamic in the management of autonomy and regional administration in the future. Some people see that this change brings hope for the improvement of local government coordination in the future.

During this time, as accurately diagnosed by ACI, the weak provincial role and ineffective local government coordination (provinces to districts/cities within their jurisdictions) have become a major institutional issue of decentralised governance in Indonesia. The problem is affecting weak government effectiveness, including the formation of business climate and regional competitiveness. Indonesia is not only facing central government's inconsistency, local government's incompetency, but also weak capacity control and vertical coordination in which the province should play a key role.

The root causes are, among other things, related to the governmental design and construction of zoning administration[2] contained in the autonomy regulations in this reform era. At the policy level (Law No. 22/1999 to Law No. 32/2004), it is clear that the hierarchy between governments has indeed been made disconnected. The province, as an intermediate government, is experiencing a loss of role as if no longer linked directly to the district/city. The governor's authority is limited and supporting institutions have not been solidly constructed, so that in practice, the dysfunction of the governor and the provincial government has been happening when dealing with the district/city.

Referring to the provisions of Law No. 22/1999 and its amendments in Law No. 32/2004 and Government Regulation No. 19/2010 *juncto* Government Regulation No. 23/2011, the implementation of deconcentration principle has not been followed up by clarity of types of implementation tasks delegated by the central government to its representatives, so that the fundamentals of position and authority of the governor in the region are not strongly placed. The birth of Government Regulation No. 7/2008 on the implementation of deconcentration principle also does not help much to improve the situation, because it is trapped by the same narrow thought, so that the relationship between the construction of deconcentration and the governor's position as the representative of the central government remains explicitly invisible.

In the other dimensions, for the purpose of the implementation of national programmes in the region, governor's dysfunction is causing non-coordination of many local activities (regional-based development) with the sectoral projects of the technical-ministries (sectoral-oriented development), which even tends to overlap and has the impression of conquest. It also cannot be separated from the majority opinion that the governor often has different perspectives from the minister regarding development practices in the region that he/she leads, or regarding sectoral

[2]In addition to administrative design issues, other reasons are also related to political factors. The recruitment system or filling the governor's post through direct elections seems just built on the logic of local democratisation and tends to give priority to the position of governor as head of the region, not as the representative of the central government in the region. In addition, the fragmented administration has also been influenced by a divided government rooted in local political asymmetry, in which the regional heads in the province along with the districts/cities come from different political parties. In such a context, governance discipline and ethics are often defeated by political party interests.

Figure 1: Provincial Strengthening Framework in Law No. 23/2014

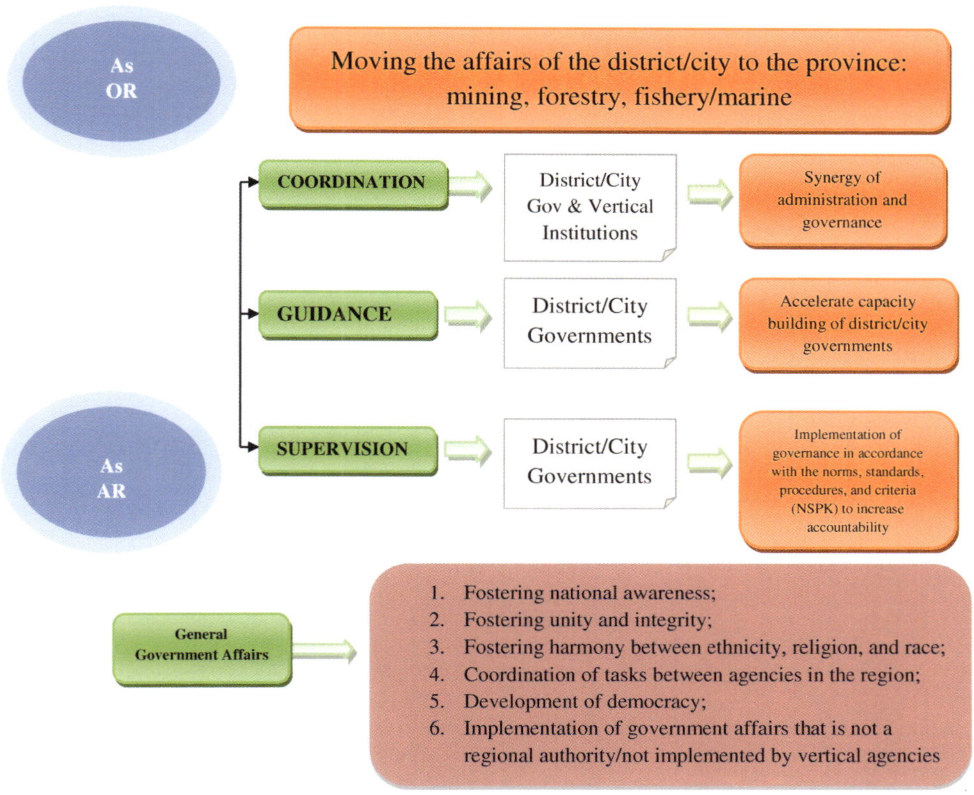

Source: KPPOD.

projects located and implemented in the province. Shortcuts are then taken by the central government by coordinating directly with vertical institutions (*Kantor Wilayah*) in the region and contacting directly the local government institutions (*Badan/Dinas Daerah*) that have a related nomenclature or function in the region without the knowledge of the governor.

Along with the revision of the Law on Local Government (Law No. 23/2014), the agenda on provincial strengthening has become a principal clause. The government is currently preparing for an elucidation of the law into a regulation of a lower level, namely a Government Regulation on Provincial Role. Briefly, the setting of provincial affairs in the new Law can be summarised in Figure 1. The position of the governor is set within the dual status framework of the province as an Autonomous Region (OR) and as an Administrative Region (AR).

As an OR, setting forth the status of the province is in the form of reaffirmation (arrangement) of concurrent government affairs, and the addition of forestry, marine, and mining affairs which used to be within the domain of districts/cities. On the one hand, this is indeed a dilemma, because the autonomy principles that close the gap between the bureaucracy and the public, and shorten the government's span of control are clearly ignored. This has marked a partial recentralisation in the substance of the new policy framework. However, given the bad licensing practices in the regions so far and a real need for economies of scale and ecological considerations (extensively based external affairs), the transfer of such affairs could be understood in the expectation of further ensuring business process (licensing to control/supervision and licensing for protection) efficiency and certainty by the government towards businesses.

While in terms of the provincial status as an AR, the new Law embodies the position setting of the governor as the representative of the central government in the following number of articles. First, setting the particulars related to the implementation of general government affairs related to practices of the Pancasila, national unity, social harmony and so on. Second, setting the particulars of the governor's role as the central government's representative in the region in terms of guidance and supervision of districts/cities; coordination and facilitation of districts/cities; monitoring, evaluation and supervision of districts/cities; evaluation of a number of draft local regulations concerning the local budget, spatial planning, development planning and local taxes/user charges; and supervision over local regulations of the districts/cities.

Figure 2: Example of Governor's Authority as the Central Government's Representative in Cancelling Local Regulation

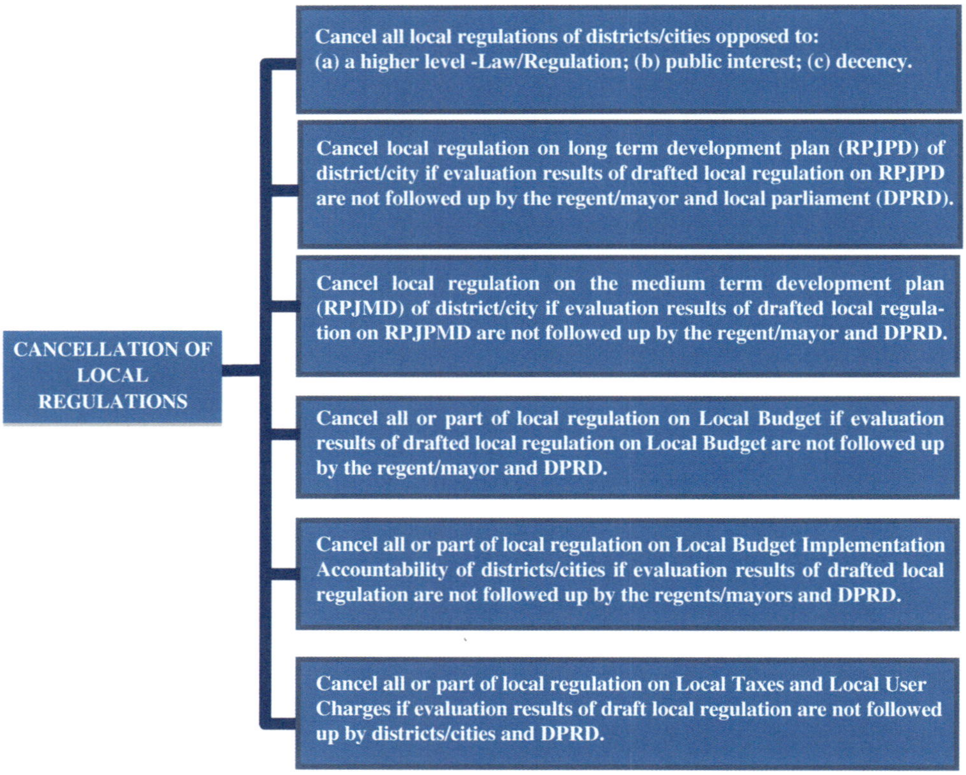

Source: KPPOD.

To run the affairs of the provincial status as AR, to the governor is given a number of authorities, among others, in the form of approval for the formation of vertical agencies, cancellation of local regulations, requesting the regent/mayor to follow up on a number of urgent matters, rewarding and sanctioning the regent/mayor, and so on. The number of provincial authorities can be seen in the example of local government obligations in carrying out licensing services, by establishing the one stop service (OSS) office. Any district that failed to carry out these obligations will be subject to consecutive sanctions in the form of administrative sanctions such as written reprimands to the regent/mayor. If an administrative sanction had been presented two times in a row and is still not implemented by the regent/mayor, the governor shall take over the licensing authority that has previously been the authority of the regent/mayor.

At first glance, the direction of this change shows a distinct step forward. Compared with the two previous Laws, Law No. 23 of 2014 has paved the way to strengthening the province as the AR. The governor will become more powerful in enforcing discipline through the role of government guidance and supervision of the districts/cities, as we can see from the setting of sanctions against the regents/mayors or the authority of the governor to overturn local regulations.

However, the new Law also raises crucial issues such as the addition of provincial authority over a number of matters: forestry, marine/fishery, plantation and mining coming from the districts/cities. This means that the emphasis of autonomy is shifted to the provinces and the emphasis is not from the transfer of a portion of the affairs of the central government to the provincial governments, but a recall (partial re-centralisation) of partial core business of districts/cities to the central government which are then transferred to the provinces as OR.

The approach taken by the government in order to strengthen the provinces is prone to become a blunder when not limited to AR but also as OR. Such an approach suggests a partial recentralisation or micro centralised tendency at the provincial level. In addition, increasing the province's autonomy given through a partial withdrawal of district/city affairs would certainly harm the construction of the province as a government entity in charge of covering cross-border affairs; "only relevant authority over cross-border affairs (externalities principle), as well as matters that could not be carried out by districts/cities (subsidiarity principle)."

According to the writer, in essence, nearly all sectoral affairs clearly have a strong locality dimension of scale/area, span of control, and accountability. The range of impacts (externalities) that could have been cross-border should only require the presence of the provinces in the form of coordination authority (deconcentration scheme) or at least treat them as concurrent affairs (partial decentralisation), not as an exclusive authority implemented in the decentralisation principle framework (absolute). Please note that experience so far has shown that the loyalty of the district/city to the province is also affected by the mixed status of the province and the position of the governor.

The approach should have been directed to the strengthening of the province as an AR and the position of the governor as a representative of the central government in the region. In that context the governor should be strengthened in the following elements:

(1) **Scale of authority:** The governor as the representative of the central government has the authority to determine policy issues in the scope of his/her jurisdiction. Most authority is already contained in the new Law, but should not be limited even opened to all coordination and supervision purposes by the province to the various affairs run by the districts/cities.

(2) **Limits of authority:** As the right to decide something, the authority of the governor should be final-authoritative in the executive environment, unless there is a rebuttal to the judicial path. By law, the authority of the policy should be stated in the form of legal basis issued by the governor, such as Governor Decree.

(3) **Synchronisation of authority setting:** This Law is potentially at odds with the existing regulations. Referring to Law No. 28 of 2009, for example, the supervisory authority against local regulations (tax/user charges) is in the hands of the Ministry of Finance and the Ministry of Home Affairs. Meanwhile, the power to overturn any local regulations is in the hands of the President pursuant to Presidential Decree. The issue here is not merely a synchronisation problem between regulations but the authority of the President to delegate cancellations to the governor as central government's representative in the region. The task to supervise local regulations can only be realised effectively on the basis of this authority.

(4) **Administrative elements:** Institutional support is not only limited to the Secretariat, but also requires the formation of deconcentration working units and budgeting allocated in the state budget. In the matter of budgeting, there should be the concept of one budgeting exit door in the central government (not broken down by ministry/agency but integrated into one ministry) and one budgeting entrance in the region (not directly distributed to local government agencies but coordinated through the cash account of the region).

3. FUTURE IMPROVEMENT AGENDA

In the interests of the economy, the focus of autonomy certainly needs to consider a greater economies of scale so as to encourage economic efficiency and public services. Therefore provincial strengthening is carried out with the (extensive) scale of approach on affairs and effectiveness. Local scale matters are left with the district/city, while cross-border affairs are handed over to the province (externalities principle) as well as affairs that could not be executed by the district/city. Furthermore, the organisation of various affairs in the district/city and province is supervised, guided and coordinated by the governor as the representative of the central government in the region.

At the dimensional relationship between the province and the central government, the deconcentration setting and the position of the governor as the representative of the central government should be put into the implementation mandate of general governmental tasks (tutelage power). Here the governor's authority and scope of work is constructed as an integral part of: (1) The authority inherent in the position as the representative of the central government in carrying out deconcentration tasks in the form of guidance, supervision, and coordination of districts/cities (attributive authority); (2) The authority delegated to inherent sectoral ministries in the position as representatives of the central government to guide, supervise and coordinate various vertical agencies as well as the districts/cities as the recipients of transfer of affairs from the ministries (delegative authority).

While in terms of funding support, the Law on Local Government has not reinforced clauses related to costing sourced from the state budget (through the deconcentration fund scheme) in order to support the governor's tasks as — the central government's representative in the region and operations of the governor's secretariat. Direction settings in the future should at least be at government regulation level, to assert financing sources (state budget), obligations of each ministry to allocate and disburse funds in a timely manner for the implementation of the delegated tasks (money follows function) and classification of funds for attributive affairs for personal/salary financing (indirect expenditure) and capital/activity spending (direct expenditure). Additionally, delegative affairs are more dominated by non-physical activity spending given the facilitative nature of the type of affairs being funded to smooth the tasks of guidance, supervision and coordination.

In the political dimension, given that in the realm of governance practices, the above various aspects would be tested in the power game in which political reality is often playing a bigger role. In that context, according to my opinion, the strengthening of governor's position is prone to "disturbance" if the political recruitment process (filling the post of governor/deputy governor) is entirely based on direct elections. Of course, the discourse of governor's appointment by the President is considered too extreme and opposed to the Constitution (1945 Constitution Article 18, paragraph 4), but fully submitting the recruitment process within the framework of direct elections as currently in practice is also felt asymmetrical with the concept of the governor as the representative of the central government. Going forward, we need to ponder about the central government's engagement space and mechanisms on a certain process and level, such as concerning the approval for candidates proposed by the political parties to be elected by the people. At another level, it may be useful to assure the "Jakarta Flavour" alignment in ensuring the presence of the central government through the figure of the governor-elect to become a more reliable identification of the governor, regional obedience, and "equality" with the Ministers who are all important to deliver an "effective deconcentration construction" for the successful implementation of general government affairs in the regions in the future.

4. ENDNOTES

The evidence suggests that the effectiveness of decentralisation in Indonesia is not only influenced by weak governance capacity of affairs by the district/city governments, but also the lack of coordination and control by the province over the implementation of the autonomy. Governor dysfunction should be revitalised and further re-positioned appropriately towards strengthening the province, particularly the province as an AR and the governor as the representative of the central government. In the interests of establishing a business and development climate, economic decentralisation should be meaningful as an opportunity structure for the local government in order to capitalise on its resources by improving governance capacity and strengthening local government coordination.

Apart from the improvement agenda in the long-term as mentioned above, whatever our attitude to the substance of the Law, in front of our eyes has come into effect a Law (Law No. 23 of 2014) which is valid and binding. This means that the provincial government should prove its ability to bear the double burden as an OR and AR which are equally reinforced in the new Law. As an OR, the province should build governance capacity in granting permits that are clear and clean and free of graft and rent-seeking in the regulation and management of large and strategic economic sectors, such as mining, forestry, and marine which have now been submitted to the province. Our study, KPPOD (2008), showed no guarantee that investment affairs at the provincial level are automatically managed effectively, as well as licensing and the business climate in general, which can vary widely across region.

On the other hand, the province must develop a capacity to guide, supervise, and control all decentralisation affairs both in their respective districts/cities and the province itself, and even coordinate vertical agencies in the region. So far anxiety has appeared that a large authority in the hands of the province could not be matched by adequate capacity, plus integrity of public officials who suddenly get a great authority at the same time. The province must prove that the investment climate and regional competitiveness can be built through the establishment of decentralised governance that is effective and accountable. It is a big job ahead. We are all on a new challenge, with a high uncertainty level of proving a new experiment.

REFERENCE

Komite Pemantauan Pelaksanaan Otonomi Daerah (KPPOD). 2008. *Pemeringkatan iklim investasi 33 provinsi di Indonesia tahun 2008* [Ranking of investment climate for 33 Indonesian provinces in 2008]. Jakarta: KPPOD. http://www.kppod.org/datapdf/laporan/rating33prov2008.pdf.

Chapter 5

Agricultural Productivity in Indonesian Provinces

5.1 INTRODUCTORY REMARKS

Indonesia is a vast archipelagic country with tremendous potential in its agricultural output. Although agriculture's contribution to the country's gross domestic product (GDP) had been steadily decreasing from 35.3% in 1960 to 11.3% in 2014, the sector still employed about 35% of Indonesia's labour force as of 2012 (World Bank 2016). Within the agricultural sector, in terms of the contribution of each sub-sector, farm food crops and horticulture dominated the agricultural output from 2000 to 2014. According to Biro Pusat Statistik (BPS) (2016), the share of food crops and horticulture declined marginally from 51.8% of agricultural output in 2000 to 46.8% in 2014, as depicted in Figure 5.1. Another declining trend was also observed in the forestry sub-sector, from 7.5% in 2000 to 5% in 2014. Meanwhile, the remaining sub-sectors displayed an increasing trend in terms of their share to total agricultural GDP. The share of estate crops[1] increased from 15% in 2000 to 16.3% in 2014; from 11.6% in 2000 to 13.1% in 2014 for livestock; and from 14% in 2000 to 18.8% in 2014 for fishery.

Figure 5.1: Share of Sub-Sector to Agricultural GDP

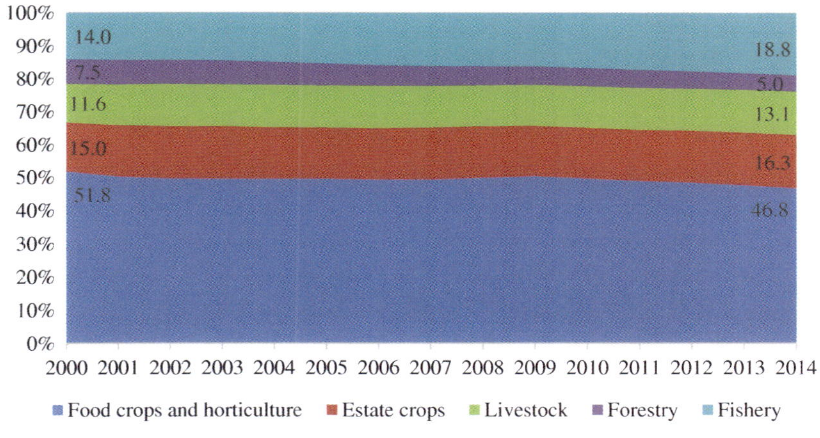

Source: Asia Competitiveness Institute with data sources from Indonesia's Central Statistical Agency (BPS).

[1]Estate crops, called *perkebunan* in local term, refer to rubber, coconut, palm oil, coffee, tea, pepper, clove, cocoa, cashew nut, sugar cane, tobacco and cotton.

Table 5.1: Agricultural Trade Balance (2010–2013)

No.	Sub-sector	Year (Million US Dollar) 2010	2011	2012	2013
1	Food crops				
	— Export	478	585	151	967
	— Import	3,894	7,024	6,307	5,659
	— Trade balance	–3,416	–6,439	–6,156	–4,692
2	Horticulture				
	— Export	391	491	505	784
	— Import	1,293	1,686	1,813	1,469
	— Trade balance	–902	–1,195	–1,309	–685
3	Estate crops				
	— Export	30,703	40,690	33,119	30,687
	— Import	6,028	8,844	3,112	2,686
	— Trade balance	24,675	31,846	30,007	28,002
4	Livestock				
	— Export	494	907	557	1,243
	— Import	1,232	1,191	2,698	3,015
	— Trade balance	–737	–284	–2,142	–1,772
5	Total				
	— Export	32,065	42,673	34,331	33,680
	— Import	12,447	18,744	13,931	12,828
	— Trade balance	19,619	23,928	20,400	20,852

Source: Ministry of Agriculture.

Indonesia's trade surplus in agriculture is mainly a result of its exports of estate crops, while its major imports include wheat, cotton, sugar, soybeans and maize. In fact, Indonesia is one of the world's major producers and exporters of palm oil, rubber, palm kernel, coffee, coconut (copra), cocoa, tea and spices. Table 5.1 provides trends of export and import for food crops, horticulture, estate crops and livestock from 2010 to 2013. From these sub-sectors, only estate crops consistently reported a trade surplus that contributed to overall surplus of agricultural trade balance. Persistent import for Indonesia's food staple (rice) and other strategic commodities such as sugar, maize, soybean and beef frequently makes news headline and push for their self-sufficiency becomes the top priority of the past and current Indonesian leaders.

Agricultural development policy in Indonesia has evolved in four significant phases (Fuglie 2010). During 1961–1967, Indonesia experienced rather poor macroeconomic performance, characterised by slow output growth with very few modern inputs and small improvements in productivity. Based on Figure 5.2, value added for agriculture was a mere 9 billion US Dollars

Figure 5.2: Agricultural Value Added in Indonesia (1960–2014)

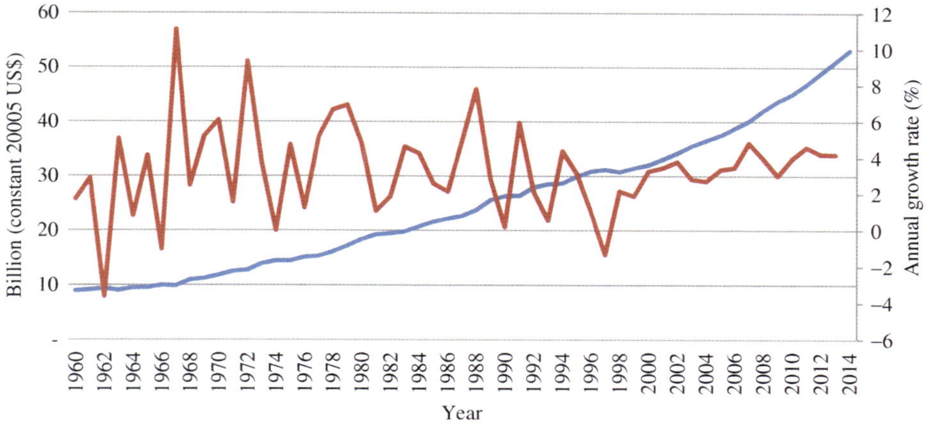

Source: World Development Indicators, World Bank.

in 1960 (World Bank 2016).[2] From 1968 to 1992, a green revolution took place and agriculture was the top priority in the economic development agenda, giving rise to the invention and wide dissemination of a number of high-yielding varieties as well as implementation of pro-agricultural policies. During this period, agricultural value added grew more than double, from 11 billion to 28 billion US Dollars (World Bank 2016).[3]

From 1993 to 2001, the agricultural sector faced stagnation, coupled with the Asian Financial Crisis (AFC) in 1997, and fewer sources for public spending in agriculture. In 1998, the annual growth of agricultural value added decreased by 1.3% before steadily climbing up to pre-crisis level. Post AFC, the period of 2002–2006 marked the liberalisation era of Indonesia's agricultural sector, where import restrictions on food crops were removed. This was a period of significant diversification of agricultural output with land expansion mostly for estate crops. The agricultural value added in Indonesia expanded by more than one-third from 1993 to 2006.

The trend for agricultural output continued to remain positive as strong macroeconomic performance translated into more resources to pursue pro-agricultural policies. In only eight years, the agricultural value added rose from 40.1 billion in 2007 to 53.2 billion US Dollars in 2014, an increase of more than 30% (World Bank 2016).[4] This was intertwined with the government's pro-poor policy as agricultural growth and productivity were often cited as the means to reduce rural poverty. According to the OECD (2012), incidence of poverty in rural areas was twice as high as in urban areas and almost three-fifth of the poor depended on agriculture as the main source of income. Hence, agricultural policy has another goal of improving the welfare of farmers through higher incomes in order to reduce the level of rural poverty. Indonesia has been recognised as a country with significant potential in agriculture, not only to be self-sufficient in

[2] Figures are in 2005 constant price.

[3] *Ibid.*

[4] Figures are in 2005 constant price.

terms of food, but also to be the "food basket" for ASEAN in particular and Asia in general.[5] However, given limited and competing use of resources, raising agricultural productivity is of paramount importance.

While most of the existing work on Indonesia's agriculture is at the national level, a provincial-level analysis of the country's agricultural sector would prove to be more useful from a policy perspective. As will be explained in Section 5.2, there is a diversity in terms of agricultural characteristics in each province. Each province has its own unique potential and challenges which have to be tapped and addressed, offering a rich information to learn from the success and failure of one another. In this light, this chapter examines agricultural productivity growth in Indonesian provinces during 2000–2011 and draws policy implications from such an empirical analysis.[6]

The remainder of the chapter is structured as follows. Section 5.2 provides a broad overview of agricultural diversity across Indonesian provinces. Section 5.3 outlines the agricultural policies in Indonesia, especially during the recent period. Section 5.4 provides a brief literature review on Indonesia's agricultural productivity to date. Section 5.5 details the methodology and data to be used in this chapter. Section 5.6 discusses the findings. Section 5.7 concludes the chapter with some policy implications.

5.2 AGRICULTURAL DIVERSITY ACROSS INDONESIAN PROVINCES

Indonesia has a highly diverse agricultural sector and it is most evident when one compares the relative resource endowments and commodities across islands. The country is blessed with fertile land, with almost every province having their own commodity mix of agricultural output. Rice as a staple crop is widely cultivated in Java Island, with Sumatra being well known for its vast palm oil plantations and Sulawesi for cocoa. Beyond that, diversity persists in terms of the size of their agricultural sector in their own economy and also their contribution to the national agricultural output.

Agricultural output as a share of provincial GDP largely varies, being a reflection of the level of economic development in the province. The most industrialised provinces located in Java Island have witnessed a declining share of agricultural output over time. In fact, for DKI Jakarta as the capital city where the urbanisation rate is close to 100%, its share of agricultural output was a negligible 0.1% in 2011, as illustrated in Figure 5.3. For the remaining provinces in Java Island, the agricultural share of their provincial GDP hovered between 7.4% for Banten and 17.9% for Central Java. The figures in outside Java Island were much higher as land for agricultural cultivation is still abundant and industrialisation has not fully kicked-off.

---

[5] Indonesia joined the Brunei Darussalam–Indonesia–Malaysia–Philippines East ASEAN Growth Area (BIMP–EAGA) which committed to become the food basket of ASEAN and Asia (Hajramurni 2010). The four countries have a number of initiatives to strengthen the collaboration in agriculture and fisheries.

[6] Our institute, Asia Competitiveness Institute (ACI), also has broad interests of conducting analysis on ASEAN countries in the context of rising China and India. As a result, similar agricultural productivity studies have also been undertaken by the ACI at the national level for ASEAN countries and at subnational level for China and India (Tan, Suo and Rajan forthcoming, Tan, Rao and Rajan 2015).

Figure 5.3: Relative Size of Agricultural Sector, by Province (2011)

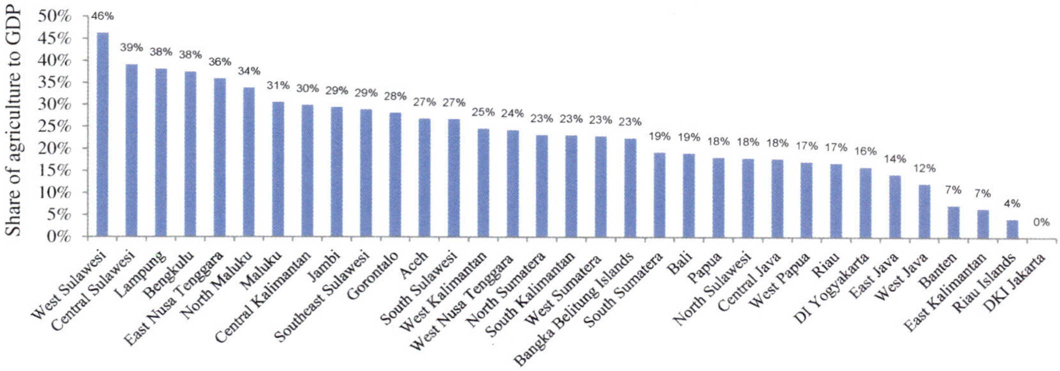

Source: Asia Competitiveness Institute with data sources from Indonesia Database for Policy and Economic Research (INDO-DAPOER), World Bank.

Table 5.2: Regional Characteristics of Agricultural Development

	Bali–Nusa Tenggara	Java	Kalimantan	Maluku–Papua	Sulawesi	Sumatra
Percentage of contribution to national agricultural output	4.6%	42.2%	8.7%	2.5%	9.8%	32.2%
Percentage of contribution to national agricultural employment	7.1%	44.9%	7.9%	4.5%	8.6%	27.0%
Average share of agricultural employment	44.9%	22.2%	46.3%	55.8%	44.7%	42.7%
Average share of agricultural output in the economy	26.5%	11.3%	21.1%	24.9%	31.2%	24.1%

Source: Asia Competitiveness Institute with data sources from INDO-DAPOER, World Bank.

For agriculture-based provinces such as West Sulawesi, Central Sulawesi and Lampung, their agricultural output shares were as high as 46.3%, 39.1% and 38.2%, respectively. Coincidentally, these three provinces are also well known for their food resiliency given that they consistently maintain surplus in rice.

Despite lower share of agricultural output among provinces in Java Island, they contributed to 42.2% of national agricultural output in 2011 (Table 5.2). East Java contributed the most with 15.7% of national agricultural output, followed by West Java (12.6%) and Central Java (10.6%). As a region, Sumatra contributed to 32.2% of national agricultural output, attributed mostly to its estate crops which dominated Indonesia's agricultural export. It is interesting that national agricultural output is still driven by Java which has transformed its economy towards manufacturing and service-based industry. The remaining land abundant regions such as Kalimantan, Sulawesi, Maluku–Papua and Bali–Nusa Tenggara only contributed to one-fourth of national agricultural output.

This is another example of imbalanced regional development that favours more established regions such as Java and Sumatra and the fact that inadequate infrastructure and lack of connectivity across Indonesian islands further undermine the efforts of eastern part of Indonesia to unleash their potential in agriculture. In spite of abundant agricultural output being produced outside Java and Sumatra regions, the poor connectivity tends to increase their price to uncompetitive level once they are shipped to another island. Anecdotal evidence suggests that it is cheaper to import oranges from China than for Indonesian farmers to sell them outside of their own islands. Additionally, fishermen in Papua can only earn four US Dollars for a kilogram of their top grade tuna, which is less than one-tenth of the price if it is sold abroad (World Bank 2015).

Despite variations in agricultural contribution to GDP for each province, one thing persists, namely, a sizeable share of employment in agricultural sector across provinces. In West Sulawesi for example, 59% of its labour force worked in agricultural sector in 2011. Sizeable agricultural employment was also found in East Java and Central Java, at about 40% and 34%, respectively, even though the share of agriculture in their respective GDP was relatively small at 14% and 18%. When illustrated in a scatter plot in Figure 5.4, an upward slope representing positive correlation emerges between the share of agriculture in provincial GDP and share of agricultural employment. At the far right of the scatter plot, domination of agricultural sector in West Sulawesi's economy also translated into high employment in this sector. In Papua, more than 70% of its workforce was absorbed in agricultural sector, though its contribution to Papua's economy was only 18.2% and the contribution to national agricultural output was a mere 1.2% in 2011. This has further implication in terms of its overall productivity in agriculture.

Figure 5.4: Correlation between Share of Agriculture in Provincial GDP and Share of Agricultural Employment

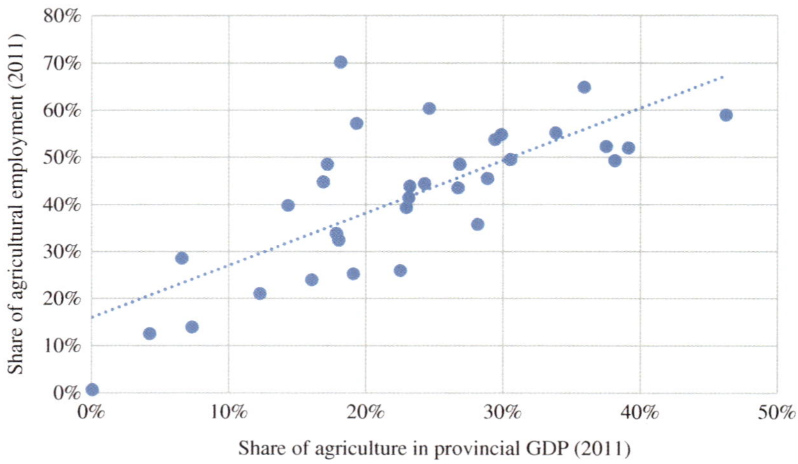

Source: Asia Competitiveness Institute with data sources from INDO-DAPOER, World Bank.

5.3 AGRICULTURAL POLICIES IN INDONESIA

Having discussed the state of Indonesia's agriculture, both at national and provincial-levels, this section aims to provide brief description of the recent agricultural policies in Indonesia. Agricultural productivity is often cited as means towards the ends, with the end goal of achieving food sovereignty. In every national medium term development plan (RPJMN), there has been a production target set for each strategic commodity. The goal of self-sufficiency, especially in terms of rice, has been an ambition of every Indonesian leader. Under President Soeharto in 1984, Indonesia earned a global acclaim from Food and Agricultural Organisation (FAO), by transforming itself "from rice importer to self-sufficiency." Then in 2008, Indonesia achieved self-sufficiency in rice for the second time.[7] In 2009, the former president Susilo Bambang Yudhoyono introduced more ambitious self-sufficiency targets but many have not been met, partly attributed to red tape, corruption cases related to import quotas and inability to keep up with the country's fast-growing demand of food as population continued to rise (*The Jakarta Post* 2015).

Under President Joko Widodo's leadership, the government aims to achieve rice self-sufficiency by 2017. To achieve such goal, the government has made available the required inputs such as tractors, fertilisers and seeds for farmers as well as access to the required water infrastructure by repairing, rehabilitating and building irrigation networks and dams. As part of the president's vision to position Indonesia as the global maritime axis, the importance of fishery sector as the backbone of Indonesia's economy has also been highly acknowledged. Table 5.3

Table 5.3: Development Target for Food Sovereignty

	2014 Baseline	2019 Target	Percentage Change
Domestic Production			
— Rice (million ton)	70.6	82.0	16.1%
— Corn (million ton)	19.1	24.1	26.2%
— Soybean (million ton)	0.9	2.6	188.9%
— Sugar (million ton)	2.6	3.8	46.2%
— Beef (thousand ton)	452.7	755.1	66.8%
— Fish (million ton)	12.4	18.8	51.6%
Development, Improvement and Rehabilitation of Irrigation Networks			
— Construction and improvement of irrigation networks: using surface water and groundwater (million hectares)	8.9	9.9	11.2%
— Rehabilitation of irrigation networks: using surface water and groundwater (million hectares)	2.7	3.0	11.1%
— Construction and improvement of irrigation of dike (thousand hectares)	189.8	304.8	60.6%
— Construction of dam	21	49	133.3%

Source: Ministry of National Development Planning/BAPPENAS (2015).

[7]Preliminary analysis from World Bank (2010) suggested that such an achievement was driven more by the increased intensification of the existing farm land, improved irrigation management, favourable weather conditions supported by input subsidies from the government, rather than an increase in productivity.

provides the exact target of accomplishment for each strategic commodity as well as efforts to restore agricultural infrastructure, to be achieved by 2019 when President Joko Widodo ends his first term in the office (Ministry of National Development Planning/BAPPENAS 2015).

In Indonesia, there are three ministries overseeing the broad agricultural sector, namely, Ministry of Agriculture for crops and livestock; Ministry of Marine Affairs and Fisheries for fishery; and Ministry of Environment and Forestry for forestry. Initially, based on 2015 budget, Ministry of Agriculture received annual budget of 15.9 trillion Rupiahs, of which 20.2% were allocated to directorate of horticulture, followed by 17.2% to directorate of farm crops (Ministry of Agriculture 2015a). When President Joko Widodo took office, the 2015 budget was revised and 32.8 trillion Rupiahs were allocated to Ministry of Agriculture, showcasing a strong signal to provide ample resources to increase agricultural production.

As listed in the 2015 revised budget published by Ministry of Finance (2015), below is a concise list of high priority programmes dedicated to achieve the goal of food sovereignty:

1. Optimisation of land use by adding 530,000 hectares to reach up to 730,000 hectares.
2. Provision of fertiliser and seeds to increase rice and corn production which initially allocated to integrated crop management (PTT) of 885,000 hectares to also be expanded to four million hectares outside PTT location.
3. Increase of fish production to reach 13.6 million ton, emphasising the improvement in production quality.
4. Increase of sugar production by providing sugarcane seeds for 12,000 hectares.
5. Increase of livestock production by artificial insemination for two million head of cattle and provision of 1,200 head of breeding cattle and 30,000 head of brood stock cattle.
6. Development of horticulture, especially chili production in 33 provinces and shallots in 25 provinces.
7. Provision of agricultural machinery of 49,200 units to support production and post-harvest stage.
8. Rehabilitation and development of 700,000 hectares tertiary irrigation network; development of 23,000 units of shallow groundwater, surface water, retention basin (locally known as *embung*) and channel reservoir; development and rehabilitation of 9,400 kilometres farm road.

Fertiliser subsidy remains a main policy instrument in Indonesia, amounting to as much as 35.7 trillion Rupiahs according to 2015 revised budget, bigger than the ministry's annual budget (Ministry of Finance 2015). The subsidy is granted to fertiliser manufacturers, which produce fertilisers at a capped price set by the government. Only farmers producing on less than two hectares are able to buy fertilisers at subsidised prices. Under this framework, the fertiliser industry is heavily regulated and relying on availability of subsidy programme and access to gas supplies, which dominate the fertiliser production cost structure, at regulated prices. In the event of rising gas prices in the international market, domestic gas supply may be negatively affected as most gas producers opt for exporting gas for higher returns. This serves as another constraint that leads to stagnating domestic production despite growing demand for fertilisers. Coupled with lack of competition and obsolete technologies, inefficiency is inevitable, leading to low capacity use and high production costs (OECD 2012). Despite various efforts to improve the distribution system and revitalise the fertiliser industry, the question to what extent the existing expensive scheme is still relevant in pushing for higher agricultural productivity and achieving food sovereignty still persists. Another concern includes the notion of trade-off that such budget can be reallocated to other dire needs to revamp agricultural infrastructure such as irrigation networks.

Most publicly announced agricultural programmes, such as the above-mentioned fertiliser subsidy, relate more to the policies affecting resource utilisation or deployment. Meanwhile, use of technology and innovation belong to factors that can shift the production frontier. Research and development (R&D) and innovation for crops and livestock are still centrally administered by Indonesian Agency for Agricultural Research and Development (IAARD) under Ministry of Agriculture, which will then pass their findings to Assessment Institutes for Agricultural Technology (AIATs) in each province whose mandate is to test the suitability of the research results for adoption at the local level.[8]

For other ministries, the research agencies are Forestry Research and Development Agency of the Ministry of Environment and Forestry (FORDA) and Agency for Marine and Fisheries Research of the Ministry of Marine Affairs and Fisheries (AMFR). Based on World Bank (2010), in real terms, public agricultural R&D spending — which was calculated based on annual budget realisation reported by the three stipulated R&D agencies and higher education institutions — experienced an increasing trend from 2001 (240 billion Rupiahs) to 2007 (507 billion Rupiahs).[9] However, the R&D spending declined in 2008 to 401 billion Rupiahs and only increased slightly in 2009 to 466 billion Rupiahs, as illustrated in Figure 5.5.[10]

Figure 5.5: Public Agricultural R&D Spending (2001–2009)

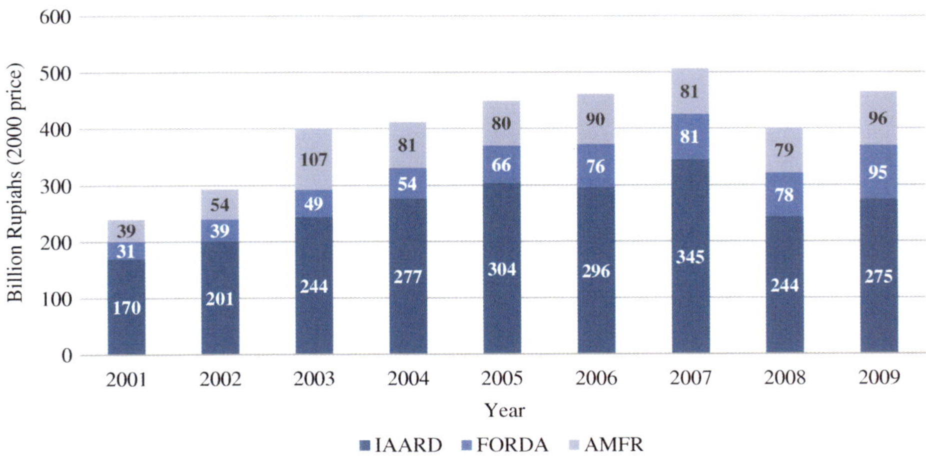

Source: World Bank (2010).

[8] In terms of organisational structure, AIATs are under the purview of Indonesian Centre for Agricultural Technology Assessment and Development (ICATAD) which belongs to IAARD.

[9] All figures are in 2000 constant price.

[10] *Ibid.*

According to Ministry of Agriculture (2015b), R&D activities for 2010–2014 produced 49 newly improved varieties of rice; 27 newly improved varieties of corn and cereal; 114 newly improved varieties of horticultural plants; 38 newly improved varieties/clones of estate crops; 47 newly improved varieties of livestock; and 44 post-harvest technologies. Dissemination is also crucial in ensuring that the technology and innovation are properly adopted by the relevant stakeholders. From 2010 to 2014, Ministry of Agriculture disseminated 1,307 technologies to end users. During that period, there were 453 innovations from IAARD whose intellectual properties had been registered, of which 294 had received intellectual property certificates.

To understand better how these agricultural policies affect the dynamics of agricultural productivity across provinces in Indonesia, the following sections will start building up the corresponding analysis, starting from literature review, followed by description of methodology, data and eventually the findings from the study.

5.4 LITERATURE REVIEW

Various literatures have examined agricultural productivity in Indonesia with largely varied findings owing to the use of different methodologies, time periods, specification of variables and data sources. "Productivity" is often interpreted in several ways. In its annual agricultural statistics, Ministry of Agriculture (2014) reported productivity figure based on total agricultural production in kilogram per hectare of land. To account for labour productivity, the calculation will take into account the agricultural output per worker. In Table 5.4, we only summarised the studies on agriculture in Indonesia that have specifically estimated Total Factor Productivity (TFP) which is the portion of output not explained by the amount of inputs used in production. As such, its level is determined by how efficiently and intensely the inputs are utilised in production.

Relying on more than four decades of time series data, Avila and Evenson (2010) and Fuglie (2010) reported a relatively modest TFP growth, 2% and 1.8%, respectively. They further decomposed the TFP growth into different periods of analysis. In Avila and Evenson (2010), the TFP growth was higher in 1961–1980 at around 4.4% than during 1981–2001 with a negative productivity growth of –0.4%. Similar trends can be found in Fuglie (2010) who reported decadal TFP growth rates and found them to be around 3% during 1961–1970; followed by about 2% growth in the next decade; a little more than 1% during 1981–1990 and a little less than 1% in 1991–2000; and finally about 2.4% between 2001 and 2006. In a follow-up study in Fuglie (2012), close to five decades of data were covered and TFP growth results were broken down into five periods. The most recent period of 2001–2009 charted the highest TFP growth at around 3.7%. The steep decline in TFP growth from the 1980s till 2000 compared to the period between 1960 and 1980 was triggered by period of economic stagnation, while the turnaround since 2001 could be attributed to more resources devoted to agriculture, as well as diversification towards estate crops.

The literature listed in Table 5.4 employed either growth accounting or Tornqvist–Theil or Malmquist Index. They also used different sets of output and input. For instance, Mundlak, Larson and Butzer (2004) and Warr (2009) used broad agricultural GDP as their output that typically also included forestry and fishery from BPS. Meanwhile, Fuglie (2010) limited the output

Table 5.4: Summary of Literature

Author	Methodology	Time Period	Specification of Variables	Data Source	TFP Growth
Suhariyanto and Thirtle (2001)	Malmquist Index	1965–1996	*Output*: Total value of agricultural production in crops and livestock; *Input*: land, labour, livestock, fertiliser and machinery;	USDA World Agricultural Trends and Indicators; FAO Agrostat Database	0.17
Mundlak, Larson and Butzer (2004)	Aggregate production function similar to Cobb–Douglas with a major difference from constant coefficients function in that the coefficients in equation are functions of the state variables and possibly of the inputs.	1971–1998	*Output*: log of agricultural GDP; *Input*: irrigated land, rainfed land, fertilisers, capital and labour; The state variables: roads, measures of education, health and incentives;	BPS; FAO	1.49
Coelli and Rao (2005)	Malmquist Index	1980–2000	*Output*: crops and livestock output; *Input*: land, tractors, labour, fertiliser, livestock and irrigation;	FAO Agrostat Database	0.98
Warr (2009)	Growth accounting	1980–2006	*Output*: agricultural GDP; *Input*: land, labour, human capital and physical capital;	BPS; SAKERNAS; Ministry of agriculture	0.90
Avila and Evenson (2010)	Growth accounting	1961–2001	*Output*: Output growth from FAO Laspeyres indexes using FAO Dollar price; *Input*: for crops – cropland, labour, fertiliser, animal power and machine services (tractors plus harvesters); for livestock: pasture land, labour, fertiliser, animal capital and feed;	FAO	2.02
Fuglie (2010)	Tornqvist-Thiel TFP Index	1961–2006	*Output*: crops, livestock, and aquaculture output; *Input*: land in crops and ponds, agricultural labour, education, wages, fertiliser, chemicals, machinery, livestock, poultry, feed and seed;	Van der Eng (1996); FAO; BPS; SAKERNAS	1.82
Fuglie (2012)	Growth accounting	1961–2009	*Output*: crop and livestock commodity production; *Input*: land, labour, livestock capital, fertiliser and machinery resources;	FAO	1961–1970 (1.75); 1971–1980 (1.40); 1981–1990 (0.59); 1991–2000 (0.99); 2001–2009 (3.68)

Source: As compiled by Asia Competitiveness Institute.

to only include crops, livestock and aquaculture. Avila and Evenson (2010), Coelli and Rao (2005) and Suhariyanto and Thirtle (2001) used only production of crops and livestock to measure output. For inputs, these literature generally included land, labour, fertiliser and machinery. National-level data were often sourced from FAO database, BPS and/or estimated by the authors using available proxies.

The literature listed in Table 5.4 revealed that most of the existing studies measuring agricultural TFP growth for Indonesia has been done at national level. However, given the significant regional differences in Indonesia, as explained earlier, this chapter will contribute to this growing literature by shedding light on the dynamics of agricultural TFP growth across provinces in Indonesia.

5.5 METHODOLOGY AND DATA SOURCES

TFP growth can be measured using two major approaches, parametric and non-parametric. While more widely used, the accuracy of the parametric approach such as Cobb–Douglas heavily depends on the specification of the production function form. An inaccurate specification of the production function could likely result in a misinterpretation of TFP. Parametric approaches also make strict assumptions on the functional form, such as constant returns to scale and technological efficiency, which are difficult to justify in practice. In contrast, non-parametric approaches such as the Malmquist index methodology is sensitive to outliers and data quality (Tong, Fulginiti, and Sesmero 2009) but not dependent on model specification.

This chapter applies both methodologies to gain a comprehensive understanding of the agricultural TFP growth in Indonesia. Given lack of observations to conduct panel analysis at the provincial level, we applied the growth accounting method only at national and regional levels. The regional grouping is island-based and aligned with Master Plan for Acceleration and Expansion of Indonesia's Economic Development (MP3EI).[11] In order to gain a deeper understanding of the driving factors of TFP growth, we adopted the Malmquist index method at provincial level, which allowed us to decompose TFP change into technological change (TC) and technical efficiency change (TEC).

5.5.1 Growth Accounting Methodology

The production function for Indonesia's agriculture sector is defined as taking a Cobb–Douglas functional form.

$$Y_{it} = A_{it}X_{it}^{\beta_1}, \tag{1}$$

where i and t indicate economy and time, respectively. Y_{it} represents the agricultural value added per labour for economy i at time t. X_{1it} indicates land per labour for economy i at

[11] More description about MP3EI can be found in Chapter 3.

time t, respectively. A_{it} is defined as the measure for TFP, which includes technology factors and efficiency factors. By taking natural logarithm on both sides of Equation (1), one can obtain Equation (2), which determines the contribution of input to output and is used in calculating TFP growth.

$$\ln Y_{it} = \beta_0 + \beta_1 \ln X_{1it} + \varepsilon_{it}. \quad (2)$$

TFP growth is the difference between real agricultural output growth and the weighted sum of input. Hence, TFP growth is calculated as the residual change in output. Therefore TFP growth can be measured by Equation (3).[12]

$$\text{TFP growth}_{it} = y_{it} - \hat{\beta}_1 x_{1it}. \quad (3)$$

5.5.2 Malmquist Index Data Envelopment Analysis

Considering the various limitations of parametric approaches to estimate TFP noted above and given limited time series, this chapter also applied the non-parametric approaches to measure agricultural TFP growth in Indonesia in the form of the Malmquist index.[13]

According to Färe *et al.* (1994), the change of TFP can be decomposed into TEC and TC through Malmquist Index. Details of this approach are given below.

Every time point has its specific technology level. Therefore, if a selected time point is represented by t, its corresponding technology level can be labelled as S^t. In this context, x^t can be used to represent all inputs of the production activity and y^t can be used to represent all outputs of the production activity. Under this circumstance, S^t can be defined in the form of Equation (1) which means all the possible combination of input x^t and output y^t under available technology at time t.

$$S^t = \{(x^t, y^t), x^t \text{ produce } y^t\}. \quad (1)$$

Since the agricultural production activity in the real world can hardly fully achieve and implement all cutting edge technologies in a specific time point t, a differentiation between the actual output and the ideal output could be spotted. According to Färe *et al.* (1994), the differentiation can be defined as Equation (2).

$$D_y^t = \inf\{\theta:(x^t, y^t/\theta) \in S^t\} = \{\sup[\theta:(x^t, \theta y^t) \in S^t]\}^{-1}. \quad (2)$$

[12] $y_{it} = \ln Y_{it} - \ln Y_{i,t-1}$.

[13] The other commonly used non-parametric measure is the Törnqvist Index. However this methodology has rather strict data requirements, including prices and quantitative data of both inputs and output. In addition, it also has some assumptions such as a perfectly competitive market and profit maximisation, which are not suitable for agricultural studies.

Equation (2) is an output-oriented distance function, in which D_y^t represents the reciprocal of the maximum change in output y through fully exploiting the input x. Given the input level x^t at time t, Equation (2) can be used to measure the maximum expansion θ of the output y^t. Meanwhile, D_y^t can also be interpreted as the reciprocal of the maximum efficiency change of the output y^t through fully exploiting the input x^t.

Similarly, as shown in Equation (3), the input-oriented distance function can measure the change of inputs given output level. For this research, the focus will be put on the output-oriented distance function.

$$D_x^t = \sup\{\lambda : (x^t/\lambda, y^t) \in S^t\}, \tag{3}$$

$$D_y^t = \inf\{\theta : (x^{t+1}, y^{t+1}/\theta) \in S^t\} = \{\sup[\theta : (x^{t+1}, \theta y^{t+1}) \in S^t\}^{-1}. \tag{4}$$

Equation (4) represents the reciprocal of maximum change of output, given input x^{t+1}, to make y^{t+1} feasible at time t. Hence, Malmquist Index can be written in the form of Equations (5) and (6).

$$M_y^t = \frac{D_y^t(x^{t+1}, y^{t+1})}{D_y^t(x^t, y^t)}, \tag{5}$$

$$M_y^{t+1} = \frac{D_y^{t+1}(x^{t+1}, y^{t+1})}{D_y^{t+1}(x^t, y^t)}. \tag{6}$$

If a specific time t is selected, the corresponding technology level will become the reference technology level. Under these circumstances, Equation (5) can be used to measure the necessary change to generate the output y^{t+1} through utilising the input x^{t+1} with the feasible technology S^t. In order to avoid choosing an arbitrage benchmark, the geometric mean of two Malmquist Indexes can be calculated to form a benchmark as Färe *et al.* (1994) did in his previous research.

$$\begin{aligned} M_y = (x^t, x^{t+1}, y^t, y^{t+1}) &= \sqrt{M_y^t * M_y^{t+1}} \\ &= \left[\left(\frac{D_y^t(x^{t+1}, y^{t+1})}{D_y^t(x^t, y^t)}\right)\left(\frac{D_y^{t+1}(x^{t+1}, y^{t+1})}{D_y^{t+1}(x^t, y^t)}\right)\right]^{1/2}. \end{aligned} \tag{7}$$

Equation (7) can be decomposed into two parts through mathematical transformation as illustrated by Equation (8).

$$M_y = (x^t, x^{t+1}, y^t, y^{t+1}) = \frac{D_y^{t+1}(x^{t+1}, y^{t+1})}{D_y^t(x^t, y^t)} \left[\left(\frac{D_y^t(x^{t+1}, y^{t+1})}{D_y^{t+1}(x^{t+1}, y^{t+1})} \right) \left(\frac{D_y^t(x^t, y^t)}{D_y^{t+1}(x^t, y^t)} \right) \right]^{1/2}. \quad (8)$$

Equation (8) can be perceived as two components. The first component represents the TEC between time t and time t+1, and the second component represents the TC between time t and time t+1. The practical meaning of this transformation is that, the change of TFP (TFPC) can be decomposed into TEC and TC, as shown in Equation (9).

$$\text{TFPC} = \text{TEC} \times \text{TC}. \quad (9)$$

TEC is broadly related to better resource utilisation or deployment as well as more efficient management. TC broadly refers to the technology innovation or progress, which can shift the production frontier. For example, an invention of new technology could shift the agricultural production frontier. Thereafter, the true driving factor could be identified through the decomposition of TFPC, which may potentially draw valuable lessons for future development of the agricultural sector.

Linear Programming approach is used to calculate the Malmquist Index in this empirical chapter. At time $t = 1,\ldots,T$, inputs of the target economy can be indicated *by* $m = 1,\ldots,M$, the corresponding production output and regions can be indicated by $n=1,\ldots,N$, and $i = 1,\ldots,I$, respectively. According to Färe *et al.* (1994), the reference technology at time t can be constructed as the form of Equation (10) under this context.

$$S^t = \left\{ \begin{array}{ll} (x^t, y^t) : y_n^t \le \sum_{i=1}^{I} z^{i,t} y_n^{i,t}, & n = 1,\ldots 1, N; \\ \text{where,} \sum_{i=1}^{I} z^{i,t} x_m^{i,t} \le x_m^t, & m = 1,\ldots, M; \\ z^{i,t} \ge 0, & i = 1,\ldots I \end{array} \right\}. \quad (10)$$

The intensity variable $z^{i,t}$ indicates the intensity application of a particular activity. For this chapter, one economy only has one such activity. It is worth to note that, by adding constrains on z, the Malmquist index can be computed under variable returns to scale (VRS). For instance, the technology can be relaxed to non-increasing returns to scale by adding Equation (11), or variable returns to scale can also be allowed by adding Equation (12).

$$\sum_{i=1}^{I} z^{i,t} \leq 1, \tag{11}$$

$$\sum_{i=1}^{I} z^{i,t} = 1. \tag{12}$$

Based on the definition of output-oriented distance function, which is exhibited in Equation (2), the distance function can be computed through available data. In order to compute the productivity change of a region i between time t and time t+1, six distance functions should be calculated. For a specific time t, with the corresponding input and output, the output distance can be calculated by the following linear programming formulation as illustrated by Equation (13).

$$\begin{aligned} &\left[D_y^t\left(x^{i',t}, y^{i',t}\right)\right]^{-1} = \max \theta^{i'}, \\ &\text{subject to } \theta^{i'} y_n^{i',t} \leq \sum_{i=1}^{I} z^{i',t} y_n^{i',t}, \quad n=1,\ldots,N, \\ &\sum_{i=1}^{I} z^{i',t} x_m^{i',t} \leq x_m^{i',t}, \quad m=1,\ldots,M, \\ &\mathrm{z}^{i,t} \geq 0, \quad i=1,\ldots,\mathrm{I}. \end{aligned} \tag{13}$$

Furthermore, the mix-period distance function at time t, corresponding to the input and output at time t+1, can be calculated through applying Equation (14).

$$\begin{aligned} &\left[D_y^t\left(x^{i',t+1}, y^{i',t+1}\right)\right]^{-1} = \max \theta^{i'} \\ &\text{subject to } \theta^{i'} y_n^{i',t+1} \leq \sum_{i=1}^{I} z^{i',t} y_n^{i',t}, \quad n=1,\ldots,N, \\ &\sum_{i=1}^{I} z^{i',t} x_m^{i',t} \leq x_m^{i',t+1}, \quad m=1,\ldots,M, \\ &\mathrm{z}^{i,t} \geq 0, \quad i=1,\ldots,\mathrm{I}. \end{aligned} \tag{14}$$

Equation (12) can be added as a constraint into the linear programming problem, in order to calculate the distance function under variable returns to scale. Up to this point, the Malmquist index value can be obtained after all calculated variables are substituted into Equation (8).

5.5.3 Data Sources

Finding relevant data at provincial level is challenging as there is no central database that provides all indicators. The data are collected from 2000 to 2011 to account for the latest changes in provincial level TFP growth in Indonesia. For output, the chapter uses provincial agricultural GDP from World Bank's INDO-DAPOER that captures crops, livestock, forestry and fishery. Labour and land are used as inputs. For labour, the data are also sourced from INDO-DAPOER which refers to a number of people employed in crops, livestock, fishery and forestry sector. The land indicator covers wetland, garden, dry land, shifting cultivation, temporary/fallow land and utilised land for main estate crops, sourced from BPS (various issues) and Ministry of Agriculture.

Data on machinery are not available on a consistent time series basis. Fuglie (2010) relied on the number of tractors in use adjusted for size; 12 horsepower (hp) for two-wheel-tractor and 20, 33 and 50 hp per small, medium and large four-wheel tractor, respectively. *Statistical Yearbook of Indonesia* only published these indicators up to 2002. The data became available again in 2011, but did not report the four-wheel tractor. The Ministry of Agriculture also reported the number of tractors but only documented those that were part of government assistance.

For fertilisers, Ministry of Agriculture only released the statistics on subsidised fertiliser for recent period, from 2009 onwards. The publication on *Farm Cost Structure of Paddy and Secondary Food Crops* gave fertiliser application rates per hectare for rice and secondary food crops. However, such data were only available in 2008 publication for paddy, 2009 for corn and 2010 for soybean. Nevertheless, they were only available for half of the provinces. Since the goal of the chapter was to cover as many provinces as possible and finding proxies to fill in unavailable data across provinces over time could further distort the results, the data used in the chapter were limited to two input variables including labour and land, which had comprehensive time series and provincial coverage.

As of 2016, Indonesia has 34 provinces. The newest province is North Kalimantan, firstly established in 2012 and hence, is not included in our analysis. During the period of analysis — 2000–2011 — there were seven newly created provinces: North Maluku (carved out from Maluku in 1999); West Papua (carved out from Papua in 1999); Banten (carved out from West Java in 2000); Bangka Belitung (carved out from South Sumatra in 2000); Gorontalo (carved out from North Sulawesi in 2000); Riau Islands (carved out from Riau in 2002); and West Sulawesi (carved out from South Sulawesi in 2004). For some indicators that were not adjusted at source reflecting these changes, data points were estimated based on their past growth trend and relative proportion to their parent province. DKI Jakarta was also not included in the analysis due to the negligible share of its agricultural sector in its economy (0.1%).

5.6 EMPIRICAL FINDINGS

5.6.1 Labour Productivity

In the case of Indonesia from 2000 to 2011, there were significant disparities across provinces in terms of labour productivity in agriculture. Labour productivity was calculated by dividing agricultural GDP by employment in agricultural sector. For average annual growth rate in labour productivity from 2000 to 2011 in Table 5.5, most provinces in Java Island grew faster than the average rate of 4.5%, except East Java where more than seven million people were still employed in agricultural sector.

Table 5.5: Labour Productivity Across Provinces (2000–2011)

		Average Annual Growth Rates (%)
Region	**Province**	**Output per Worker**
Sumatra	Aceh	2.3
	North Sumatra	4.8
	Riau	4.0
	Riau Islands	5.0
	West Sumatra	6.2
	Jambi	4.2
	Bengkulu	5.8
	South Sumatra	4.8
	Bangka Belitung Islands	7.3
	Lampung	5.9
Java	West Java	5.6
	Banten	8.3
	Central Java	4.7
	DI Yogyakarta	5.5
	East Java	2.9
Kalimantan	West Kalimantan	2.3
	Central Kalimantan	1.3
	South Kalimantan	5.1
	East Kalimantan	5.0
Sulawesi	North Sulawesi	6.0
	Central Sulawesi	6.9
	Southeast Sulawesi	5.6
	Gorontalo	9.2
	West Sulawesi	3.7
	South Sulawesi	3.3
Bali–Nusa Tenggara	Bali	5.6
	West Nusa Tenggara	3.4
	East Nusa Tenggara	3.2
Maluku–Papua	North Maluku	4.1
	Maluku	1.3
	West Papua	2.3
	Papua	0.4

Source: Asia Competitiveness Institute's calculation.

There were wide variations of labour productivity within provinces in each region. When the figures were aggregated at the regional level, labour productivity in Java was actually lower than that of Kalimantan, Sumatra and Sulawesi where expansions in high value estate crops such as palm oil, rubber and cocoa took place. On the other hand, labour productivity growth rates for Bali–Nusa Tenggara and Maluku–Papua were lower than the national average. From these two regions, Bali was the only province with higher than average labour productivity growth. In fact, International Fund for Agricultural Development (2011) has cited a number of ingrained issues found in Maluku and North Maluku that led to poor productivity in agricultural sector such as local conflicts, poor marketing and infrastructure and insufficient natural resource management.[14]

5.6.2 TFP

Based on panel data analysis using growth accounting method, as shown in Table 5.6, TFP growth for 2000–2011 was 3.1% for Indonesia as a whole. Further analysis at regional level revealed that Sulawesi had the highest TFP growth at about 3.5%. Other regions which reported higher than national TFP growth were Sumatra (3.3%), Java (3.3%) and Bali–Nusa Tenggara (3.2%). Due to limited sample size, we did not calculate TFP growth at provincial level using the growth accounting method. Kalimantan and Maluku–Papua were the laggards with 2.0% and 1.5% TFP growth, respectively. The recent initiative to push for Merauke Integrated Food and Energy Estate (MIFEE) that will cover over a million hectares of plantations and industrialised agriculture may contribute to higher TFP growth in Maluku–Papua Region in the future.[15]

Table 5.6: TFP Growth Using Growth Accounting Method (2000–2011)

	β_0	β_1	**TFP Growth**
National	0.030***	0.602***	3.06%
Sulawesi	0.033***	0.579**	3.47%
Sumatra	0.032***	0.674***	3.34%
Java	0.032***	0.921***	3.26%
Bali–Nusa Tenggara	0.030***	0.453	3.24%
Kalimantan	0.024***	0.568***	1.98%
Maluku–Papua	0.015***	0.564*	1.48%

Note: ***, **, and * indicate statistically significant at the 1%, 5% and 10% levels, respectively.
Source: Asia Competitiveness Institute's calculation.

[14]On top of that, other issues included limited knowledge of modern agricultural practices and lack of effective extension services, research outreach, supply of production input and financing. As a result, most agricultural output was of poor quality with low market value as there was no local value addition through processing and marketing. Hence, it was not surprising that most food crop production solely aimed for meeting subsistence needs.

[15]MIFEE is part of the MP3EI projects which designate Merauke as the centre of food and energy reserves in Eastern Indonesia. Yulisman (2015) reported that the programme has attracted a dozen of domestic and foreign investors who were interested in growing rice, corn, soybean, sugar cane and palm oil.

Table 5.7: Average TFPC and Its Decomposition from 2000–2011 for 32 Provinces

Province	TEC	TC	TFPC
Banten	1.022	1.041	1.064
South Kalimantan	1.028	1.026	1.055
Lampung	1.012	1.039	1.051
Central Sulawesi	1.032	1.019	1.051
Southeast Sulawesi	1.024	1.024	1.049
North Sulawesi	1.024	1.023	1.047
Bali	1.003	1.043	1.046
Bengkulu	1.022	1.023	1.046
West Sumatra	1.018	1.025	1.044
Gorontalo	1.021	1.02	1.042
North Sumatra	1.006	1.034	1.04
West Java	1.000	1.039	1.039
South Sumatra	1.012	1.026	1.039
Bangka Belitung Islands	1.022	1.016	1.038
Jambi	1.013	1.024	1.037
South Sulawesi	1.002	1.032	1.034
Central Java	1.002	1.03	1.032
Riau	1.003	1.028	1.031
East Nusa Tenggara	0.995	1.033	1.028
DI Yogyakarta	0.997	1.03	1.027
West Kalimantan	1.000	1.026	1.026
East Java	0.994	1.03	1.025
Riau Islands	1.000	1.025	1.025
West Nusa Tenggara	0.983	1.043	1.025
Central Kalimantan	0.988	1.031	1.019
Aceh	0.997	1.021	1.018
West Papua	0.996	1.019	1.015
Maluku	0.99	1.019	1.008
East Kalimantan	0.988	1.019	1.007
West Sulawesi	0.977	1.03	1.007
North Maluku	0.98	1.027	1.006
Papua	0.977	1.023	1.000

Note: TEC: Total Efficiency Change; TC: Technological Change; TFPC: Change of TFP.
Source: Asia Competitiveness Institute's calculation.

For Malmquist–DEA results, as Table 5.7 reveals, TFP grew at an annual average rate of 3.2% from 2000 to 2011, which was somewhat aligned with the estimation using growth accounting method. The TC's contribution was 2.9%, while TEC's contribution was 0.3%. While this likely overstated the importance of TFP (since we have excluded other inputs for which data were not available), the TFP estimate was slightly below the 3.7% found by Fuglie (2012) during 2001–2009.[16]

[16]Another study by Fuglie (2010) found 2.4% TFP growth from 2001 to 2006.

There remained significant variations in TFP growth across provinces, with Banten the highest — a 6.4% increase — and Papua the lowest — attaining a status quo or zero change. The majority of provinces with high labor productivity growth also reported high TFP growth. Looking at the provinces which reported the ten-highest TFP growth, four provinces were from Sulawesi, three provinces from Sumatra and the remaining provinces were from Java, Kalimantan and Bali–Nusa Tenggara regions.

Across the provinces, results suggested that TFP growth could be predominantly attributed to TC, with the growth in TEC being marginal and even negative in most provinces (Papua and West Sulawesi being the lowest, registering a decrease by 2.3%). The fact that TC was relatively similar across provinces might be mainly due to the fact that R&D and innovation were still driven by the central government. The funding would typically be allocated to IAARD under Ministry of Agriculture, and then distributed to its local offices in each province. For estate crops, Indonesian Research Institute for Estate Crops (IRIEC) has mainly been funded by the plantation sector itself, through Indonesian Planters Association for Research and Development (IPARD). IRIEC was relatively better funded as research expenditure per scientist was about four times higher than that of IAARD (Fuglie and Piggott 2006). TEC has largely lagged in provinces with profound infrastructure bottlenecks, such as East Nusa Tenggara, West Nusa Tenggara, West Sulawesi, West Papua, Maluku and North Maluku, all of which reported negative growth.

Robustness checks were also conducted by only including 16 highest contributors to national agricultural output. Based on Table 5.8, the results showed that the overall rankings of the

Table 5.8: Average TFPC and Its Decomposition for Selected Provinces

Province	TEC	TC	TFPC
Banten	1.021	1.045	1.067
South Kalimantan	1.019	1.032	1.052
Central Sulawesi	1.026	1.026	1.052
Lampung	1.007	1.044	1.051
West Sumatra	1.015	1.035	1.050
South Sumatra	1.006	1.035	1.041
North Sumatra	1.001	1.040	1.041
West Java	1.000	1.040	1.040
Central Java	1.002	1.030	1.032
South Sulawesi	0.993	1.040	1.032
West Kalimantan	1.003	1.026	1.029
East Java	0.994	1.030	1.025
Central Kalimantan	1.000	1.024	1.024
Riau	1.003	1.019	1.022
Aceh	0.988	1.030	1.018
East Kalimantan	1.000	1.007	1.007

Note: TEC: Total Efficiency Change; TC: Technological Change; TFPC: Change of TFP.
Source: Asia Competitiveness Institute's calculation.

Table 5.9: Average TFPC and Its Decomposition from 2000–2011 for Six Regions

Region	TEC	TC	TFPC
Sulawesi	1.012	1.027	1.039
Sumatra	1.008	1.029	1.038
Bali–Nusa Tenggara	0.994	1.040	1.034
Java	0.996	1.030	1.030
Kalimantan	1.001	1.025	1.026
Maluku–Papua	0.984	1.022	1.006

Note: TEC: Total Efficiency Change; TC: Technological Change; TFPC: Change of TFP.
Source: Asia Competitiveness Institute.

provinces remained fairly consistent when the analysis was performed for smaller sample size. The top four as well as the bottom provinces largely retained their positions in the absence of less significant provinces (based on the size of their agricultural output).

The regional TFPC, TEC and TC were calculated based on the weighted average of provincial contribution to the region's agricultural output. Based on Table 5.9, Sulawesi outperformed the rest, with TFP growth of 3.9%, with 1.2% coming from improvements in TEC and 2.7% from TC. The results corroborated the findings using the growth accounting method. Four out of six provinces in Sulawesi Region were also part of those that registered the 10-highest TFP growth rates. This supports the region's designated role as a centre for production and processing of national agricultural, plantation and fishery, as stipulated in MP3EI (Coordinating Ministry of Economic Affairs 2011).

5.7 CONCLUSIONS AND POLICY IMPLICATIONS

The new leadership under President Joko Widodo has emphasised the importance of achieving food sovereignty in Indonesia. The MP3EI also stresses agriculture as one of the eight main programmes, with the production of palm oil, rubber, cocoa, animal husbandry, timber, fishery and food crops as part of 22 main economic activities. Such policies signal the importance of agricultural productivity to the country, especially given the significant regional variations in terms of productivity. In this light, this chapter has provided the most recent analysis on estimating agricultural productivity in Indonesia, focusing on the dynamics at the provincial level.

From 2000 to 2011, TFP grew on average by 3.1 to 3.2% using both growth accounting and Malmquist methods, respectively. TFP growth at regional level is also broadly consistent, indicating the robustness in the estimates. According to the Malmquist index, TFP growth was predominantly due to improvements in TC which was broadly uniform across provinces. This uniformity is not very surprising as TC is driven primarily by R&D, new innovations and technology under the provision of central government. It is important to recognise the role of the IAARD in this context, especially for food crops and livestock research, as IRIEC has been driving the research in estate crops. Going forward, IAARD should continue building its technological capacity to gradually strengthen its focus on non-staple foods with higher value added and its interaction with the private sector.

For estate crops that are still dominated by small farms, the challenge is to address the low productivity of smallholders with limited access to high quality inputs. Developing effective systems for small farms is key to improving productivity in estate crops such as in the case of nucleus–plasma programme based on partnerships between large estates and smallholders.[17] This kind of programme is not only restricted to state-owned enterprises but also private companies. For instance, collaboration between Unilever and local farmers in Java to produce black soybeans, both providing win-win solution for Unilever to secure their supplies of raw materials and for farmers to receive access to credit and improved incomes as well as a guaranteed market for their products (OECD 2012).

With regards to R&D, World Bank (2010) reported that the intensity with which Indonesia invests in agricultural research is relatively low (0.22%) even after adding the R&D spending from private sector. With such low R&D spending, Indonesia is on par with Lao PDR (0.24%), and much lower than Malaysia (1.92%) and the Philippines (0.44%), as can be seen in Figure 5.6. The budget allocation for agricultural R&D in Indonesia tends to be volatile, especially when time gets tough, as in the case of AFC when the budget was cut by more than 60% (Fuglie and Piggott 2006). In this case, more can be learned from India where there is a consistent positive trend of public research funding stemmed from strong political commitment to research across electoral cycles (Pal and Byerlee 2006).

Figure 5.6: Public Agricultural R&D Spending Among Asian Countries

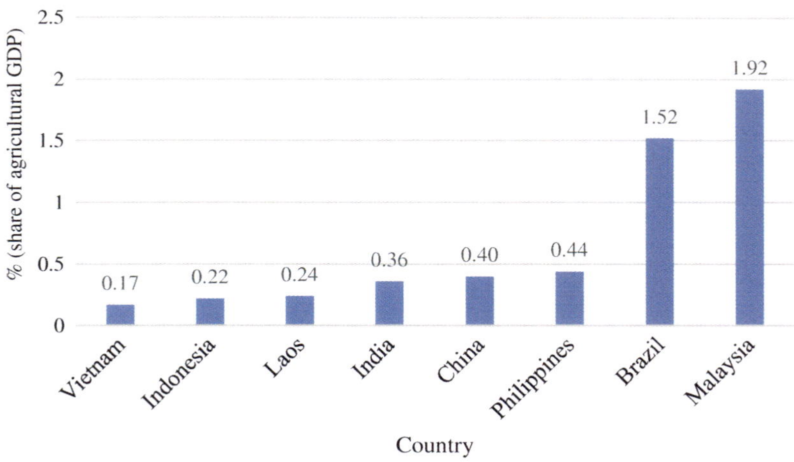

Source: World Bank (2010).

[17] Under this programme, large estates (nucleus) will be provided subsidised capital and long-term leases to state land for crop production with the conditions that they provide inputs, credit, and other services such as technical and marketing services to smallholders (plasma) surrounding their plantations.

On top of that, it is important to forge greater collaborations with the private sector, involvement of universities, and linkages with those of international R&D providers. Various incentives can be set by the government to encourage private investment in agriculture, such as intellectual property protection to ensure that companies can retain rights to their research findings, enabling them to recover their investment on generating knowledge. Other incentives can be in the form of tax concession or matching grants to make private investment in agricultural R&D and knowledge creation in better farming techniques more appealing.

Agricultural R&D system in Indonesia has a unique feature where research activities are centrally administered by IAARD consisting of a number of centres clustered around commodities,[18] while dissemination efforts in terms of application of the research outcomes are relatively decentralised, operated by AIATs located in every province. This is in contrast to the highly decentralised approach by China where agricultural R&D activities are organised parallel to the country's administrative system comprising national agricultural academies under Ministry of Agriculture, provincial agricultural academies, and prefectural agricultural research institutes. As a result, duplications and overlapping of resources are inevitable as well as unrealised economies of scale and scope (Fan, Qian and Zhang 2006).

In the case of India, the dominant players in agricultural R&D ecosystem are Indian Council of Agricultural Research (ICAR) at the national level and state agricultural universities (SAUs). In both countries, technology transfer tends to take a back seat, mostly due to the fact that extension services are managed separately by a different institution with little or no coordination with the respective research centres; and incentive system for the researchers are skewed towards publication with no rewards for technology transfer (Fan, Qian and Zhang 2006; Pal and Byerlee 2006).

Despite of the fact that Indonesia has an integrated structure that connects researchers and extension workers, there is plenty room for improvement. The success of extension services largely depends on the quality of extension workers. The Agency of Agricultural Human Resource Development (AAHRD) at the central level can assume a leadership role in the provision of appropriate training at the entry level as well as in continuous training updates both to refresh and provide the latest information on new technologies and innovative agricultural research to the extension workers (World Bank 2010). Furthermore, both extension workers and farmers need to have access to agricultural R&D centres and knowledge networks to be able to successfully adopt the new technology.

As the empirical results point out, the main differences of TFP growth across provinces arise from TEC which can be improved in lagging provinces through better resource utilisation. With provincial-level analysis, there is an opportunity for inter-province learning to ensure more efficient resource deployment and management techniques. For many lagging provinces, if they are

[18] In total, there are 13 research centres under IAARD, locally known as *pusat penelitian* or *balai besar.* They are as follows: Centre for Food Crops R&D; Centre for Rice Research; Centre for Horticulture R&D; Centre for Estate Crops R&D; Centre for Animal Science R&D; Centre for Agricultural Land Resources R&D; Centre for Biotechnology and Genetic Resources R&D; Centre for Socio Economic and Policy Studies; Centre for Agricultural Engineering R&D; Centre for Post-Harvest R&D; Centre for Veterinary Sciences; Centre for Agricultural Technology Assessment and Development; Centre for Agricultural Library and Technology Dissemination.

able to learn from high-performing provinces and enhance TEC, overall agricultural sector can be expanded with minimal increases in resources.

The bottom three provinces, Papua, North Maluku and West Sulawesi, all suffered from 2% to 2.3% decline of TEC over the period of 2000–2011. All three provinces have substantial share of agricultural sector which absorbs significant proportion of their labour force. North Maluku and Papua are located at the far eastern part of Indonesia which are infamous for their rudimentary infrastructure. On the other hand, provision of infrastructure in West Sulawesi, a newly created province in 2004, is also still behind its peers in Sulawesi Region. Hence, it is not surprising that they are all falling behind in terms of competitiveness, particularly for quality of life and infrastructure development environment, as can be seen from Chapter 2. Their relatively poor infrastructure creates another layer of bottleneck, making it harder to get access to the much-needed inputs such as fertiliser and seeds while post-harvest distribution and marketing become more challenging. Improvement in this area requires not only commitment from provincial government but also central government to redirect funding for more connectivity with the eastern region.

Given limited resources, the government has to be cognisant of prioritising agricultural policies that have the most impact on agricultural productivity. With regards to public spending in agriculture, Armas, Osorio and Moreno-Dodson (2010) found that in 2009, 56% of agricultural resources in Indonesia (34.4 trillion Rupiahs) were allocated toward subsidising private goods; most went to fertiliser subsidies (18.5 trillion). There is an opportunity cost of such subsidies, how the resources for subsidising input is done at the expense of providing public goods such as funding R&D and improving irrigation network. Their research found that public spending in providing agricultural public goods led to a positive effect on growth rate of agricultural GDP per capita. On the other hand, spending on fertiliser subsidies reported a significant negative effect. Further discussion on the needs to reallocate public spending from subsidising private inputs to providing agricultural public goods and services needs to be taken into account. Additionally, it is important to implement strategies to increase the spending effectiveness by putting in place a comprehensive monitoring and evaluation system.

Lastly, it is essential to improve the provision of reliable and timely statistics across provinces and over time. As mentioned in Section 5.5.3, provincial-level agricultural data are at best patchy and not available in consistent time series. There were instances that statistical publications for certain variables were stopped halfway and reinstated at later year with different ways of defining and calculating the variables. While improvements in terms of data collection are welcomed, it is equally important to ensure consistency across the years by providing back casting of the previous year data should the definition has been altered. At the international level, FAO has played a role as a main source of reliable data for cross-country analysis and put substantial efforts in harmonising agricultural data across countries and years. Similar efforts should be taken by Ministry of Agriculture to ensure high quality panel data to allow for richer provincial-level analysis. With better quality and availability of appropriate data, more evidence-based policy decisions can be made and eventually enhance policy performance.

REFERENCES

Armas, Enrique B., Camilo G. Osorio and Blanea Moreno-Dodson. 2010. "Agriculture Public Spending and Growth: The Example of Indonesia." *Economic Premise, Poverty Reduction and Economic Management Network (PREM), World Bank* No. 9.

Avila, Antonio F.D. and Robert E. Evenson. 2010. "Total Factor Productivity Growth in Agriculture: The Role of Technological Capital." In *Handbook of Agricultural Economics Volume 4*, edited by Prabhu L. Pingali and Robert E. Evenson, 3769–3822. Amsterdam: Elsevier.

Biro, Pusat Statistik. 2016. "GDP in 2000 Constant Price Based on Industrial Origin." http://www.bps.go.id/linkTabelStatis/view/id/1200 (accessed January 15, 2016).

Biro, Pusat Statistik. various issues. *Land Size According to Its Utilisation*. Jakarta: Biro Pusat Statistik.

Coelli, Tim J. and D.S. Prasada Rao. 2005. "Total Factor Productivity Growth in Agriculture: A Malmquist Index Analysis of 93 countries, 1980–2000." *Agriculture Economics* 32: 115–134.

Coordinating, Ministry for Economic Affairs. 2011. *Masterplan for Acceleration and Expansion of Indonesia's Economic Development*. Jakarta: Coordinating Ministry for Economic Affairs.

Fan, Shenggen, Keming Qian and Xiaobo Zhang. 2006. "China: An Unfinished Reform." In *Agricultural R&D in the Developing World: Too Little, Too Late?* edited by P. G. Pardey, J. M. Alston and R. R. Piggott, pp. 29–63. Washington: International Food Policy Research Institute.

Färe, Rolf, Shawna Grosskopf, Mary Norris and Zhongyang Zhang. 1994. "Productivity Growth, Technical Progress, and Efficiency Change in Industrialised Countries." *American Economic Review* 84(1): 66–83.

Fuglie, Keith O. 2010. "Sources of growth in Indonesian agriculture." *Journal of Productivity Analysis* 33: 225–240.

Fuglie, Keith O. 2012. "Productivity Growth and Technology Capital in the Global Agricultural Economy." In *Productivity Growth in Agriculture: An International Perspective*, edited by Keith O. Fuglie, V. Eldon Ball and Sun Ling Wang, pp. 335–368. Oxfordshire: C.A.B. International.

Fuglie, Keith O and R.R. Piggott. 2006. "Indonesia: Coping with Economic and Political Instability." In *Agricultural R&D in the Developing World: Too Little, Too Late?* edited by P. G. Pardey, J. M. Alston and R. R. Piggott, pp. 65–104. Washington: International Food Policy Research Institute.

Hajramurni, Andi. 2010. "East ASEAN Set to Become 'Food Basket' in Asia." *The Jakarta Post*, November 27. http://www.thejakartapost.com/news/2010/11/27/east-asean-set-become-%E2%80%98food-basket%E2%80%99-asia.html (accessed January 15, 2006).

International Fund for Agricultural Development. 2011. *Smallholder Livelihood Development Project in Maluku and North Maluku*. Project design report, Asia and the Pacific Division Programme Management Department.

Ministry of Agriculture. 2014. *Agricultural Statistics*. Jakarta: Ministry of Agriculture.

Ministry of Agriculture. 2015a. *Budget Allocation (APBN) of Ministry of Agriculture 2013–2015*. Jakarta: Ministry of Agriculture.

Ministry of Agriculture. 2015b. *Strategic Planning of Ministry of Agriculture 2015–2019*. Jakarta: Ministry of Agriculture.

Ministry of Finance. 2015. *Budget in Brief: APBNP 2015*. Jakarta: Ministry of Finance.

Ministry of National Development Planning/BAPPENAS. 2015. *National Medium Term Development Plan 2015–2019.* Jakarta: Ministry of National Development Planning/BAPPENAS.

Mundlak, Yair, Donald Larson and Rita Butzer. 2004. "Agricultural Dynamics in Thailand, Indonesia and the Philippines." *The Australian Journal of Agricultural and Resource Economics* 48(1): 95–126.

OECD. 2012. *OECD Review of Agricultural Policies: Indonesia 2012.* Paris: OECD Publishing.

Pal, Suresh and Derek Byerlee. 2006. "India: The Funding and Organisation of Agricultural R&D — Evolution and Emerging Policy Issues." In *Agricultural R&D in the Developing World: Too Little, Too Late?* edited by P. G. Pardey, J. M. Alston and R. R. Piggott, 155–193. Washington: International Food Policy Research Institute.

Suhariyanto, Kecuk and Colin Thirtle. 2001. "Asian Agricultural Productivity and Convergence." *Journal of Agricultural Economics* 52(3): 96–110.

Tan, Khee Giap, Kartik Rao and Ramkishen Rajan. 2015. "How Productive is the Agricultural Sector across Indian States?" *International Journal of Development Issues* 14(3): 231–248.

Tan, Khee Giap, Suo Haoran and Ramkishen Rajan. Forthcoming (a). "How Productive is the Agricultural Sector in ASEAN?" *International Journal of Technological Learning, Innovation and Development.*

Tan, Khee Giap, Suo Haoran and Ramkishen Rajan. Forthcoming (b). "Estimating Provincial Agricultural Total Factor Productivity in Mainland China." *International Journal of Business Performance Management.*

The Jakarta Post. 2015. "Jokowi Wants Farmers to Work Harder for Food Sufficiency." March 7. http://www.thejakartapost.com/news/2015/03/07/jokowi-wants-farmers-work-harder-food-sufficiency.html (accessed January 18, 2016).

Tong, Haizhi, Lilyan E. Fulginiti and Juan P. Sesmero. 2009. Chinese Regional Agricultural Productivity: 1994–2005. *Agricultural Economics Department*, University of Nebraska-Lincoln, Nebraska, 21 July, Working paper 89.

Warr, Peter. 2009. Aggregate and Sectoral Productivity Growth in Thailand and Indonesia. *The Arndt-Corden Division of Economics*, ANU College of Asia and the Pacific, Australian National University, Canberra, September, Working papers in Trade and Development No. 2009/10.

World Bank. 2010. *Indonesia Agriculture Public Expenditure Review 2010.* Jakarta: World Bank.

World Bank. 2015. "The Tale of Two Ports in Indonesia." *World* Bank, May 26. http://www.worldbank.org/en/news/feature/2015/05/26/the-tale-of-two-ports-in-indonesia (accessed January 21, 2016).

World Bank. 2016. *World Development Indicators.* Washington, DC: World Bank.

Yulisman, Linda. 2015. "Govt to Revive Food Estate Project in Papua." *The Jakarta Post.* April 16. http://www.thejakartapost.com/news/2015/04/16/govt-revive-food-estate-project-papua.html (accessed January 21, 2016).

Discussant Notes: Agricultural Productivity in Indonesian Provinces: Overview and Review of Research Results

Agung Hendriadi

Executive Secretary of Indonesian Agency for Agricultural Research and Development (IAARD)

I will present two things today, first is the overview of agricultural development in Indonesia, and second, my review on the Asia Competitiveness Institute's (ACI) research findings. Overview of agricultural development and its challenges in Indonesia are very important in order to draw policy implication based on ACI's research findings. I tried to compare the ACI's research findings on Total Factor Productivity (TFP) in agriculture with the facts of what we have achieved.

Similar to neighbouring countries, the contribution of agricultural sector to national GDP is lower than that of industrial and service sector. Instead of the contribution of the agricultural sector to GDP, I would like to propose three important parameters in evaluating agricultural development which include contribution of agriculture to the total export, total import and also employment. It is proven from the ACI's studies presented today, the agricultural contribution to the GDP was around 14.7% in 2011. Another feature that we have to consider is the agricultural employment. The agricultural employment in Indonesia is starting to decrease year by year. Within periods of 1970–2010, the total households working in agricultural sector decreased from 64% to 33%. In order to evaluate the agricultural development in Indonesia, it is also very important to consider the density of population in Indonesia which very much differs from island to island. Java Island represents only 7% of the total land area but hosts 57% of the population with density around 1,000 person/km,^{2} while Papua occupies 22% of the land area but is habited by less than 2% of the total population with density of around 7 person/km.^{2}

Regarding the growth of production of five major agricultural commodities (rice, corn, soybean, sugar and beef), currently, it is shown that production of rice and corn has achieved national self-sufficiency target. Sugar and beef have almost reached self-sufficiency, while soybean is still far below the national consumption.

To sum up the issues and challenges, the development of agriculture in Indonesia is facing: (1) Increasing demand of imported agricultural products, (2) Climate changes, agricultural land being converted to other purposes, lack of water resources, (3) Pressure of globalization, (4) Low private sector investment in agriculture (in 2011, domestic investment in agriculture was around 9.6 trillion Rupiahs, while foreign investment was around 1.2 million US Dollars), (5) Insufficient agricultural infrastructure, (6) Inefficiency in supply-chain input and product, (7) Increasing cost for fertiliser and energy and (8) Weak coordination among government institutions.

In relation to the methodology of study conducted by ACI on TFP, I would suggest to have a separate group evaluation among sub-sector in agriculture. Food crop, horticulture and livestock could be in one group and should be separated from forestry and also fishery. The reason was the character of those sub-sectors is much different in terms of land holding and number of employment involved.

Based on the ACI's research findings on TFP, it is surprising that Banten is in the top rank, while in fact, agricultural production for the five major commodities for Banten is relatively much lower than other provinces such as West Java, East Java, Central Java, South Sulawesi and West Sumatra. Similarly for the findings of technical efficiency change (TEC) and technological change (TC), the results shown do not match with the fact based on agricultural production by province. This contradictive findings need further analysis leading to policy formulation.

From the conclusion drawn, the rank of TFP was based on two indicators, (1) agricultural GRDP and (2) agricultural policies (with clear road map on agribusiness development). Based on the two indicators, Banten was concluded as the top performing province, while in fact, Banten has agricultural GRDP that is lower than South Kalimantan and also other provinces. In order to have more representative conclusion to align with the fact, I would suggest to conduct deeper analysis.

The use of agricultural policies which includes roadmap on agribusiness development is significant and correct to draw the conclusion. My previous study concluded that there were three top leverage of agricultural development in Indonesia. These include agricultural infrastructure development, opening new agricultural land and technology innovation and distribution and readiness including seed fertiliser and services.

Chapter 6

Concluding Remarks and Future Research Agenda

6.1 CONCLUDING REMARKS

The Asia Competitiveness Institute (ACI) has been committed to evaluate the competitiveness of countries that are part of Association of Southeast Asia Nations (ASEAN),[1] in the context of rising China[2] and India.[3] Analysis at the provincial level has been ACI's forte, an approach that is more relevant given the vast and diverse characteristics of big countries such as Indonesia, China, and India. This book is a continuance of our deep interest to track provincial and regional competitiveness in Indonesia, as well as put forward other evidence-based topical research findings based on our rich provincial and regional database.

Chapter 1 provides a mapping of what the book is about and also its overall structure. The chapter includes brief discussion on Indonesia's latest fixation to strengthen its maritime supremacy, going as far as to claim the goal of transforming Indonesia into a global maritime axis.[4] To be materialised, such grand vision requires a systematic and comprehensive plan of actions that transcends all relevant ministries; foreign affairs, defence, finance and many more. However, there is little evidence that such plan has been formulated.[5] At best, each ministry defines its role in the grand vision and formulates the relevant policies to make it happen. For instance, Ministry of National Development Planning/BAPPENAS put together a framework to develop a sea toll[6] connecting all islands from western to eastern part of Indonesia. According to Ministry of National Development Planning/BAPPENAS (2015, 26–28), elements of sea toll include (i) an excellent sea toll for cargo that is supported by effective inland access, shipping industry, regular and scheduled shipment and adequate loading for west to east and east to west routes; (ii) a sea toll for passengers and cruise which provides specialised services, integrated

[1]The ACI's publications of competitiveness analysis for ASEAN countries can be found in Tan *et al.* (2013b, 2015d) and Tan and Tan (2014). Among ASEAN countries, ACI also published competitiveness studies of Indonesia at provincial and regional level. For more details, see Tan *et al.* (2013c, 2015b, 2015c); Tan and Amri (2013) and Tan and Merdikawati (2015).

[2]The ACI's publications of competitiveness analysis for China can be found in Tan *et al.* (2013d); Tan, Yuan and Yoong (2015a, 2015b, 2015c).

[3]The ACI's publications of competitiveness analysis for India can be found in Tan *et al.* (2013a, 2015a); Tan, Rao and Gopalan (forthcoming); Tan and Rao (2015).

[4]Witular (2014) elaborates more on the five pillars of President Joko Widodo's maritime-axis doctrine.

[5]See Damuri and Day (2015, 6) for more details.

[6]Development of sea toll had been frequently mentioned by President Joko Widodo during his presidential campaign. Sea toll refers to an effective sea connectivity that provides routine and scheduled shipment from western to eastern part of Indonesia (Ministry of National Development Planning/BAPPENAS 2015, 25).

transport, and connectivity to various tourist and commercial destination for travel and leisure; (iii) a well-developed shipping industry which has excellent maritime policies, human resource services, logistic systems, environmental standards, shipping classification services, shipping insurance and finance, efficient fisheries and offshore oil and gas.

Indonesia's reorientation to be more maritime focus is not new. As far back as in 1957, then Prime Minister Djuanda proclaimed that all waters between the islands of Indonesia were under Indonesian sovereignty. Such concept as an archipelagic state only gained international approval in 1982 during the United Nations Convention on the Law of the Sea (Cribb and Ford 2009). Indonesia's first maritime-related ministry was established in Djuanda's cabinet, which was continued during Soekarno's era in 1959–1967 (Sato and Damayanti 2015). However, such ministry was abolished under Soeharto's regime, as his focus pivoted to development centred on land connectivity. Only during *reformasi* era under Abdurrahman Wahid that maritime-related ministry was re-established.

As a result, it is not surprising that development is more advanced in the area close to the capital city, most notably provinces located in Java Island. From Chapter 2, our Overall Competitiveness findings further enhance Java's supremacy as all of its six provinces are part of the top 10. On the contrary, competitiveness of all easternmost provinces tend to lag behind. They have suffered not only from poor connectivity to the epicentre of economic development in the western part of Indonesia, but also from the lack of connectivity within the province. The government's various initiatives such as revitalising and building various ports to boost connectivity with the eastern region bring hope to narrow the gap in regional development. More collective efforts are necessary to bring Papua to the level playing field as the province is far behind the rest of Indonesia in terms of Quality of Life and Infrastructure Development environment.

The stellar performance of provinces in Java Island and poor performance of easternmost provinces are also reflected in Chapter 3 on regional competitiveness analysis. Java Region occupies the top spot while Maluku–Papua Region is at the last. As the regions which heavily rely on natural resource endowment, Kalimantan tends to perform better than Sumatra.[7] For instance, in Overall Competitiveness, Kalimantan Region becomes the runner-up while Sumatra Region is at fourth. The range of ranking among provinces in Kalimantan Region is between third (East Kalimantan) to 19th (West Kalimantan), while Sumatra Region has a wider range with Riau Islands at seventh and Bangka Belitung Islands at 30th. Various efforts to diversify economic reliance away from merely extractive industry have been in place, though their success level relatively varied.

The government introduced substantial set of reforms through a number of economic policy packages starting in September 2015 to attract investment and stimulate domestic demand amidst external pressure of plummeting commodity prices and China's economic slowdown. While the effectiveness of these policies depends largely on their implementation, such policies are the steps in the right direction. The most crucial aspect is to what extent they bring transformative power to revive the manufacturing sector which plays a significant role in

[7]Going forward, it will be interesting to track how those provinces that rely heavily on extractive industry navigate the future as commodity prices plunged with no sign of bouncing back.

pushing the Indonesia's economic development and growth. The central government recently established National Economic and Industry Committee (KEIN) who would be in-charge of creating a re-industrialisation roadmap to boost domestic manufacturing (Amindoni 2016).

Our rich database also allows us to go deeper to sub-environment level where we can pinpoint the strengths and weaknesses of each province and region. For instance, even though Sumatra Region earns a runner-up position in Macroeconomic Stability environment, the region struggles to perform well in Attractiveness to Foreign Investors sub-environment. On the other hand, we can also find best practices as in the case of Kalimantan and Sulawesi regions for Institutions, Governance and Leadership.

In Chapter 4, our empirical analysis provides insights on how provinces may attract business investment. There are four fundamental governing conditions involved. First, providing a secured environment and stable political order to support business operations. A series of explosions taken place in Jakarta in January 2016 by Islamic State of Iraq and Greater Syria (ISIS) affiliated militants is a reminder of the need to heighten the security to prevent militants from launching major terrorist acts in Indonesia.[8] Densus 88, a counter-terrorism squad, should strengthen its capability in foiling the radicalisation of young men and continue to dismantle terror cells (Beech 2016). Given such small and amateurish scale of Jakarta attack, there was no substantial disruption to economic activities following the incident. Nevertheless, the government at all levels should make it a priority to ensure the safety and stability of the country, in order to make Indonesia as an attractive investment destination. Second, building capable and trusted institutional measures to ensure good governance is in place. Third, creating a conducive operational environment by providing basic physical infrastructure and well-functioning governmental system. Fourth, providing an efficient administrative process such as streamlining business processes.

Chapter 5 sheds light on the state of agricultural productivity in Indonesia. The analysis found that total factor productivity (TFP) grew by around 3% from 2000 to 2011. The TFP growth was largely attributed by improvement in technological change (TC) which tended to be broadly uniform across provinces. This further emphasises the importance of research and development (R&D), new innovation, and technology use in productivity improvement. On top of that, a number of provinces will also benefit from improvement in technical efficiency change (TEC) through better resource utilisation. Given limited resources, the government has to be cognisant of prioritising agricultural policies that have the most impact on agricultural productivity.

Apart from chapters written by ACI's researchers, we also received contributions from our reviewers. The first reviewer for Chapters 2 and 3, Ir Alma Karma, MEM, Director of Regional Potential Development at Investment Coordinating Board (BKPM), outlined a number of initiatives by the central, provincial and district/city governments in attracting investment in order to improve the competitiveness of Indonesia and their respective localities. The second reviewer for Chapter 4, Dr Agung Wicaksono, Assistant Professor at School of Business and

[8] Indonesia has a long and painful history of jihadist activity and as the world's largest Muslim population, ISIS aggressively recruits supporters there. Before Jakarta attack, the most recent large-scale strike was in 2009 when suicide bombers attacked Ritz-Carlton and J.W. Marriott hotels in Jakarta.

Management — Institut Teknologi Bandung and Special Assistant to Head of President's Delivery Unit for Development Monitoring and Oversight (UKP4), provided a brief account of how decentralisation and direct election gave rise to new capable local leaders and how multiple layers of government brought upon multiple challenges.

The third reviewer, also for Chapter 4, Mr Robert Na Endi Jaweng, MAP, Executive Director of Regional Autonomy Watch (KPPOD), shared in greater details on various changes arising from the newly enacted Law No. 23/2014 on local government. The fourth reviewer for Chapter 5, Dr Agung Hendriadi, Executive Secretary of Indonesian Agency for Agricultural Research and Development (IAARD), gave his thoughts on the TFP results from ACI's research and linked that with trends of agricultural sector in Indonesia, as well as its issues and challenges.

6.2 FUTURE RESEARCH AGENDA

In the following section, brief introduction on ACI's future research agenda will be provided, which consists of (i) ease of doing business index on attractiveness to investors, business friendliness and competitive policies (EDB Index ABC) for Indonesian provinces and (ii) growth slowdown analysis by income thresholds, potential and challenges encountered by provinces in Indonesia.

6.2.1 Ease of Doing Business Index on Attractiveness to Investors, Business Friendliness and Competitive Policies (EDB Index ABC) for Indonesian Provinces

Aligning with Indonesia's ambitious goal of achieving 7% annual growth rate by 2018 and meeting the much needed infrastructure development that costs the country 5,519.4 trillion Rupiah, attracting both domestic and foreign investment has become a top priority agenda of the government under the leadership of President Joko Widodo. It is therefore necessary to create conducive investment climate to make Indonesia as an attractive investment destination. Such challenging task should be shared among central and local governments. Hence, it is as crucial for each provincial government to play its part in improving the ease of doing business in their respective province.

While business friendliness in terms of facilitating business operations and responsive to businesses are crucial advantages, these are just the necessary but not sufficient conditions to attract investment. Even if these reform measures were taken into account with substantial improvement in ease of doing business, there is no guarantee that investment will be forthcoming because attractiveness to investors in terms of infrastructure resilience, market potential, profitability and cost effectiveness are the Sine Quo Non for a vibrant industry cluster. The pro-business role of the government in formulating and implementing competitive policies are paramount, without which very often market forces are either slow or too weak to act. Hence, ACI is advocating a holistic and comprehensive approach to evaluate under investment and addressing capital shortfall.

This is in contrast to the World Bank's *Ease of Doing Business Ranking* which only focuses on 10 business process comprising starting a business, dealing with construction permits, getting electricity, registering property, getting credit, protecting minority investors, paying taxes, trading across borders, enforcing contracts and resolving insolvency. For each economy being studied, the World Bank took examples of business processes in certain cities, such as Jakarta and Surabaya for the case of Indonesia. From the latest result, Indonesia's ranking has improved to 109th in 2016 from 114th in 2015 (World Bank 2016). Efforts to deep dive into subnational analysis has undertaken in 2012 when the World Bank covered 20 cities for three *Doing Business* indicators, namely starting a business, dealing with construction permits and registering property (World Bank 2012).

The ACI's EDB Index ABC will provide a fresh perspective by using a comprehensive subnational and recurrent analysis covering all Indonesian's provinces. This is a bottom-up approach that takes into account business perspectives at the micro level by survey data, combining it with publicly available hard data and assessment of one-stop services' (PTSP) performances. From such analysis, ACI can generate insights on which province is doing well, drawing best practices for fertile learning ground to learn from one another's success.

6.2.2 Growth Slowdown Analysis by Income Thresholds: Potential and Challenges Encountered by Provinces in Indonesia

Most literature on growth slowdown focuses on national-level analysis. The size and diversity of each country, such as in the case of Indonesia, warrant the study of growth slowdown at subnational level. This research will offer insights to academics and policy makers as we can make plausible predictions about the possibilities of certain provinces experiencing growth slowdowns assuming they continue on their current economic growth trajectories. We aim to reveal potential threats, weaknesses or impediments to continued economic growth based on the Gross Regional Domestic Product (GRDP) per capita level they are currently at.

For different income groups including low, lower middle, upper middle and high income provinces, they may understandably face different problems and issues in dissimilar aspects. Thus different policy implications called for specific policy formulations which more often than not involved no short term solutions especially if impediments or weaknesses are structural in nature. Based on the findings of our model specifications, we shall perform a statistical prediction for each province in its respective income group on the probability of it experiencing growth slowdown. This probability can be used as a preliminary caution for the local government so that they could take targeted actions in order to minimise the chances of economic slowdown.

This growth analysis is very timely as Indonesia seeks to grow at higher rate. For that to happen, each province should optimise its own potential. The existing practice of relying on extractive industry should be replaced by diversification towards other alternative growth engines, such as spearheading the industrialisation. Manufacturing sites in Java can be further spread out towards the eastern part of island, for instance, making East Java as another national manufacturing hub. The province is strategically located as a gateway and logistic hub for eastern part of Indonesia. Tanjung Perak Port will be the most important node in the *Pendulum Nusantara* network, a plan to accelerate connectivity among major islands and west–east corridors of Indonesia. As such, East Java's port capacity has to be expanded to facilitate higher inter-provincial trade, paving the way for rapid pace of growth. As economic structure moves towards higher value added chain, ensuring availability of capable human capital to support the transition is of paramount importance, especially to meet the rising demand of workers equipped with technical skills. In 2013, ACI has signed letter of intent (LOI) with East Java provincial government to cooperate in enhancing the competitiveness of human resources as well as research activities to facilitate economic interchanges and improvement of the local economy. In the future, we hope to expand the collaboration with East Java provincial government and also other provincial governments from other provinces. After all, it is in ACI's interest to see Indonesia's growing at faster rate as given more intra-ASEAN trade, a rising Indonesia will lead to a rising ASEAN in the global economy.

REFERENCES

Amindoni, Ayomi. 2016. "New Committee to Provide Second Opinion on Industrialisation in Indonesia." *The Jakarta Post*, February 11. http://www.thejakartapost.com/news/2016/02/11/new-committee-provide-second-opinion-industrialization-indonesia.html (accessed February 11, 2016).

Beech, Hannah. 2016. "ISIS Opens a New Battlefront in Asia with Jakarta Attacks." *Time*, January 15. http://time.com/4182127/indonesia-jakarta-attacks-isis-is-terrorism/ (accessed February 11, 2016).

Cribb, Robert and Michele Ford, eds. 2009. *Indonesia beyond the Water's Edge: Managing an Archipelagic State*. Singapore: Institute of Southeast Asian Studies.

Damuri, Yose R. and Creina Day. 2015. "Survey of Recent Developments." *Bulletin of Indonesian Economic Studies* 51(1): 3–27.

Ministry of National Development Planning/BAPPENAS. 2015. *Development of the Sea Toll in the National Medium-Term Development Plan 2015–2019 and its Implementation in 2015*. Jakarta: Ministry of National Development Planing/BAPPENAS.

Sato, Yuri and Arie Damayanti. 2015. "Survey of Recent Developments." *Bulletin of Indonesian Economic Studies* 51(2): 165–188.

Tan, Khee Giap and Kartik Rao. 2015. "Sub-national Competitiveness Analysis and Simulation Studies for 35 States and Union Territories of India." *International Journal of Indian Culture and Business Management* 10(4): 476–493.

Tan, Khee Giap, Kartik Rao and Sasidaran Gopalan. 2015. "Assessing Regional Competitiveness in the Five Regions of India." *International Journal of Business Competition and Growth* 4(3/4): 192–219.

Tan, Khee Giap, Linda Low, Kartik Rao and Tan Kong Yam. 2015a. *2014 Regional Competitiveness Analysis and a Master Plan on Regional Development Strategies for India*. Singapore: World Scientific.

Tan, Khee Giap, Linda Low, Tan Kong Yam and Kartik Rao. 2013a. *Annual Analysis of Competitiveness, Simulation Studies and Development Perspective for 35 States and Federal Territories of India: 2000–2010*. Singapore: World Scientific.

Tan, Khee Giap, Linda Low, Tan Kong Yam and Lim Lijuan Amanda. 2013b. *Annual Analysis of Competitiveness, Development Strategies and Public Policies on ASEAN-10: 2000–2010*. Singapore: Pearson.

Tan, Khee Giap and Mulya Amri. 2013. "Subnational Competitiveness and National Performance: Analysis and Simulation for Indonesia." *Journal of CENTRUM Cathedra: The Business and Economics Research Journal* 6(2): 173–192.

Tan, Khee Giap, Mulya Amri, Linda Low and Tan Kong Yam. 2013c. *Competitiveness Analysis and Development Strategies for 33 Indonesian Provinces*. Singapore: World Scientific.

Tan, Khee Giap and Nurina Merdikawati. 2015. "Assessing Regional Competitiveness in Indonesia." *International Journal of Business and Systems Research* 9(3): 273–296.

Tan Khee Giap, Nurina Merdikawati, Mulya Amri and Blake Harley Berger. 2015b. *2014 Annual Competitiveness Analysis and Development Strategies for Indonesian Provinces*. Singapore: World Scientific.

Tan, Khee Giap, Nurina Merdikawati, Mulya Amri and Tan Kong Yam. 2015c. *2014 Provincial and Inaugural Regional Competitiveness Analysis: Safeguarding Indonesia's Growth Momentum*. Singapore: World Scientific.

Tan, Khee Giap, Sangiita Yoong Wei Cher, Sasidaran Gopalan and Nguyen Le Phuong Anh. 2015d. *2014 Annual Competitiveness Ranking and Simulation Study for ASEAN-10 and Development Strategies to Enhance Asia Economic Connectivity*. Singapore: World Scientific.

Tan, Khee Giap and Tan Kong Yam. 2014. "Assessing Competitiveness of ASEAN-10 economies." *International Journal of Economics and Business Research* 8(4): 377–398.

Tan, Khee Giap, Yuan Randong, Sangiita Yoong Wei Cher and Yang Mu. 2013d. *Annual Analysis of Competitiveness, Simulation Studies and Development Perspective for 34 Greater China Economies: 2000–2010*. Singapore: World Scientific.

Tan, Khee Giap, Yuan Randong and Sangiita Yoong Wei Cher. 2015a. *2014 Annual Provincial and Regional Competitiveness Analysis for Greater China Economies: Development Strategies under the New Normal*. Singapore: World Scientific.

Tan, Khee Giap, Yuan Randong and Sangiita Yoong Wei Cher. 2015b. "Assessing Competitiveness and Development Strategies in 34 Greater China economies." *International Journal of Chinese Culture and Management* 3(4): 323–350.

Tan, Khee Giap, Yuan Randong and Sangiita Yoong Wei Cher. 2015c. "Assessing Regional Competitiveness in Greater China." *ACI Policy Paper* No.6.

Witular, Rendi A. 2014. "Jokowi Launches Maritime Doctrine to the World." *The Jakarta Post*, November 13. http://www.thejakartapost.com/news/2014/11/13/jokowi-launches-maritime-doctrine-world.html (accessed February 11, 2016).

World Bank. 2012. *Doing Business in Indonesia 2012*. Washington, DC: World Bank.

World Bank. 2016. *Doing Business 2016: Measuring Regulatory Quality and Efficiency*. Washington, DC: World Bank.

Appendix 1

List of Indicators: 2015 Provincial and Regional Competitiveness Ranking and Simulation for Indonesia

No.	Indicator	Unit	Reversed Indicator
1	MACROECONOMIC STABILITY		
1.1	***Regional Economic Vibrancy***		
1.1.01	Gross Regional Domestic Product (GRDP)	Rupiah (Million), 2000 Constant Prices	
1.1.02	GRDP, Non-oil and gas	Rupiah (Million), 2000 Constant Prices	
1.1.03	GRDP Growth	Percentage Change Per Annum, 2000 Constant Prices	
1.1.04	GRDP Per Capita	Rupiah (Million), 2000 Constant Prices	
1.1.05	GRDP Per Capita, Non-oil and gas	Rupiah (Million), 2000 Constant Prices	
1.1.06	GRDP of Primary Industry	Rupiah (Million), 2000 Constant Prices	
1.1.07	GRDP of Secondary Industry	Rupiah (Million), 2000 Constant Prices	
1.1.08	GRDP of Tertiary Industry	Rupiah (Million), 2000 Constant Prices	
1.1.09	Gross Domestic Fixed Capital Formation	Rupiah (Million), 2000 Constant Prices	
1.1.10	Inflation	Percentage Change Per Annum	R
1.2	***Openness To Trade and Services***		
1.2.01	Exports	Rupiah (Million), 2000 Constant Prices	
1.2.02	Exports, Non-oil and gas	Rupiah (Million), 2000 Constant Prices	
1.2.03	Imports	Rupiah (Million), 2000 Constant Prices	
1.2.04	Imports, Non-oil and gas	Rupiah (Million), 2000 Constant Prices	
1.2.05	Openness To Trade	Ratio	
1.3	***Attractiveness To Foreign Investors***		
1.3.01	Foreign Direct Investment, Last 3 Year Average	US Dollars (Million), Current Market Prices	
1.3.02	Domestic Direct Investment, Last 3 Year Average	Rupiah (Billion)	
1.3.03	Investment Promotion and Management	Index (Survey Data)	

(Continued)

Appendix 1 *(Continued)*

No.	Indicator	Unit	Reversed Indicator
2	**GOVERNMENT AND INSTITUTIONAL SETTING**		
2.1	***Government Policies and Fiscal Sustainability***		
2.1.01	Government Revenue	Rupiah (Thousand), 2000 Constant Prices	
2.1.02	Tax Revenue	Rupiah (Thousand), 2000 Constant Prices	
2.1.03	Tax Revenue per Government Revenue	Ratio	
2.1.04	Government Expenditure	Rupiah (Thousand), 2000 Constant Prices	
2.1.05	Fiscal Balance	Rupiah (Thousand), 2000 Constant Prices	
2.2	***Institutions, Governance and Leadership***		
2.2.01	Lack of Corruption	Index (Survey Data)	
2.2.02	Crime Rate	Rate Per 100.000 population	R
2.2.03	Security	Index (Survey Data)	
2.2.04	Government Inclusiveness and Accountability	Index (Survey Data)	
2.2.05	Government Progress & Expectation	Index (Survey Data)	
2.2.06	Government Efficiency	Index (Survey Data)	
2.2.07	Coordination of Local Governments	Index (Survey Data)	
2.2.08	Provincial Governing Capacity	Index (Survey Data)	
2.3	***Competition, Regulatory Standards and Rule of Laws***		
2.3.01	Regulatory Governance	Index (Survey Data)	
2.3.02	Rule of Law	Index (Survey Data)	
2.3.03	Vibrancy of Competition and Collaboration	Index (Survey Data)	
3	**FINANCIAL, BUSINESSES AND MANPOWER CONDITIONS**		
3.1	***Financial Deepening and Business Efficiency***		
3.1.01	Bank Deposits	Rupiah (Million), 2000 Constant Prices	
3.1.02	Bank Loans	Rupiah (Million), 2000 Constant Prices	
3.1.03	Non-Performing Loans	Rupiah (Million), 2000 Constant Prices	R
3.1.04	Non-Performing Loans per Total Bank Loans	Ratio	R
3.1.05	Number of Bank Branches or Offices	Number	
3.1.06	Population per Number of Bank Branches or Offices	Ratio	R

(Continued)

Appendix 1 *(Continued)*

No.	Indicator	Unit	Reversed Indicator
3.1.07	Ease of Dealing With Banks	Index (Survey Data)	
3.1.08	Firms' Performance	Index (Survey Data)	
3.1.09	Firms' Strategy	Index (Survey Data)	
3.1.10	Firms' Human Resource Capacity	Index (Survey Data)	
3.1.11	Firms' Equipment Capacity	Index (Survey Data)	
3.1.12	Firms' Application of IT	Index (Survey Data)	
3.1.13	Firms' Innovation	Index (Survey Data)	
3.2	***Labour Market Flexibility***		
3.2.01	Labour Force	Number	
3.2.02	Labour Force Participation Rate	Ratio	
3.2.03	Employment	Number	
3.2.04	Employment in Primary Industry	Number	
3.2.05	Employment in Secondary industry	Number	
3.2.06	Employment in Tertiary Industry	Number	
3.2.07	Unemployment Rate	Percentage	R
3.2.08	Minimum Wage per Month	Rupiah, Current Market Prices	R
3.2.09	Labour Relations	Index (Survey Data)	
3.3	***Productivity Performance***		
3.3.01	Overall Labour Productivity	Rupiah (Million) per person-year, 2000 Constant Prices	
3.3.02	Overall Labour Productivity, Non-oil and gas	Rupiah (Million) per person-year, 2000 Constant Prices	
3.3.03	Primary Industry Productivity	Rupiah (Million) per person-year, 2000 Constant Prices	
3.3.04	Secondary Industry Productivity	Rupiah (Million) per person-year, 2000 Constant Prices	
3.3.05	Tertiary Industry Productivity	Rupiah (Million) per person-year, 2000 Constant Prices	
4	**QUALITY OF LIFE AND INFRASTRUCTURE DEVELOPMENT**		
4.1	***Physical Infrastructure***		
4.1.01	Population	Persons, Year-end	
4.1.02	Population Growth	Percentage Change Per Annum	

(Continued)

Appendix 1 (*Continued*)

No.	Indicator	Unit	Reversed Indicator
4.1.03	Urban Population	Percentage of Total Population	
4.1.04	Length of Paved Roads	Kilometres	
4.1.05	Registered Motor Vehicles	Number	
4.1.06	Registered Motor Vehicles per KM of paved road	Ratio	R
4.1.07	Cargo at Inter-island Seaport	Tons	
4.1.08	Cargo at International Seaport	Tons	
4.1.09	Passengers of Domestic Air Traffic	Number	
4.1.10	Passengers of International Air Traffic	Number	
4.1.11	Households with pipe water services	Percentage of households	
4.1.12	Households with state electricity services	Percentage of households	
4.1.13	Ease of Acquiring Property	Index (Survey Data)	
4.1.14	Quality of Physical Infrastructure	Index (Survey Data)	
4.2	***Technological Infrastructure***		
4.2.01	Telephone Ownership	Percentage of households	
4.2.02	Handphone Ownership	Percentage of households	
4.2.03	Desktop Computer Ownership	Percentage of households	
4.2.04	Laptop Computer Ownership	Percentage of households	
4.2.05	Internet Access at Home	Percentage of households	
4.2.06	Internet Access at Office	Percentage of households	
4.2.07	Internet Access at School	Percentage of households	
4.2.08	Internet Access in Handphone	Percentage of households	
4.2.09	Quality of Technological Infrastructure	Index (Survey Data)	
4.3	***Standard of Living, Education and Social Stability***		
4.3.01	Adult Illiteracy Rate	Percentage of Adults	R
4.3.02	Mean Years of Schooling	Years	
4.3.03	School Enrolment Rate (Primary)	Percentage	
4.3.04	School Enrolment Rate (Junior High)	Percentage	
4.3.05	School Enrolment Rate (Senior High)	Percentage	
4.3.06	Student-Teacher Ratio (Primary)	Ratio	R
4.3.07	Student-Teacher Ratio (Junior High)	Ratio	R

(*Continued*)

Appendix 1 *(Continued)*

No.	Indicator	Unit	Reversed Indicator
4.3.08	Student-Teacher Ratio (Senior High)	Ratio	R
4.3.09	Human Development Index	Index	
4.3.10	Life Expectancy at Birth	Years	
4.3.11	Gini Ratio	Ratio	R
4.3.12	Urban Population Growth	Percentage Per Annum	
4.3.13	Population per Health Facility	Ratio	R
4.3.14	Population per Medical Worker	Ratio	R
4.3.15	Environmental Quality Index	Index	
4.3.16	Fatalities due to Natural Disaster	Number	R
4.3.17	Quality of Education	Index (Survey Data)	
4.3.18	Quality of Healthcare	Index (Survey Data)	
4.3.19	Affordability and Accessibility of Goods	Index (Survey Data)	

Source: Asia Competitiveness Institute.

Appendix 2

Computation of Rankings: The Algorithm

A step-by-step description of the ranking process is described below for N regions (or provinces respectively), M indicators and C environments, with each environment comprising S sub-environments.

Algorithm: Ranking Methodology

(1) Compute the mean value of indicator j ($j = 1, \ldots, M$),

$$\bar{X}_j = \frac{1}{N}\sum_{i=1}^{N} X_{ij},$$

where X_{ij} represents the value that region i ($i = 1, \ldots, N$) takes for indicator j.

(2) For each indicator j ($j = 1, \ldots, M$), calculate its standard deviation (SD),

$$\text{SD}_j = \sqrt{\frac{1}{N}\sum_{i=1}^{N}(X_{ij} - \bar{X}_j)^2}.$$

(3) Compute the standardised value of indicator (SVI) that each region i ($i = 1, \ldots, N$) takes under each of the indicators j ($j = 1, \ldots, M$),

$$\text{SVI}_{ij} = \frac{X_{ij} - \bar{X}_j}{SD_j}.$$

(4) Compute the 'ranked' standardised value of indicator (RSVI) that each region i ($i = 1, \ldots, N$) takes under each of the indicators j ($j = 1, \ldots, M$):

$$\text{RSVI}_{ij} = \begin{cases} \text{SVI}_{ij}, & \text{if a higher value is better} \\ -\text{SVI}_{ij}, & \text{if a lower value is better.} \end{cases}$$

(5) For each indicator, j ($j = 1, \ldots, M$), a ranking can be obtained for regions: regions with a higher value of RSVI for indicator j are ranked ahead of those with a lower value.

(6) For each region i ($i = 1, \ldots, N$), calculate the RSVI for each sub-environment k ($k = 1, \ldots, S$) belonging to environment l ($l = 1, \ldots, C$),

$$\text{Raw\_RSVI}_{i,lk} = \frac{1}{y_{lk}} \sum_{p=1}^{y_{lk}} \text{RSVI}_{i,jlk,p},$$

$$\text{Mean\_RSVI}_{lk} = \frac{1}{N} \sum_{i=1}^{N} \text{Raw\_RSVI}_{i,lk},$$

$$\text{SD\_RSVI}_{lk} = \sqrt{\frac{1}{N} \sum_{i=1}^{N} (\text{Raw\_RSVI}_{i,lk} - \text{Mean\_RSVI}_{lk})^2},$$

$$\text{RSVI}_{i,lk} = \frac{\text{Raw\_RSVI}_{i,lk} - \text{Mean\_RSVI}_{lk}}{\text{SD\_RSVI}_{lk}}.$$

where y_{lk} is the total number of indicators under sub-environment k of environment l and ($\text{RSVI}_{i,jlk,1}$, …, $\text{RSVI}_{i,jlk,ylk}$) are the RSVIs for region i that make up sub-environment k of environment l.

(7) For each region i ($i = 1, \ldots, N$), calculate the RSVI for each environment l ($l = 1, \ldots, C$),

$$\text{Raw\_RSVI}_{i,l} = \frac{1}{S_l} \sum_{k=1}^{S_l} \text{RSVI}_{i,lk},$$

$$\text{Mean\_RSVI}_{l} = \frac{1}{N} \sum_{i=1}^{N} \text{Raw\_RSVI}_{i,l},$$

$$\text{SD\_RSVI}_{l} = \sqrt{\frac{1}{N} \sum_{i=1}^{N} (\text{Raw\_RSVI}_{i,l} - \text{Mean\_RSVI}_{l})^2},$$

$$\text{RSVI}_{i,l} = \frac{\text{Raw\_RSVI}_{i,l} - \text{Mean\_RSVI}_{l}}{\text{SD\_RSVI}_{l}},$$

where ($\text{RSVI}_{i,l1}$, …, $\text{RSVI}_{i,lS}$) are the RSVIs for the S sub-environments under each environment l.

(8) Overall rank score of region i ($i = 1, \ldots, N$),

$$\text{Raw\_}R_i = \frac{1}{C} \sum_{l=1}^{C} \text{RSVI}_{i,l},$$

$$\text{Mean\_}R = \frac{1}{N} \sum_{i=1}^{N} \text{Raw\_}R_i,$$

$$\text{SD\_}R = \sqrt{\frac{1}{N}\sum_{i=1}^{N}(\text{Raw\_}R_i - \text{Mean\_}R)^2},$$

$$R_i = \frac{\text{Raw\_}R_i - \text{Mean\_}R}{\text{SD\_}R}.$$

Regions with a higher R_i are ranked ahead of those with lower value of R_i, and the region with the highest R_i is the most competitive region.

Step (5) provides the ranking of each region for each individual indicator. To achieve this ranking, Step (4) adjusts the value of the SVIs so that a higher value will lead to a better ranking in terms of 'competitiveness'. Depending on the nature of the indicator in question, a higher or lower value may reflect a more 'competitive' region. Take for instance the sub-indicators 'Gross Regional Domestic Product (GRDP)' and 'Unemployment Rate'. A higher GRDP but a lower 'unemployment rate' suggest better economic performance, which makes a region more 'competitive'. In most cases where a higher value is better (e.g. GRDP), the SVIs of regions are considered, and those with a higher SVI value will have a better ranking. However, for indicators where the inverse is true (e.g. Unemployment Rate), the 'negative SVI' values are compared between regions and a lower SVI value will lead to a better ranking. Step (4) thus seeks to make all standardised values of all indicators consistent for ranking purposes.

Step (6) determines the sub-environment rankings of each region. The average RSVI of all the indicators in the sub-environment are calculated, re-standardised across all the regions and compared to other regions. Regions with a higher average RSVI rank better in the sub-environment. Although the number of indicators varies for each sub-environment, there are three sub-environments for each of the four environments. The aggregate score for each sub-environment is given an equivalent weighting: 33.33% of their respective environment's score.

To arrive at the ranking for each environment, the RSVIs of the sub-environments are averaged and re-standardised across all the regions as detailed by Step (7). Finally, Step (8) requires the RSVI values of each environment to be averaged and re-standardised across all the regions to determine the overall ranking of the region. Regions with a higher RSVI are ranked ahead of those with a lower RSVI.

Identical weights are assigned to each environment as they represent equivalent significance to the computation of Overall Competitiveness Index. This method is repeated and applied consistently across all the regions to ensure precision of the rankings. Mathematically, this can be illustrated as follows:

Overall Competitiveness Index
= 25% × (Macroeconomic Stability)
+ 25% × (Government and Institutional Setting)
+ 25% × (Financial, Businesses and Manpower Conditions)
+ 25% × (Quality of Life and Infrastructure Development)

Appendix 3

Notes on Data Aggregation from Provincial Level to Regional Level

No.	Indicator	Unit	Reversed Indicator	Calculated as in
1	**MACROECONOMIC STABILITY**			
1.1	***Regional Economic Vibrancy***			
1.1.01	Gross Regional Domestic Product (GRDP)	Rupiah (Million), 2000 Constant Prices		Approach 1
1.1.02	GRDP, Non-oil and gas	Rupiah (Million), 2000 Constant Prices		Approach 1
1.1.03	GRDP Growth	Percentage Change Per Annum, 2000 Constant Prices		Approach 2
1.1.04	GRDP Per Capita	Rupiah (Million), 2000 Constant Prices		Approach 2
1.1.05	GRDP Per Capita, Non-oil and gas	Rupiah (Million), 2000 Constant Prices		Approach 2
1.1.06	GRDP of Primary Industry	Rupiah (Million), 2000 Constant Prices		Approach 1
1.1.07	GRDP of Secondary Industry	Rupiah (Million), 2000 Constant Prices		Approach 1
1.1.08	GRDP of Tertiary Industry	Rupiah (Million), 2000 Constant Prices		Approach 1
1.1.09	Gross Domestic Fixed Capital Formation	Rupiah (Million), 2000 Constant Prices		Approach 1
1.1.10	Inflation	Percentage Change Per Annum	R	Approach 3
1.2	***Openness To Trade and Services***			
1.2.01	Exports	Rupiah (Million), 2000 Constant Prices		Approach 1
1.2.02	Exports, Non-oil and gas	Rupiah (Million), 2000 Constant Prices		Approach 1
1.2.03	Imports	Rupiah (Million), 2000 Constant Prices		Approach 1
1.2.04	Imports, Non-oil and gas	Rupiah (Million), 2000 Constant Prices		Approach 1
1.2.05	Openness To Trade	Ratio		Approach 2
1.3	***Attractiveness To Foreign Investors***			
1.3.01	Foreign Direct Investment, Last 3 Year Average	US Dollars (Million), Current Market Prices		Approach 1
1.3.02	Domestic Direct Investment, Last 3 Year Average	Rupiah (Billion)		Approach 1
1.3.03	Investment Promotion and Management	Index (Survey Data)		Approach 3

(Continued)

Appendix 3 (*Continued*)

No.	Indicator	Unit	Reversed Indicator	Calculated as in
2	**GOVERNMENT AND INSTITUTIONAL SETTING**			
2.1	***Government Policies and Fiscal Sustainability***			
2.1.01	Government Revenue	Rupiah (Thousand), 2000 Constant Prices		Approach 1
2.1.02	Tax Revenue	Rupiah (Thousand), 2000 Constant Prices		Approach 1
2.1.03	Tax Revenue per Government Revenue	Ratio		Approach 2
2.1.04	Government Expenditure	Rupiah (Thousand), 2000 Constant Prices		Approach 1
2.1.05	Fiscal Balance	Rupiah (Thousand), 2000 Constant Prices		Approach 1
2.2	***Institutions, Governance and Leadership***			
2.2.01	Lack of Corruption	Index (Survey Data)		Approach 3
2.2.02	Crime Rate	Rate Per 100.000 population	R	Approach 3
2.2.03	Security	Index (Survey Data)		Approach 3
2.2.04	Government Inclusiveness and Accountability	Index (Survey Data)		Approach 3
2.2.05	Government Progress and Expectation	Index (Survey Data)		Approach 3
2.2.06	Government Efficiency	Index (Survey Data)		Approach 3
2.2.07	Coordination of Local Governments	Index (Survey Data)		Approach 3
2.2.08	Provincial Governing Capacity	Index (Survey Data)		Approach 3
2.3	***Competition, Regulatory Standards and Rule of Laws***			
2.3.01	Regulatory Governance	Index (Survey Data)		Approach 3
2.3.02	Rule of Law	Index (Survey Data)		Approach 3
2.3.03	Vibrancy of Competition and Collaboration	Index (Survey Data)		Approach 3
3	**FINANCIAL, BUSINESSES AND MANPOWER CONDITIONS**			
3.1	***Financial Deepening and Business Efficiency***			
3.1.01	Bank Deposits	Rupiah (Million), 2000 Constant Prices		Approach 1
3.1.02	Bank Loans	Rupiah (Million), 2000 Constant Prices		Approach 1
3.1.03	Non-Performing Loans	Rupiah (Million), 2000 Constant Prices	R	Approach 1

(*Continued*)

Appendix 3 (*Continued*)

No.	Indicator	Unit	Reversed Indicator	Calculated as in
3.1.04	Non-Performing Loans per Total Bank Loans	Ratio	R	Approach 2
3.1.05	Number of Bank Branches or Offices	Number		Approach 1
3.1.06	Population per Number of Bank Branches or Offices	Ratio	R	Approach 2
3.1.07	Ease of Dealing With Banks	Index (Survey Data)		Approach 3
3.1.08	Firms' Performance	Index (Survey Data)		Approach 3
3.1.09	Firms' Strategy	Index (Survey Data)		Approach 3
3.1.10	Firms' Human Resource Capacity	Index (Survey Data)		Approach 3
3.1.11	Firms' Equipment Capacity	Index (Survey Data)		Approach 3
3.1.12	Firms' Application of IT	Index (Survey Data)		Approach 3
3.1.13	Firms' Innovation	Index (Survey Data)		Approach 3
3.2	***Labour Market Flexibility***			
3.2.01	Labour Force	Number		Approach 1
3.2.02	Labour Force Participation Rate	Ratio		Approach 2
3.2.03	Employment	Number		Approach 1
3.2.04	Employment in Primary Industry	Number		Approach 1
3.2.05	Employment in Secondary industry	Number		Approach 1
3.2.06	Employment in Tertiary Industry	Number		Approach 1
3.2.07	Unemployment Rate	Percentage	R	Approach 2
3.2.08	Minimum Wage per Month	Rupiah, Current Market Prices	R	Approach 3
3.2.09	Labour Relations	Index (Survey Data)		Approach 3
3.3	***Productivity Performance***			
3.3.01	Overall Labour Productivity	Rupiah (Million) per person-year, 2000 Constant Prices		Approach 2
3.3.02	Overall Labour Productivity, Non-oil and gas	Rupiah (Million) per person-year, 2000 Constant Prices		Approach 2
3.3.03	Primary Industry Productivity	Rupiah (Million) per person-year, 2000 Constant Prices		Approach 2
3.3.04	Secondary Industry Productivity	Rupiah (Million) per person-year, 2000 Constant Prices		Approach 2
3.3.05	Tertiary Industry Productivity	Rupiah (Million) per person-year, 2000 Constant Prices		Approach 2

(*Continued*)

Appendix 3 (*Continued*)

No.	Indicator	Unit	Reversed Indicator	Calculated as in
4	**QUALITY OF LIFE AND INFRASTRUCTURE DEVELOPMENT**			
4.1	***Physical Infrastructure***			
4.1.01	Population	Persons, Year-end		Approach 1
4.1.02	Population Growth	Percentage change per annum		Approach 3
4.1.03	Urban Population	Percentage of total population		Approach 3
4.1.04	Length of Paved Roads	Kilometres		Approach 1
4.1.05	Registered Motor Vehicles	Number		Approach 1
4.1.06	Registered Motor Vehicles per KM of paved road	Ratio	R	Approach 2
4.1.07	Cargo at Inter-island Seaport	Tons		Approach 1
4.1.08	Cargo at International Seaport	Tons		Approach 1
4.1.09	Passengers of Domestic Air Traffic	Number		Approach 1
4.1.10	Passengers of International Air Traffic	Number		Approach 1
4.1.11	Households with pipe water services	Percentage of households		Approach 3
4.1.12	Households with state electricity services	Percentage of households		Approach 3
4.1.13	Ease of Acquiring Property	Index (Survey Data)		Approach 3
4.1.14	Quality of Physical Infrastructure	Index (Survey Data)		Approach 3
4.2	***Technological Infrastructure***			
4.2.01	Telephone Ownership	Percentage of households		Approach 3
4.2.02	Handphone Ownership	Percentage of households		Approach 3
4.2.03	Desktop Computer Ownership	Percentage of households		Approach 3
4.2.04	Laptop Computer Ownership	Percentage of households		Approach 3
4.2.05	Internet Access at Home	Percentage of households		Approach 3
4.2.06	Internet Access at Office	Percentage of households		Approach 3
4.2.07	Internet Access at School	Percentage of households		Approach 3
4.2.08	Internet Access in Handphone	Percentage of households		Approach 3
4.2.09	Quality of Technological Infrastructure	Index (Survey Data)		Approach 3
4.3	***Standard of Living, Education and Social Stability***			
4.3.01	Adult Illiteracy Rate	Percentage of Adults	R	Approach 3
4.3.02	Mean Years of Schooling	Years		Approach 3

(*Continued*)

Appendix 3 (*Continued*)

No.	Indicator	Unit	Reversed Indicator	Calculated as in
4.3.03	School Enrolment Rate (Primary)	Percentage		Approach 3
4.3.04	School Enrolment Rate (Junior High)	Percentage		Approach 3
4.3.05	School Enrolment Rate (Senior High)	Percentage		Approach 3
4.3.06	Student-Teacher Ratio (Primary)	Ratio	R	Approach 3
4.3.07	Student-Teacher Ratio (Junior High)	Ratio	R	Approach 3
4.3.08	Student–Teacher Ratio (Senior High)	Ratio	R	Approach 3
4.3.09	Human Development Index	Index		Approach 3
4.3.10	Life Expectancy at Birth	Years		Approach 3
4.3.11	Gini Ratio	Ratio	R	Approach 3
4.3.12	Urban Population Growth	Percentage per annum		Approach 3
4.3.13	Population per Health Facility	Ratio	R	Approach 3
4.3.14	Population per Medical Worker	Ratio	R	Approach 3
4.3.15	Environmental Quality Index	Index		Approach 3
4.3.16	Fatalities due to Natural Disaster	Number	R	Approach 3
4.3.17	Quality of Education	Index (Survey Data)		Approach 3
4.3.18	Quality of Healthcare	Index (Survey Data)		Approach 3
4.3.19	Affordability and Accessibility of Goods	Index (Survey Data)		Approach 3

Source: Asia Competitiveness Institute.